Paradigm Lost

Paradigm Lost

State Theory Reconsidered

Stanley Aronowitz and Peter Bratsis, Editors

University of Minnesota Press
Minneapolis
London

Published by the University of Minnesota Press
111 Third Avenue South, Suite 290
Minneapolis, MN 55401-2520
http://www.upress.umn.edu

Library of Congress Cataloging-in-Publication Data

Paradigm lost : state theory reconsidered / Stanley Aronowitz and Peter Bratsis, editors.
p. cm.
Based on the conference "Miliband and Poulantzas : In Retrospect and Prospect," held in April 1997.
Includes bibliographical references and index.
ISBN 978-0-8166-3293-0 (HC : alk. paper) — ISBN 978-0-8166-3294-7 (PB : alk. paper)
1. State, the. 2. Miliband, Ralph—Contributions in political science. 3. Poulantzas, Nicos—Contributions in political science. I. Aronowitz, Stanley. II. Bratsis, Peter.
JC11 .P37 2002
320.1—dc21 2002002333

Printed in the United States of America on acid-free paper

12 11 10 09 08 10 9 8 7 6 5 4 3 2

This book is dedicated to the memory of Joseph Murphy

Contents

Acknowledgments

The inspiration for and most of the contents of this collection derive from the conference "Miliband and Poulantzas: In Retrospect and Prospect," held in April 1997. We would like to thank the Ph.D. program in political science of the CUNY Graduate School and the Center for Byzantine and Modern Greek Studies, Queens College, for their sponsorship and support of this conference. We would like to thank and acknowledge all those who were involved in the organization of this conference and without whom the conference would not have been possible: Nicos Alexiou, Jose Eisenberg, Joao Feres Jr., Hollis France, Andreas Karras, Andrew Lawrence, Chris Malone, Roland Marden, Irving Leonard Markovitz, Eleni Natsiopoulou, W. Ofuatey-Kodjoe, Constantine Panayiotakis, and Frances Fox Piven. We would also like to thank, in addition to those represented in this collection, those who participated in the conference and greatly contributed to its success: Ira Katznelson, Mark Kesselman, John Mollenkopf, Bertell Ollman, and Robert Ross. Finally, we wish to note the importance of Joseph Murphy. Not only was he involved in all aspects of the conference, but his friendship, advice, humor, and intellect were invaluable to us and to the success of this project.

State Power, Global Power

Stanley Aronowitz and Peter Bratsis

The ability to rise from the dead is unique to that which has been improperly buried. From Freud's *Totem and Taboo* to Stephen King's *Pet Sematary*, a lack of proper burying protocol results in the return of that which had been thought dead. Marxist state theory and, increasingly, the state as an analytical object have been the victims of an improper burial. They have been buried by a conservative shift inside and outside of the academy. They have been buried by an assumed decline of the state in the face of globalizing and localizing forces. They have been buried by a shift of emphasis, within the left, away from the study of "political power" to a more disaggregated vision of power as a dispersed and undifferentiated phenomenon (from Foucault and Habermas to Deleuze and Guattari).

The main goal of the essays collected here is to assist state theory in its resurrection from the dead. The essays are organized around three broad themes: to introduce readers to some foundational aspects of Marxist state theory, to evaluate the relevance of state theory in relation to contemporary political phenomena and theoretical tendencies, and to identify the limits to state theory that must be overcome for its continued development. All three themes are developed while focusing on the contributions of Ralph Miliband and Nicos Poulantzas. Focusing on Miliband and Poulantzas allows us to frame and understand state theory as a whole because they occupy the methodological extremes within the range of theorists particular to state theory and because their debate is more often than not the point of departure for subsequent attempts to produce a Marxist theory of the state. To understand the utility and limits of Miliband and Poulantzas is thus to understand the utility and limits of state theory in a broader sense.

This introduction attempts to situate the issues examined in the subsequent essays to broader empirical and theoretical concerns. We will focus on identifying those aspects of state theory that distinguish it from competing theoretical tendencies and we will illustrate the utility of state theory in relation to questions about the changes of the state in the face of globalization and in relation to questions regarding the affects of state institutions.

The Specificity of State Theory

As many of the essays in this collection attest (especially Barrow and Panitch), state theory enjoyed a fair amount of attention in the 1970s not only from Marxist theorists but also from more mainstream sects within social science. State theory had in a few short years constituted itself as an important and viable alternative to the orthodoxy of pluralism and structural functionalism/systems theory within political science and political sociology. By 1985, *Bringing the State Back In,* the presumed benchmark for the return of the state as an object of inquiry to social science, had relegated theorists such as Miliband, Offe, Block, Therborn, and Poulantzas to a couple of paragraphs and footnotes. What is paradoxical about this startling loss of currency and popularity is its lack of justification. State theory was never the object of a rigorous and sustained critique that would properly "bury" it and clear the way for alternative approaches.[1] Slavoj Žižek's comment on the peculiar decline of the Althusserian school fits well in this context: "It is more as if there were . . . a traumatic kernel which had to be quickly forgotten, 'repressed'; it is an effective case of theoretical amnesia" (Žižek 1989, 1).

A related and equally paradoxical phenomenon is the initial attraction to the Miliband–Poulantzas debate. Within the Marxist commentaries on the debate we find two recurring and conflicting observations. It is noted that the debate received much attention and constituted the point of departure and frame of reference for most, if not all, subsequent attempts for a Marxist theory of the state; and, it is also noted that the debate was a caricature of Miliband's and Poulantzas's true positions, offering no substantive insight into a theory of the state (cf. Jessop 1985, xiv; Barrow in this volume; and Levine in this volume). The obvious question is, how can this be? How can what we may assume to be informed and intelligent people spend so much time discussing and debating what is ultimately a vulgar and substance-lacking opposition? Our answer to this paradox is that though it may be the case that the debate was lacking in its explicit focus (as a debate about what constitutes the Marxist theory of the state), the real significance of the debate was its repetition of the Lenin–Luxemburg debate. After all, what is Miliband's "instrumentalist" claim that the state has been captured by the capitalist class by way of its political organization other than a repetition of Lenin's argument that the state is an instrument of the capitalist class and, necessarily, his defense of organization and the role of the revolutionary party (a result of the instrumentalist concept of power common to both)? What is Poulantzas's "structuralist" claim that the state is capitalist by virtue of its functions and acts to disorganize the working class other than a repetition of Luxemburg's argument that the state apparatuses are by function bourgeois and, necessarily, her defense of self-organized and autonomous working-class movements (that is, outside the formal and legal logic of "the state" and hierarchical organization)?

The "traumatic kernel" of state theory may well be its connection to political strategy. That which initially was the source of attraction to state theory may ultimately have served as the source of its rejection. On a superficial level, this connection can be seen by the attention given to state theory by various political movements; this is especially true of Eurocommunism (cf. Carrillo 1978). On a more substantive level, this connection is present in the strategic value of the questions state theory tends to pose. Whereas systems theory/behaviorism conformed to and supported the pluralist fiction of a fragmented society with more or less equal shares of political power among its factions, and whereas the state-centered/neo-institutionalist approach chooses to reject the question of the social foundations of political power in favor of the assumption that political power is autonomous from society, state theory of all denominations begins with the very strategic focus of explaining the social foundations and dominating effects of political power. Where political analysis once spoke the language of "domination" and "class antagonism," it now speaks in the language of "state capacities" and "conflict resolution."

Our contention is that although the popularity of state theory has declined, the importance of the questions specific to it has increased. As

Leo Panitch notes in his essay, the popularity and decline of state theory are directly related to the vicissitudes of class struggles and political conditions.[2] As radical movements from below ebbed in the past two decades or so, state theory and its protagonists became increasingly marginal to the shifting political climate and its corresponding academic fashions. The reflexive effect of this decline has been that alternative understandings of the present and their respective concepts, necessary weapons for a renewed and strategically informed class struggle, have all but disappeared from the intellectual scene. The resultant neutering of political analysis has accompanied an increasing technicalization of politics and the ways it presents itself. The increased importance assumed by the Federal Reserve, the International Monetary Fund, the World Bank, and the European Union has accompanied a transformation of what used to be overtly political questions of fiscal policy and social welfare into what are now technical questions associated with monetary policy—interest rate and debt management. The actions of political institutions increasingly appear as more or less inevitable and determined by the logic of the free market or as the outcome of legal mandates.[3] In this context of politics appearing more and more separated from social agency, the problematic of state theory becomes more and more necessary for revealing the relation of the state to social interests and actors and for serving as a tool for the future manifestations of the political struggle of the dominated classes.

The decline of state theory not only has political ramifications, but also has led to a conceptual regression within social inquiry. We examine two related areas of inquiry in what follows—the study of institutions and the study of globalization—that we think can greatly benefit from a reapplication of state theory. Of course, these themes are central to many of the essays included in this collection in that the problematic of state theory has suffered at the hands of contemporary discussions of globalization and the assumed decline of state autonomy as well as at the hands of state-centered theories that assert that they have overcome the simple-mindedness of society-centered theories by taking institutions and their agency seriously. Beginning with an analysis of Michael Hardt and Antonio Negri's recent work *Empire* (2000), we attempt to show how Marxist state theory can assist contemporary efforts on the left to come to terms with current political changes and demonstrate that contemporary political theory, in spite of its "amnesia," needs to rethink the potential analytical and strategic value of Miliband, Poulantzas, and state theory as a whole.

Globalization, Institutions, and the Vicissitudes of State Power

We are in the midst of a veritable avalanche of descriptive and theoretical writing on globalization. From William Greider's journalistic accounts of the spread of transnational corporate power to all corners of the globe to the dense theoretical work of Hardt and Negri, and almost everything in between, there is general agreement that world capitalism has entered a new era, marked by the partial or complete displacement of the old regulatory institutions and the sovereignty of the nation-state. Some, such as Claus Offe (1985) and Scott Lash and John Urry (1987), call attention to the end of regulation and foresee the possibility of new forms of interstate rivalries, but most of the significant works of the 1990s on globalization insist that the crucial characteristic of globalization is a radical reconfiguration of economic and, especially, political space. Since the mid-1970s, it is argued, transnational corporations based largely in the advanced capitalist states have taken economic and political power, undercutting the sovereignty of nation-states and subverting the very concept of citizenship. Although the old arrangements, based on the rivalry of capitals situated in, and supported by, sovereign nation-states, which seek raw materials and markets for the export of capital, survive in vestigial form, Hardt and Negri (2000), following Gilles Deleuze, adopt the thesis of "deterritorialization" and "reterritorialization" to describe the changes; the concept corresponds to themes enunciated by the popular literature on globalization, left and right, as well as the more scholarly work.

The thesis goes something like this: States construct social space in the metaphor of "striated" space, an allusion to centralization of power and the organization of the social world in the model of hierarchy and domination. Thus, they conceive of the apparent decentralization of material production into the far reaches of the globe as a moment followed by reterritorialization, the return to centralization. In their rich, complex, and immensely influential book *A Thousand Plateaus,* Deleuze and his collaborator Félix Guattari elaborate these ideas in a theory of the state and of political agency. As they put it: "We are compelled to say there has always been a State, quite perfect, quite complete. . . . The state dates back to the most remote ages of humanity" (Deleuze and Guattari

1987, 360). Far from tracing the development of the state form within the evolution of human societies, between an earlier stage of so-called primitive communism and ancient societies, most often modes of production grounded in slave labor, Deleuze and Guattari insist on the *Urstate*, property of all human associations. In their conception, the state is not an efflux of classes and of class struggle; they conceive the state as the repository of self-reproducing power, as a form of knowledge, especially scientific knowledge based on the same centralizing assumptions of its unquestioned universality: "by right... [the state acquires] a consensus raised to the absolute" (375–76). The state and its science have always claimed the mantle of reason and, in their quest for power over social space and social thought, systematically suppress alternative social movements and knowledges. The characteristic form of state politics is molar; its centralization is immanent to its power. To this transhistorical power Deleuze and Guattari pose the alternative of smooth space, the molecular politics of the nomad in which deterritorialization is not followed by centralization; with the nomadic, the state's power itself, not just a particular form of it, is contested. In political terms, this is a new anarchist manifesto.

Underlying this discourse is the view that territory, as the foundation of social power, is identical with the state. Thus, the object of political struggle is not, as some Marxists believe, to capture state power in order to dismantle it sometime in the future. Just as, following Lévi-Strauss and Pierre Clastres, they abjure the concept of the evolution of human societies, they also renounce the concept of a transitional state between capitalism and communism. Because the state is itself a form of tyranny, capturing state power will only reproduce that which the revolution is trying to overcome, tyranny.

Hardt and Negri introduce the concept of Empire as the latest form of reterritorialization. They argue that the nation-state is now largely displaced by a "network" of transnational corporations that lead the capitalist states, of which the only real superpower, the United States, holds pride of place and aggregates to itself significantly greater power than the others. The sinews of empire are an international legal system in which human rights, violations of national sovereignty, the interest of perpetual "peace," and other traditional discourses of liberal democracy trump sovereignty. But the attempt to establish a new rule of law in international affairs is not merely a ruse for advancing the interests of

Empire; it is a genuine effort to reintroduce juridical regulation in order to ensure economic and political stability. Of course, this effort is directed by the combined military and police powers of the various states. If the question of control over these forces remains a serious obstacle because residual sovereignty claims are still in force among the major powers, Hardt and Negri have no doubt that these impediments to global empire are only temporary. A new international "metastate" is in the making and the old nation-state is in its death throes.

The nation-state lives chiefly as a repressive power, but also has some purchase on maintaining a degree of ideological hegemony over what they call "the multitude." Because citizenship refers to states in full possession of national sovereignty, and the effectivity of old class movements such as trade unions and political parties presupposes this situation, under the new conditions of Empire, the labor and socialist movements, whose targets—national capital and the capitalist state—are disappearing, have lost their claim to power. Empirically, it is easy to document the decline of the opposition within the framework of the nation-state. Hardt and Negri repeat the familiar litany of defeats suffered by labor at the hands of globalization: sharp membership losses, the de facto defanging of the strike weapon, and, as a result, the capitulation of traditional working-class and socialist parties to neoliberal policies, if not to free-market doctrine (although the Labour government in the United Kingdom has gone a long way toward a full embrace). Even in power, these parties have proved all too willing supplicants of Empire. Moreover, perhaps the signal achievement of the labor and other social movements, the welfare state, is in the process of being dismantled (United States) or has been seriously eroded in erstwhile bastions of labor solidarity (Germany, France, Italy) (cf. Levine's and Cloward and Piven's essays in this volume). On the one hand, labor is reduced to a fungible commodity on the world scale; on the other hand, the new information economy has brought into being what Negri has termed a new "social" as opposed to "mass" worker, a type not dissimilar from Robert Reich's symbolic analyst in which, according to their latest version, the functions of management and the coordination of intellectual labor need no longer be a separate occupational designation. Unlike the mass worker, whose labor has been segmented and degraded, the fully qualified worker must know the entire labor process and is often scientifically as well as technically trained. But, following André Gorz's older concept, capital deprives intellectual labor of power over its own work; whereas the mass worker's rebellion against her subordination takes the form of "refusal" to work in the new economy, the socialized worker's demands are for autonomy in the performance of her work. The revolt is no less filled with intensities but, like the 2000 Boeing engineers' strike in which sixteen thousand participated, the worker wants to be left to do his work at his own pace, a preference that disrupts capital's drive for increased productivity, and its incessant demand that qualified labor be reduced to mass labor.

According to Hardt and Negri, the Empire has completely destroyed the traditional opposition; the old politics is dead and we are facing the end of history, if by that term we signify the revolution to displace one form of centralized state power by another. In *A Thousand Plateaus,* the force of molecular politics—the highly decentralized efforts of small groups to forge new social spaces at the local level—is counterposed to molar politics, the affairs of state. They point to the long-term challenges to state science as well. Their alternative sciences do not work in the solid, geometric mode but in the fluid mode: nature is not portrayed in terms of gravitas but in terms of flows. The figure of the nomad is posed against the state apparatus. Hardt and Negri take at least one step backward from these theses, which were crafted in the aftermath of the May 1968 events in France and the Italian "Hot Autumn" the following year. Deleuze and Guattari condemn the Marxist parties for failing to anticipate the May events, a failure they ascribe to Marxism's imprisonment in the politics of centralized state power. Rather than looking above, the Marxists should look below to the conditions not of formal statecraft, but of rhizomic discontent. But, echoing Foucault's notion that power is dispersed, is everywhere, Hardt and Negri posit concrete social groups as the new agents. According to them, the proletariat as political subject has disappeared. They assert the disappearance of the mediations between a severely crippled labor movement and global capital. The new agent of opposition is the "multitude"—the great mass of humanity who have been marginalized and otherwise repressed by the Empire. The characteristic form of social action is a "direct confrontation" between multitude and Empire.

In *State, Power, Socialism,* Poulantzas challenges the basic premise of this type of analysis by arguing that the true opposite of the territorial is not the nomadic, but rather the ancient Western conception of space as a homogeneous field that has a center but has no limits:

> The space of Western Antiquity is a space with a *centre:* the *polis* (which itself has a center: the *agora*). But it has no frontiers in the modern sense of the term. It is concentric, but, having no real outside, it is also open. This centre (the *polis* and *agora*) is inscribed in a space whose essential characteristics are homogeneity and symmetry, not differentiation and hierarchy. . . . In this space (which is the one represented by Euclid and the Phythagoreans) people do not change their position, they simply move around. They always go to the same place, because each point in space is an exact repetition of the previous point; when they found colonies, it is only to form replicas of Athens or Rome. (Poulantzas 1978, 101)

What is significant about this point is that modern territoriality is not opposed to the ancient conception of space based simply on logical deduction, but by looking to the historicity of political space and seeking its determinations. For Poulantzas, the mistake of Deleuze and Guattari (and thus Hardt and Negri as well) is that they fail to recognize the importance of the division of labor and everyday life to this historicity of space.[4] The space of ancient, and even feudal, societies has no territorial boundaries because the hierarchies particular to these societies are not segmented spatial ones, but rather are based on the immobility of social position given the ascribed status of class. Before the capitalist division of labor, there is no escaping to the big city to "reinvent" yourself, there is no moving to "America" for the good life, no running away to join the circus. In this preterritorial space, "Delimitations are constantly intersecting and overlapping in a series of twists and turns; and subjects, while remaining on the spot, move around in accordance with the changes of the lords and sovereigns to whom they are personally tied" (Poulantzas 1978, 103). Here, the dream of the nomadic faces its mirror image, movement without change, smooth spaces from which there is no escape.

With the rise of capitalism, the limitation and segmentation of space and its (re)production by the state become paramount.

> The direct producer, the worker, is now totally separated from the means of labour—a situation which is at the root of the social division of labour in machine production and large-scale industry. The latter involves as its precondition an entirely different spacial matrix: *the serial, fractured, parcelled, cellular, and irreversible* space which is peculiar to the Taylorist

> division of labour on the factory assembly line. Although this space also becomes homogenous in the end, it does so only through a second-degree and problematic homogenization, which arises on the basis of its essential segmentation and gaps. Already at this level, the matrix space has a twofold dimension: it is composed of gaps, breaks, successive fracturings, closures and frontiers; but it has no end: capitalist labour process tend towards world-wide application (expanded co-operation). It may be said that the separation of the direct producer from his means of labour and his liberation from personal bonds involve a process of deterritorialization. But the naturalist image peddled by this term is no more exact in this context than it is elsewhere. The whole process is inscribed in a fresh space, which precisely involves closures and successive segmentations. In this modern space, people change *ad infinitum* by traversing separations in which each place is defined by its distance from others; they spread out in this space by assimilating and homogenizing new segments in the act of shifting their frontiers. (Ibid., 103–4)

This means that territoriality is a property not simply of a "state," but of the capitalist state. It means that the dialectic of the inside and the outside, so basic to territoriality as we know it and as Deleuze and Guattari define it, is fundamentally and necessarily tied to capitalist exploitation and its organization/reproduction by the state. It also means that arguments such as those given by Hardt and Negri are fundamentally flawed because there is no space "outside" of the nation-state in which power can reside (for additional arguments against the globalization thesis, see the essays by Jessop, Panitch, and Tsoukalas in this volume). The inside-outside dialectic is only proper to one of the spatial dimensions that Poulantzas speaks of—the fractured, segmented, that is, vertical, space of capitalist society and its division of labor. The horizontal space of capitalism has no limits, no "beyond" the nation-state and its organs of power. It is simply a question of what nation-state you happen to be in and what your position is within the spatial hierarchies of that class society. The metaphorical statements of Hardt and Negri about power residing "above" or "over" or "beyond" the territoriality of the state are necessarily incorrect unless some space other than that of the state and its corresponding rhythms of everyday life can be identified as being the generator and locus of alternative political power. This is not to say that territoriality is here to stay; it is to say that unless there are alternative spatial and institutional organizations of power, there can be no question of going beyond the centrality of the state.

The nation-states remain a mainstay of global arrangements. To take a contemporary example, the executive committees of the main institutions of globalization—the International Monetary Fund (IMF) and the World Bank (WB)—are composed of the finance ministers of the leading capitalist powers, who in turn retain close ties with the chief transnational corporations. In Hardt and Negri's analysis, there are no mediations because they have eluded performing the necessary work of investigating the institutional basis of the Empire's power. Just as the French and Italian Communist parties could not anticipate the movements from below that disrupted ordinary life and state power in their respective countries in the late 1960s because they were looking in the wrong direction, Hardt and Negri could not anticipate the protests that occurred in Seattle in December 1999, in April 2000 in Washington, D.C., and in Genoa in 2001 precisely against the institutions of the Empire. As we write these lines, groups all over the world greet every meeting of the IMF, WB, and World Trade Organization (WTO) with militant protests, often using direct action to make their presence felt and to articulate their demands. In December 1999, a march of fifty thousand demonstrators, most of whom were trade unionists, successfully shut down the WTO meetings and everyday life for several days in Seattle, sounding a gong that has been heard around the world. The alliances that are being forged in these struggles are, indeed, molecular: they are composed of environmentalists, trade unionists, women's groups, sex radicals, anarchists, New Leftists, and other unlikely partners. But the struggles, although international in scope and the alliances, are conducted with the political culture, as well as the borders, of the nation-states. In Seattle and Washington, the slogans were incurably American, the pledge and practice of "nonviolence" was a direct legacy of the 1960s civil rights movement, and the call for democratic access to institutional decision making was in the tradition of New Left participatory democratic discourse. To the extent that rhetoric always contains a strong cultural dimension, the internationalist protests against the Empire's key institutions were distinct national mediations.

The failure to see the possibilities is directly related to the theory: if there are no mediations such as institutions that are repositories of power; if there are no class agents; if the movements have been decimated beyond recognition, then this focused and highly organized series of demonstrations can hardly be conceived. In the end, Hardt and Negri are left with "nomadic" intellectuals linked, somewhat mystically, to multitudes without definition. This practical mélange may be connected to a deeper flaw: the sin of theoreticism. Confining itself to a highly abstract series of concepts, the discourse borders on formalism and, because references to practices, which inevitably entail analysis of the interventions of specific social groups, are absent, Negri and Hardt are left in the embarrassing position of rendering an ultimately apolitical discourse. *Empire* is bereft of practice largely because it posits the impossibility of any agency other than those who have been wrenched from territory. But, although Deleuze is right to contrast molecular to molar levels of political practice, the state remains an arena for politics because, among other reasons, its territories, both geographic and political, albeit segmented, remain pertinent to popular need.

Of course, it is not only Hardt and Negri who tend to ignore the role of institutions qua mediations. Strangely enough, self-proclaimed neo-institutionalist (or, state-centered) approaches have done the most to diminish the analysis of institutions. Neo-institutionalism tends to follow two trends. One trend (the most famous example being the work of Theda Skocpol) views state institutions as social agents. The other trend views state institutions not as actors but as constraints that encourage or discourage various policy outcomes (perhaps the best example of this tendency is the collection edited by Weaver and Rockman, 1993). Both are great retreats from the advancements in institutional analysis championed by Poulantzas and Offe with their concept of structural selectivity, Jessop and his concept of strategic selectivity, and even Miliband with his C. Wright Mills–like approach for understanding the interpersonal linkages between state and corporate institutions.[5] Now, we can either, following Skocpol, posit the autonomy of state power and, without any reference to the practices and struggles that actually take place in these settings, assume that all institutions act, whenever possible, to further their own corporate interests (thus fetishizing institutions). Or we can, following Weaver and Rockman, revert to typical systems-theory–like analysis of looking to inputs and outputs in order to find some correlations that will, presumably, tell us what kind of institutional arrangements are best for dealing with various kinds of policy areas.[6] In both cases, the spaces and practices of institutions are never studied because institutions are either assumed to be one social actor among many or they are conceived of as independent variables that are not to be explained or examined, but only used to help understand why some law was passed.

In contrast to these approaches, neo-Marxist theory always gave great importance to explaining capitalist institutional spaces and the practices within them. Take the case of education. Following Antonio Gramsci's insistence that questions of educational reform are crucial to any project of political intervention, Louis Althusser has argued that in societies ruled primarily by consent rather than by force, schooling is the main ideological state apparatus. Both were very aware that, unlike previous modes of production, capitalism with its segmented spaces and the separation of worker from means of production relies on the institutions of the state in the broad sense in order to secure the expanded reproduction of society. No longer do the economic spaces, as had been the case with slave and feudal societies, reproduce themselves in a simple way. Even the casual observer recognizes the mediating functions of schooling today. Buffeted by cultural and economic pressures—mainly the fact that women have rejected their traditional role as household manager and, in any case, are being integrated into the paid labor force—the bourgeois family (the model for all social classes in these societies) has become an unreliable institution for the social discipline of the young. Even though the traditional mythologies associated with nationalism and patriotism may have suffered damage in advanced capitalist societies and, owing to globalization and labor migration, the existence of a singular national culture is seriously in doubt, the degree to which education represents social hope for working and middle classes would confound anyone who is attracted to the romance of deterritorialized, nomadic agents. Of course, at the intellectual level, Marxist critics have been able to puncture the myth of the link between education and class mobility. Bourdieu has shown how education, especially cultural capital, actually reproduces the class system, even if a few from the lower orders are permitted to attain positions of technical authority. But these debunking activities pale in comparison to the lived experience of the striving classes: having been deprived of stable working-class jobs by the application of neoliberal economic policies, many who once disdained formal education and its curriculum have opted to spend five years or more beyond secondary school to learn how to become a socialized worker in computers, management, engineering, and other technical occupations. Moreover, most experience this decision as having been coerced by the realities of the labor market, which, with the exception of skilled trades, simply offers few well-paying industrial jobs.

No mediations? Try the steady erosion of the health care systems in advanced capitalist countries. In the United States, where there was never a universal health plan, tens of millions of people received adequate care under prepaid programs negotiated under collective bargaining agreements in the public and private sectors and emulated by nonunion companies, often as a means to keep the union at bay. The disappearance of well-paid factory jobs has placed many of these plans at risk. The advent of "managed" care, a health care austerity program aimed at cutting costs, has resulted in severe delimitation of the extent of coverage, with millions losing their benefits and a decline in the quality of care. It would surprise those who try to comprehend the effects of globalization without an institutional analysis that this question has been thrust to the center of electoral and labor struggle.

What is more surprising is that any political intellectual living in these societies at the turn of the twenty-first century could miss the significance of the mediations of education and health, especially as they affect everyday life. To theorize that the mediating institutions constructed in the era of regulated capitalism have undergone profound transformations in the past quarter century is simply not the same as declaring that they have disappeared. For example, schooling remains, among other functions, an efficient aging vat and warehouse of labor power. It is also the site of the socialization of the costs of training a qualified, increasingly flexible, and disciplined labor force for capital's use. Education remains a huge industry, absorbing tens of billions of dollars in every capitalist society, especially the most technically and economically developed. Health care is a major outlet for capital investment and is being relentlessly privatized, precisely because of its profitability.

Beyond the practical and historical argument remains a theoretical one: geographic, political, and social space has been transformed by globalization and by the demands of empire. That the transnationals constitute a parallel "metastate" with close interlocks with nation-states is highly likely, and, as we have seen, they share with the states common institutions of coordination and control over both advanced and developing countries. But, as Bob Jessop shows, Poulantzas's discussion of processes of internationalization is at once a strategic, that is, a political intervention, and a theoretical advance over earlier work in Marxist state theory. Jessop reveals the degree to which Poulantzas modifies the traditional theory of imperialism by separating out the United States, with its unique postwar international power and role, from other "imperialist powers." According to Jessop, Poulantzas's analysis anticipates later work on "Atlantic Fordism," even though in other respects he did not anticipate its subsequent crisis or the growth of East Asian capitalism. Yet, Poulantzas was acutely aware of the appearance of regional differences within an otherwise regulated global imperialism and, in this sense, continued to insist on that which the Deleuzian Empire thesis denies: the continued importance of territory administered by the state as the context for capital accumulation, international power relations, and political struggle. As he puts it:

> capital is a relationship between capital and labour; and it is because it moves in the *inter*national spatial matrix of the labour and exploitation process that capital can reproduce itself only through *trans*nationalization—however deterritorialized and a-national its various forms appear to be. (Poulantzas 1978, 106)

Indeed, regional power blocs—the most ubiquitous is undoubtedly the European Union (EU)—have altered the international landscape. Since the 1970s, they have been in conflict with their constituent nation-states over a wide range of issues: the demand for a common currency; the demand on the constituent states to weaken their welfare programs; uniform reductions in subsidies for agriculture and other state-protected sectors, even as the demand for eliminating intrastate trade barriers proceeds. As we have seen over the past couple of decades, the economic, political, and cultural implications of trying to institute the euro as even a partial replacement for the pound, mark, and franc has elicited enormous opposition and, as for the standard of reduced state welfare budgets, this proposal generated mass demonstrations in France in 1995, has resulted in victories for social-democratic and labor parties throughout Europe, and produced a new wave of anti-Americanism in many of its capitals.

The essays in this volume represent more than a sign that a discredited Marxist theory of the state refuses to lie in its grave. Although the editors are acutely aware that the traditional theory of imperialism no longer accounts for the character of international political-economic relations and that its privileging of the nation-state as a theoretical and practical site needs serious modifications, many of which are discussed by various contributors, the invocation of the work of Miliband and Poulantzas, among others, should be read as a positive intervention in an ongoing debate. Surely, for those who have abandoned class and class struggle, this book is a provocation. In sync with the theoretical underpinnings of historical materialism, we remain convinced that social struggles, equally at the international and the national planes, entail strategic as well as analytic attention to the mediations between the relations at the level of production, consumption, and distribution, the spheres of civil society where social groups discuss and fight out their worldviews, as well as contest for ideological hegemony, and the state where issues of power, including those having to do with a wide array of institutions and their bureaucracies, are contested. We believe the essays contained herein make a contribution to the revitalization of the theory of the state because, in every instance, they continue to take seriously political economy on the one side, and ideological and cultural issues on the other. At the same time, nearly all contributors are committed to a secular-radical view in which what has been surpassed by History is ruthlessly criticized and abandoned. As Marx once quipped, "to be radical is to go to the root and to make a ruthless critique of everything." The successes and shortcomings of this volume may be measured by that standard.

Notes

1. Notable among the few attempts to provide such a critique are Easton (1981), Skocpol (1980), and van den Berg (1988). None of these works, however, attained a sufficient degree of acceptance or popularity to constitute a definitive or fatal critique of state theory.
2. It is interesting to note that in Asia and Latin America, where political struggles are still overt and politics has not reached the degree of fetishization present in Europe and North America, state theory has continued to enjoy a significant following. For example, in Brazil there still exist "Poulantzasian" departments of political science (notably, the Federal University of Paraná).
3. As a corollary to this technicalization, we see the proliferation of the view that politics and the legal process are mere spectacles to be consumed (from Court TV and the Gulf War to the infatuation with the Clinton scandals). Of course, in this "society of the spectacle," the popular classes become increasingly marginal actors.
4. In this way, Poulantzas is much closer to Henri Lefebvre than to the Deleuze–Guattari school.
5. For more on these concepts, see the essays in this volume by Barrow, Bratsis, and Codato and Perissinotto.

6. It is striking that a collection with such a direct title *(Do Institutions Matter?)* spends very little time examining institutions. Rather than examine specific institutions, the book is organized around differing interinstitutional relations of the broadest level: the four "regime types" of separation of powers (the United States), coalitional (Italy), party government (France and England), and single-party dominant (Japan and Mexico) (cf. Weaver and Rockman 1993, 448). These regime types are evaluated by their policy "capabilities," which Weaver and Rockman define as "a pattern of government influence on its environment that produces substantially similar outcomes across time and policy areas" (6). Particular capabilities examined include setting and maintaining priorities, coordinating conflicting objectives, and managing political cleavages. "Capabilities" are stressed over policy content because policy preferences are not the same for different societies, and thus it becomes very misleading to compare regimes on the substance of their policies. Through a series of statistical case studies designed to show any correlations between these "regime types" and a series of "capabilities" (such as cleavage management and maintaining international agreements), the authors attempt to discover the agency of these institutional forms. At the end of more than four hundred pages of analysis, the authors conclude that institutions matter but are unable to explain exactly why they matter, for correlations do not equal causal analysis, and they must resort to speculation about possible explanations.

References

Carrillo, Santiago. 1978. *Eurocommunism and the State.* Westport, Conn.: Lawrence Hill and Company.

Deleuze, Gilles, and Félix Guattari. 1987. *A Thousand Plateaus: Capitalism and Schizophrenia.* Trans. Brian Massumi. Minneapolis: University of Minnesota Press.

Easton, David. 1981. "The Political System Besieged by the State." *Political Theory* 9(3): 303–25.

Evans, Peter, Dietrich Rueshemeyer, and Theda Skocpol, eds. 1985. *Bringing the State Back In: Contemporary and Historical Perspectives.* Cambridge: Cambridge University Press.

Hardt, Michael, and Antonio Negri. 2000. *Empire.* Cambridge: Harvard University Press.

Jessop, Bob. 1985. *Nicos Poulantzas: Marxist Theory and Political Strategy.* New York: St. Martin's Press.

Lash, Scott, and John Urry. 1987. *The End of Organized Capitalism.* Madison: University of Wisconsin Press.

Offe, Claus. 1985. *Disorganized Capitalism.* Cambridge: MIT Press.

Poulantzas, Nicos. 1978. *State, Power, Socialism.* London: Verso Books.

Skocpol, Theda. 1980. "Political Response to Capitalist Crisis: Neo-Marxist Theories of the State and the Case of the New Deal." *Politics and Society* 10: 155–201.

van den Berg, Axel. 1988. *The Immanent Utopia: From Marxism on the State to the State of Marxism.* Princeton, N.J.: Princeton University Press.

Weaver, R. Kent, and Bert A. Rockman, eds. 1993. *Do Institutions Matter?* Washington, D.C.: Brookings Institute.

Žižek, Slavoj. 1989. *The Sublime Object of Ideology.* New York: Verso Books.

I

Miliband and Poulantzas in Review

CHAPTER ONE

The Miliband–Poulantzas Debate

An Intellectual History

Clyde W. Barrow

> In the Marxist scheme, the "ruling class" of capitalist society is that class which owns and controls the means of production and which is able, by virtue of the economic power thus conferred upon it, to use the state as its instrument for the domination of society.
>
> —RALPH MILIBAND, 1969

> The state has the particular function of constituting the factor of cohesion between the levels of a social formation. This is precisely the meaning of the Marxist conception of the state as a factor of "order"... as the regulating factor of its global equilibrium as a system.
>
> —NICOS POULANTZAS, 1978b

What Is the Miliband–Poulantzas Debate?

The publication of Nicos Poulantzas's *Pouvoir politique et classes sociales* (1968) and Ralph Miliband's *The State in Capitalist Society* (1969) initiated a return to the state in political science and sociology (Easton 1981; Evans, Rueschemeyer, and Skocpol 1985; Comninel 1987; Therborn 1987; Almond 1988), but it simultaneously fractured Marxist political theory into pieces that may never be reassembled (Barrow 1993; Alford and Friedland 1985; Carnoy 1984; Jessop 1982). Miliband observes that prior to the publication of his book, Marxists had "made little notable attempt to confront the question of the state" since Lenin. The one exception to this claim was Poulantzas's *Pouvoir politique et classes sociales,* which

Miliband (1969, 6, 7 n. 1) describes favorably as "a major attempt at a theoretical elaboration of the Marxist 'model' of the state." Similarly, after the publication of Miliband's *The State in Capitalist Society*, Poulantzas (1969, 67) praised the book as "extremely substantial" and indicated that "he cannot recommend its reading too highly." However, Poulantzas's praise was qualified by "a few critical comments" that set off a series of exchanges in the *New Left Review* that became known as the Miliband–Poulantzas debate (Miliband 1970a, 1973; Poulantzas 1969, 1976).

The debate was never confined exclusively to Miliband and Poulantzas; political theorists and political sociologists quickly lined up on either side of the debate, and particularly over whether Miliband's "instrumentalist" theory of the state or Poulantzas's "structuralist" theory of the state was *the Marxist* theory of the state (Gold, Lo, and Wright 1975a, 1975b; Jessop 1977). Moreover, the debate itself remains symptomatic of unresolved epistemological issues within Marxism that have far-reaching methodological repercussions beyond state theory. Therefore, the Miliband–Poulantzas debate was never just a conceptual or empirical disagreement about the nature of the capitalist state; it was from the beginning an epistemological dispute over whether there is any such thing as a specifically Marxist methodology.[1]

Thus, on the one hand, the Miliband–Poulantzas debate is a watershed in the development of Marxist political theory. On the other hand, it brought into sharp relief a methodological impasse that has persisted since Eduard Bernstein (1961) first argued that there is no such thing as a Marxist methodology and Georg Lukács (1971, 1) replied that Marxist theory refers exclusively to a method. Consequently, the debate captured the attention of radical scholars for almost ten years, but by the end of the 1970s, the debate became sterile as Marxist theorists again found it impossible to move beyond these methodological antinomies.[2]

In reconstructing the Miliband–Poulantzas debate, I do not claim to answer the original epistemological question posed by Bernstein and Lukács as to whether there is a Marxist methodology in some abstract sense of the term. However, as a particular historical observation, I do argue that there is nothing peculiarly "Marxist" about the methodologies employed by Miliband or Poulantzas. In my book *Critical Theories of the State*, I advanced this thesis as a mere assertion and it is my intention to document that claim with more specificity in this essay.[3] At the same time, it is my contention that the conceptual aspects derived strictly from "the Marxian classics" by Miliband and Poulantzas are embedded in problems of textual interpretation that cannot be resolved by further appeals to the Marxian corpus.

Background to the Debate

The Miliband–Poulantzas debate erupted within a paradoxical historical context defined by the political rebellions of 1968 and the dominance of a social science preoccupied with "pluralism" and "system equilibrium." The two sides of this contradiction were mediated by a student, intellectual, and cultural revolt that revived Marxism inside the universities of the advanced capitalist societies (Ollman 1982). Not coincidentally, Miliband and Poulantzas were public intellectuals already engaged in this ideological struggle, and, surprising as it may sound, they both shared similar conceptions of "the Marxist tradition" and considered it the main alternative to the dominant "bourgeois social science." In fact, the two books that precipitated their initial debate appeared within a year of each other at the global apogee (1968–69) of the domestic and colonial insurrections in and against advanced capitalism.

Biographical Background: The 1960s

In a sense, Miliband and Poulantzas were both expatriates and refugees who fled repressive regimes early in their lives. Miliband was born in Brussels in 1924 to Polish-Jewish immigrants.[4] He joined his first socialist youth organization at age fifteen and fled to England with his father in 1940 literally on the last boat to leave Belgium before Nazi troops captured Ostend. Two years later, at age seventeen, Miliband entered the London School of Economics (LSE) specifically to study with Harold Laski (Miliband 1993). Miliband began teaching at LSE in the early 1950s. He remained at LSE until the late 1970s, when he left for North America to take up a series of teaching posts at Brandeis University, York University, and, finally, the City University of New York Graduate Center. He had just retired from CUNY shortly before his death in 1994 at age seventy.

Miliband was an independent socialist intellectual who never joined an established political party, but instead promoted the building of a new socialist *movement* that would steer a path between Leninist vanguardism and Labourist revisionism. Miliband's first book, *Parliamentary Socialism* (1961) was a critique of the British Labour Party and of the electoral and bureaucratic mechanisms that diverted the party from pursuing more radical objectives (Saville 1995). During this time, Miliband was a founding editor of the *New Left Review* and a cofounder of the *Socialist Register* (which he coedited with John Saville for thirty years).[5] He was also active in the British peace movement, the anti-Vietnam War movement, and numerous other campaigns against social and political oppression. In the 1980s, Miliband was a founder of the Socialist Society, which helped convene several conferences to provide a new voice for socialists outside the British Labour Party. In the final decade of his life, he was calling for a new socialist party capable of forging an alliance between labor and the new social movements (Allender 1996). Miliband's intellectual reputation derives primarily from his book *The State in Capitalist Society*, which, as George Ross (1994, 572) points out, was responsible more than any other single work for "bringing the state back into political science and sociology." Indeed, by the mid-1970s, Miliband was near the top of the American Political Science Association's list of most-cited political scientists and, at the height of his popularity, was probably "the leading Marxist political scientist in the English-speaking world" (Blackburn 1994, 15).

Nicos Poulantzas was born in Athens in 1936, where he lived through the Nazi occupation and the Greek civil war. Poulantzas received his baccalaureate from the Institut Français in 1953 and then entered the University of Athens School of Law. Although active in various political movements as a youth, it was not until the early 1960s, after Poulantzas had moved to Paris, that he became a card-carrying member of the Greek Communist Party (Jessop 1985, chap. 1). Poulantzas was a professor of legal philosophy at the Sorbonne from 1961 to 1964 and he continued teaching at French universities until his death in 1979. By the time he published *Pouvoir politique et classes sociales* in 1968, he was already well known in French intellectual circles, primarily through his association with the "existential Marxists" at *Les Temps modernes*. However, shortly after joining the editorial board of *Les Temps modernes* in 1964, Poulantzas was increasingly influenced by the British Marxists gathering around the *New Left Review*, by the works of Antonio Gramsci, but most especially by the structuralist Marxism of Louis Althusser (Hirsch 1981; Poster 1975).

Poulantzas's reputation as a state theorist was secured by the publication of *Pouvoir politique et classes sociales*, which appeared only a few days before the May days of 1968 (Jessop 1985, 9–25; see Singer 1970 and

Touraine 1971 for background). However, Poulantzas was catapulted to prominence within the English-speaking left with his review of Miliband's book in the *New Left Review* and, shortly thereafter, increasing interest in Poulantzas's work led to its translation in 1973. Goran Therborn observes that "in the first half of the 1970s, Nicos Poulantzas was arguably the most influential living political theorist in the world," whose works influenced left-wing academics and political activists throughout Europe, North America, and Latin America (Therborn 1987, 1230). Similarly, Bob Jessop (1985, 5–6), who has written the most extensive intellectual biography of Poulantzas, suggests that "it is no exaggeration to claim that Poulantzas remains the single most important and influential Marxist theorist of the state and politics in the post-war period"; for even where Poulantzas's contributions have been superseded by more recent work, he has often "set the terms of debate."[6]

Intellectual Background: Bourgeois Social Science

In the late 1960s, however, the terms of debate in social science and political theory were being defined by theories that could not account for the existence, much less the magnitude, of rebellion within the advanced capitalist societies (Young 1977). The concept of the state and state power had been replaced in academic sociology and political science by a concept of "political system" that Miliband identifies with the works of David Easton and Robert A. Dahl. David Easton (1953, 106) had played a major role in initiating the behavioral revolution more than a decade earlier with his declaration that "neither the state nor power is a concept that serves to bring together political research." In urging political scientists to abandon the analysis of state and power, Easton proposed that scholars examine instead "those interactions through which values are authoritatively allocated for a society." Furthermore, Easton (1965, 21–23) emphasized that to account for the persistence of political systems, one had to assume that they successfully generate two "system outputs": (1) the political system must be able to allocate values *for a society,* and (2) the political system must *induce* most members to accept these allocations as binding, at least most of the time. The bulk of Easton's theoretical and empirical work during the 1950s and 1960s was on the "support inputs" that stabilize and equilibrate political systems.

As Miliband (1969, 3) observes, systems analysis was tied closely to "a democratic-pluralist view" of society that came "to dominate political science and political sociology." Robert A. Dahl was certainly the single most important proponent of pluralist theory among the icons of the behavioral revolution. The significance of pluralist theory is that it seemed to explain how the political system *induces* most citizens to accept decisions as binding most of the time. As Dahl (1959, 36) pointed out, pluralist theory assumes

> that there are a number of loci for arriving at political decisions . . . business men, trade unions, politicians, consumers, farmers, voters and many other aggregates all have an impact on policy outcomes; that none of these aggregates is homogeneous for all purposes; that each of them is highly influential over some scopes but weak over many others; and that the power to reject undesired alternatives is more common than the power to dominate over outcomes directly.

Thus, as Miliband (1969, 2, 3) concludes, the state seemed unimportant to mainstream social science only because it implicitly assumed, or more often explicitly asserted, a pluralist theory of the state. Importantly, Miliband notes that because "a theory of the state is also a theory of society and of the distribution of power in that society," pluralist assumptions tended "to exclude, by definition, the notion that the state might be a rather special institution, whose main purpose is to defend the predominance in society of a particular class."

Although Miliband has often been chastised by structuralists for allowing bourgeois social science to set the methodological terms of his analysis, Poulantzas was responding to a parallel intellectual context. Poulantzas (1978b, 19) explicitly derides French political science as "underdeveloped" and, consequently, he calls explicit attention to the fact that he made "frequent recourse" to works by British and American authors. These authors include Talcott Parsons, David Easton, Gabriel Almond, David Apter, and Karl Deutsch—a virtual pantheon of the systems analysis and structural-functionalist movements in American social science. As Poulantzas was aware, in Parsonian systems analysis,

> the political component of the social system is a center of integration for all the aspects of this system which analysis can separate, not the sociological scene of a particular class of social phenomena. (Parsons 1951, 126)[7]

Similarly, although relying more on the structural functionalism of Robert K. Merton, David Apter (1958) defined the "political" as a structure with "defined responsibilities for the maintenance of the system of which it is a part." Likewise, Gabriel Almond and James Coleman (1960, 12) identified the function of the political system within the overall social system as the crucial "boundary maintenance function." Importantly, Poulantzas (1978b, 47 n. 17) cites these works favorably, even if critically, in a section titled "The General Function of the State" as examples of how contemporary political science was "beginning to emphasize the role of the political as the factor of maintenance of a formation's unity."[8] Thus, if Miliband was preoccupied with challenging bourgeois social science within the methodological parameters defined by behavioralist methodology and pluralist theory, Poulantzas was also working through a methodological position that is directly traceable to the systems analysis and structural functionalism of Parsons, Almond, and Apter. It is ironic that so much of the Miliband–Poulantzas debate came to revolve around the question of *Marxist* methodology when there was nothing peculiarly Marxist about either author's *methodological* approach.

Intellectual Background: The Marxist Tradition

Nevertheless, Miliband and Poulantzas both challenged the dominance of bourgeois social science by drawing on a Marxist tradition that each of them identified with the writings of Marx, Engels, Lenin, and Gramsci. Miliband (1969, 5) argues quite explicitly that "the most important alternative to the pluralist-democratic view of power remains the Marxist one." Miliband (1977, 1) identifies "classical Marxism" with "the writings of Marx, Engels, and Lenin and, at a different level, [with] those of some other figures such as Rosa Luxemburg, Gramsci, and Trotsky." Miliband's (1969, 5) interpretation of classical Marxism was based on his observation that Marx "never attempted a systematic study of the state." Miliband was well aware of the fact that "this was one of the tasks which he [Marx] hoped to undertake as part of a vast scheme of work which he had projected in the 1850s but of which volume I of *Capital* was the only fully finished part." Hence, most of Marx's political writings "are for the most part the product of particular historical episodes and specific circumstances; and what there is of theoretical exploration of politics . . . is mostly unsystematic and fragmentary, and often part of other work" (Miliband 1977, 1–2). Miliband identifies the *political* writings of classical Marxism primarily with Marx's *Eighteenth Brumaire of Louis Bonaparte* and *The Civil War in France* and with Lenin's *What Is to*

Be Done? and *State and Revolution.* Significantly, although references to the state in different types of society constantly recur in almost all of Marx's writings, Miliband concludes in the final analysis that

> as far as capitalist societies are concerned, his [Marx's] main view of the state throughout is summarised in the famous formulation of the *Communist Manifesto:* "The executive of the modern state is but a committee for managing the affairs of the whole bourgeoisie." (Ibid., 5)[9]

Miliband claims that this thesis "reappears again and again in the work of both Marx and Engels; and despite the refinements and qualifications they occasionally introduce in their discussion of the state . . . they never departed from the view that in capitalist society the state was above all the coercive instrument of a ruling class, itself defined in terms of its ownership and control of the means of production" (ibid.).[10] Miliband (1969, 6) considered Lenin's *State and Revolution* to be merely "a restatement and an elaboration of the main view of the state" found in *The Communist Manifesto,* and that after Lenin "the only major Marxist contribution to the theory of the state has been that of Antonio Gramsci."[11]

Miliband identifies the chief deficiency of contemporary Marxist political theory as the fact that nearly all Marxists have been content to assert the thesis articulated in *The Communist Manifesto* as more or less self-evident. Thus, for Miliband, the primary objective in renewing state theory was "to confront the question of the state in the light of the concrete socio-economic *and* political *and* cultural reality of actual capitalist societies." Miliband suggests that Marx provided a conceptual foundation for the socio-economic analysis of capitalist societies, Lenin provided guidance for a political analysis, and Gramsci supplied the conceptual apparatus for a cultural and ideological analysis of capitalist societies. Hence, Miliband was convinced that the central thesis and conceptual structure of Marxist political theory was effectively in place and that what Marxism needed was empirical and historical analysis to give concrete content to this thesis and its theoretical concepts. The intended purpose of *The State in Capitalist Society* was "to make a contribution to remedying that deficiency" (Miliband 1969, 7).

Poulantzas's *Political Power and Social Classes* (1978b, 1, 42) also claims to draw on the classical texts of Marx, Engels, Lenin, and Gramsci and "to provide a systematic political theory by elucidating implicit ideas and axioms in their practical writings." However, it will come as no surprise that Poulantzas's epistemological attitude toward these texts was far more complex and problematic than Miliband's position. In *Political Power and Social Classes*, Poulantzas cites Louis Althusser's (1969) work as the basis for his claim that Marxism consists of two united but distinct disciplines called dialectical materialism and historical materialism. According to Poulantzas (1978b, 11), dialectical materialism (i.e., Marxist philosophy) "has as its particular object the production of knowledge; that is the structure and functioning of thought." Marxist philosophy is essentially a process of reading the classic texts rigorously *to produce the concepts necessary to an understanding of history and society.*[12] Althusserian structuralists viewed the historical development of Marx's own thought as exemplary of this process and to that extent they emphasized a distinction between the young Marx and the mature Marx. For Althusserians, including Poulantzas, Marx did not become a "Marxist" until he wrote *The German Ideology*, which constituted his "epistemological break" with bourgeois categories of thought, although Marx's thought does not reach full maturity until the publication of *Capital* (Therborn 1976).

Thus, whereas Miliband places Marx and Engels's *Communist Manifesto* at the center of Marxist political theory, Poulantzas (1978b, 20) identifies *Capital* as "the major theoretical work of Marxism."[13] Nevertheless, Poulantzas's (1978b, 21) reading of *Capital* leads to the parallel conclusion that while providing "a systematic theoretical treatment of the economic region" of the capitalist mode of production (CMP), there is "no systematic theory of ideology . . . to be found in *Capital*. . . nor is there a theory of politics in it." Hence, with respect to political theory, Poulantzas understood that an Althusserian epistemology had to deal with two problems from the outset: (1) problems related to the "raw material" of theoretical production, and (2) problems concerning the status of what texts among the Marxist classics count as "political."

The chief difficulty in designating *Capital* as the central theoretical work of Marxism is that it is an unfinished work. It contains no theory of social class, no theory of the state, no theory of transition from one mode of production to another and yet it explicitly intends to address those issues. The known gap between what Marx intended in *Capital* and what he accomplished before his death leaves a text that is rife with lacunae, omissions, and stated intentions that are never fulfilled in fact. Hence, Marxist philosophers, particularly Althusserian structuralists, are faced with the task of not only clarifying the existing text, but of completing the existing text. For Althusserians, Engels's role as editor of the final volumes of *Capital*, and his role in explicating various ideas in *Anti-Dühring* and *The Origin of the Family, Private Property, and the State* provides an exemplary model of the type of intellectual production involved in completing the central text. Therefore, Poulantzas concludes that to produce a theory of the capitalist state, it is not only necessary to "Read Capital," but to "Write Capital" (or at least its political equivalent). Interestingly, Poulantzas concurs with Miliband that, after Engels, it was Lenin and Gramsci who did most to advance this task.

Unfortunately, as Poulantzas observes, these Marxist classics do not specifically discuss politics and the state at the same level of theoretical *systematicity* as one finds in Marx's *Capital*. Thus, Poulantzas (1978b, 19) emphasizes that,

> in order to use the texts of the Marxist classics as a source of information, particularly on the capitalist state, it has been necessary to complete them and to subject them to a particular critical treatment. Because of the non-systematic character of these texts, the information contained in them sometimes appears incomplete or even inexact.

Consequently, for Poulantzas (ibid., 21), the concepts required for a theory of the capitalist state are merely *implicit* in the texts of the Marxist classics. Importantly, in sorting out the issue of which classic texts count as political, he distinguishes between those theoretical texts that "deal with political science in its abstract-formal form, i.e., the state in general, class struggle in general, the capitalist state in general," and "the political texts in the strict sense of the term." Among the former, Poulantzas includes Marx's *Critique of the Gotha Programme* and *The Civil War in France*; Engels's *Anti-Dühring*; Lenin's *State and Revolution*; and Gramsci's *Notes on Machiavelli*. It is interesting that Poulantzas never clearly defines "the political texts in the strict sense of the term," although his subsequent citations indicate that they include Marx's *The Poverty of Philosophy*; Engels's *Origin of the Family, Private Property, and the State*; Lenin's *What Is to Be Done?*; Gramsci's *Prison Notebooks*; and numerous pamphlets by Lenin and personal letters by Marx. It is remarkable that the one prominent classic not included on this list is *The Communist Manifesto*—the one work that Miliband considered key to a Marxist theory of the state.[14]

Yet, not only did Miliband and Poulantzas see two different Marxes, their different epistemological conceptions of how one engages in a Marxian social science is further clarified by contrasting Miliband's preoccupation with fact gathering to Poulantzas's insistence on concept production. According to Poulantzas, historical materialism is the actual "science of history" constructed through the use and application of Marxist categories of knowledge derived through dialectical materialism. More specifically, Poulantzas (1978b, 11) suggests that historical materialism "has as its object the concept of history, through the study of the various modes of production and social formations, their structure, constitution and functioning, and the forms of transition from one social formation to another." In other words, if dialectical materialism (i.e., philosophy) is responsible for producing these concepts through a reading of the Marxian canon, historical materialism (i.e., general theory) is responsible for defining these concepts so they become the basis of so-called regional and particular theories.

For Poulantzas, regional theory is the study of the elemental structures and practices whose specific combinations constitute a mode of production and a social formation.[15] Particular theories consist of theories of particular combinations, for example, a theory of the slave mode of production, the feudal mode of production, or the capitalist mode of production. For Poulantzas, it is particular theories that allow one to understand and explain "real, concrete, singular objects" such as France at a given moment in its political development. Thus, Poulantzas was concerned with producing a particular theory of the capitalist state; namely, the production of the concept of the political superstructure in the capitalist mode of production.

Significantly, therefore, Poulantzas (ibid., 24) claims that dialectical and historical materialism do not involve the study of facts (i.e., real concrete singulars), but the study of "abstract-formal objects" (i.e., concepts). He acknowledges that abstract-formal objects (e.g., the capitalist mode of production or the capitalist state) "do not exist in the strong sense of the word, but they are the condition of knowledge of real-concrete objects." In other words, there is no such thing ontologically as "the capitalist state," but it is this category of knowledge that makes it possible for us to know and understand an actually existing capitalist state (i.e., a real concrete singular). Consequently, the methodological role of the "real concrete" in Poulantzasian theory is merely (1) to illustrate and exemplify the regional or particular theory, or (2) to provide raw material for producing the specific concepts that make concrete knowledge possible.

It is no doubt a controversial claim, but this epistemological position places structuralism squarely within the 1950s and 1960s tradition of transcendental and analytic political philosophy. The method of textual analysis and its epistemological underpinnings are again not uniquely Marxian, because one can find the same types of arguments being made in mainstream political philosophy by Leo Strauss and Joseph Cropsey, among others.[16] Viewed within the larger postwar context of academic political theory, the only thing uniquely Marxian about the Althusserian epistemology was its choice of a sacred canon: the Marxist tradition, rather the classical tradition (e.g., Plato or Aristotle), or the liberal tradition (e.g., Hobbes, Locke, Rousseau), but the *epistemology* of textual analysis is identical. In this respect, the Miliband–Poulantzas debate merely reproduced within Marxism the very same empiricist-textualist dichotomy that had divided mainstream political science since the early 1950s (Ashcraft 1980; Lukács 1971, 110–49).[17] Of course, the epistemological dichotomy at the center of the Miliband–Poulantzas debate, including the radical divergence in their definition of Marx's "political writings," is essential to understanding their different concepts of the state, state power, and the state's role in a capitalist social formation.

Miliband's Theory of the State

The most succinct summary of Miliband's (1969, 23) theory of the state is the following:

> In the Marxist scheme, the "ruling class" of capitalist society is that class which owns and controls the means of production and which is able, by virtue of the economic power thus conferred upon it, to use the state as its instrument for the domination of society.[18]

In empirical terms, Miliband identifies the corporation as the initial reference point for defining the capitalist class. In the United States, for example, the bulk of capitalist economic activity, whether measured in terms of assets, profits, employment, investment, market shares, or research and development expenditures, is concentrated in the fifty largest financial institutions and the five hundred largest nonfinancial corporations (Means 1939; Mason 1964; Baran and Sweezy 1966; Edwards, Reich, and Weisskopf 1978). Thus, members of the capitalist class are identified as those persons who occupy the managerial and ownership functions of corporations (Mintz 1989, 208; Zeitlin 1974; Useem 1984). The capitalist class is an overlapping economic network of authority based on institutional position (i.e., management) and property relations (i.e., ownership). The wealthy families who own large blocks of corporate stock and the high-ranking managers of those same corporations are usually estimated to compose no more than 0.5 percent to 1 percent of the total U.S. population (Domhoff 1978, 4).

Social Class and Political Practice

In making this claim, Miliband was directly challenging the pluralist theory of liberal democrats who were arguing that references to "*a* capitalist class" are empirically meaningless, because corporate power is diffuse and competitive, and the representation of business interests is fragmented among divergent interest groups and/or checked by countervailing centers of social, economic, and political power. Thus, Miliband's empirical documentation captured the attention of behavioral social scientists, because it questioned the assertions of political theories that claimed to be empirical (e.g., Truman 1951; Dahl 1959; Galbraith 1952). Moreover, in challenging these theories, Miliband was also debunking a widely held ideological belief, especially in the United States, that capitalist societies were more or less classless, pluralistic, egalitarian, and democratic. Thus, as bizarre as it may seem in retrospect, it was theoretically important within the Anglo-American intellectual context to reestablish the simple empirical fact that a capitalist class does exist and that numerous mechanisms can be identified that facilitate the economic cohesion of capitalists *as a class.*

However, assuming that one can document the existence of an economically dominant capitalist class, Miliband (1969, 24) contends that in conceptualizing the state, most Marxists had failed "to note the obvious but fundamental fact that this [capitalist] class is involved in a *relationship* with the state, which cannot be *assumed* in the political conditions which are typical of advanced capitalism" (i.e., political democracy). Instead, if Marxist theory is to effectively challenge the claims of bourgeois social science, then the relationship between the state and the capitalist class "has to be *determined*" with historical and empirical precision (ibid., 1969, 55).[19] Miliband emphasizes that in documenting this relationship the claim put forward by a Marxist theory of the state entails a heavy empirical burden for the political theorist. This burden derives from the fact that Marxists do not merely assert that the capitalist class exercises substantial power, or even that it exercises more power than other classes, but insists that the capitalist class "exercises a decisive degree of political power" *and* that "its ownership and control of crucially important areas of economic life also insures its control of the means of political decision-making in the particular environment of advanced capitalism" (ibid., 48).[20]

What Is the State?

However, determining the magnitude of the relationship between a capitalist class and the state requires not only a clear definition of the capitalist class, but an equally clear designation of "the means of political decision-making" that constitute the state. Yet, Miliband observes paradoxically that the state "is a nebulous entity," because the state "is not a thing, that it does not, as such, exist." Instead, the state, as Miliband (ibid., 48–50) conceives it, is merely an analytic reference point that "stands for . . . a number of particular institutions which, together, constitute its reality, and which interact as parts of what may be called the state system." For Miliband, the state system is actually composed of five "elements" that are each identified with a cluster of particular institutions (ibid., 49–53):

1. the governmental apparatus, which consists of elected legislative and executive authorities at the national level that make state policy
2. the administrative apparatus, consisting of the civil-service bureaucracy, public corporations, central banks, and regulatory commissions, which regulates economic, social, cultural, and other activities
3. the coercive apparatus, consisting of the military, paramilitary, police, and intelligence agencies, which together are concerned with the deployment and management of violence
4. the judicial apparatus, which includes courts, the legal profession, jails and prisons, and other components of the criminal justice system
5. the subcentral governments, such as states, provinces, or departments; counties, municipal governments, and special districts

According to Miliband (ibid., 54): "These are the institutions—the government [executive], the administration, the military and the police, the judicial branch, sub-central government, and parliamentary assemblies—which make up the 'the state,' and whose interrelationship shapes the form of the state system." Miliband's emphasis on the state system as a set of *interrelationships* between particular institutions warrants special attention, because he has often been accused of reducing the state to a mere "tool in the hands of the ruling class." Yet, contrary to these assertions, Miliband offers an important qualification that belies this metaphorical straw man.

Miliband chastises liberal pluralists and left-wing activists for the mistaken belief that "the assumption of governmental power is equivalent to the acquisition of state power." Although it is a simple distinction, Miliband's conflicts with the British Labour Party made him acutely aware that drawing a conceptual distinction between government and the state can have significant consequences for political strategy and tactics. Miliband understood that the accession to governmental power at various points in the twentieth century by liberal, labor, and social-democratic *governments* was accompanied generally by a simultaneous failure to conquer *state power* in its diverse forms and places within the state system. The fact that a socialist government might control the parliamentary and executive branches of government, whether by election or revolution, does not automatically entail its control of the military, the police, the intelligence agencies, the civil service, the legal system, the subnational governments, the schools and universities, regulatory agencies, public corporations, and so on. As Miliband (ibid., 49–50) notes: "the fact that the government does speak in the name of the state and is formally *invested* with state power, does not mean that it effectively *controls* that power."

What Is State Power?

Consequently, it is theoretically important to Miliband to know who actually controls state power at any given time. One of the most direct indicators of ruling-class domination is the degree to which members of the capitalist class *control* the state apparatus through interlocking positions in the governmental, administrative, coercive, and other apparatuses. Miliband (ibid., 54) emphasizes that

> It is these institutions in which "state power" lies, and it is through them that this power is wielded in its different manifestations by the people who occupy the leading positions in each of these institutions.

For this reason, Miliband (ibid., 55) attaches considerable importance to the social composition of the state elite. The class composition of a state elite creates "a strong presumption . . . as to its general outlook, ideological dispositions and political bias," and thus one way to measure the degree of *potential* class domination is to quantify the extent to which members of a particular class have disproportionately colonized command posts within the state apparatuses. In the eyes of critics, Miliband's theory of the state is considered synonymous with the concept of institutional colonization. This misrepresentation of Miliband's analysis has wildly exaggerated his empirical claims about the direct domination of the state apparatuses by members of the capitalist class.

Despite the importance of colonization to Miliband's analysis, his empirical claims about the degree to which capitalists colonize the state apparatus were always circumscribed by his recognition that capitalists have not "assumed the major share of *government*" (ibid.) in most advanced capitalist democracies. For that reason, he argues (ibid., 59) that capitalists "are not, properly speaking, a 'governing' class, comparable to pre-industrial, aristocratic and landowning classes."[21] Indeed, a fact completely ignored by Miliband's critics is that he quotes Karl Kautsky to the effect that "the capitalist class reigns but does not govern" (ibid., 55).[22] The colonization of key command posts in selected state apparatuses is merely one weapon, albeit an important one, in the larger arsenal of ruling-class domination. What Miliband (ibid., 56, 48) actually claims is that capitalists are "well represented in the political executive and in other parts of the state system" and that their occupation of these key command posts enables them to exercise *decisive influence over public policy.*[23]

The fact that finance capitalists usually control the executive branch of government and the administrative-regulatory apparatuses is considered particularly important, under normal circumstances, for both historical and theoretical reasons. In historical terms, political development of the modern state system has been marked mainly by the growth of its regulatory, administrative, and coercive institutions over the course of the last century. As these institutions have grown in size, numbers, and technical complexity, the state's various subsystems have achieved greater autonomy from government in their operations. The growth of independent administrative and regulatory subsystems within the state has occurred as governments, especially legislatures, have found it increasingly difficult to maintain any central direction over the many components of the state system. The historical result is that the preponderance of state power has shifted from the legislative to the executive branch of government and to independent administrative or regulatory agencies.

This development is theoretically important partly because the very basis of state power is concentrated in those institutions (i.e., administration, coercion, knowledge) and because it is those institutions that the capitalist class has colonized most successfully. Thus, the actual extent of power that capitalists achieve by colonizing executive, administrative, and regulatory command posts has been magnified by the asymmetrical power structure within the contemporary state system (e.g., in the United States by the imperial presidency and the emergence of independent regulatory agencies). This magnification of their state power provides capitalists with strategic locations inside the state system from which to initiate, modify, and veto a broad range of policy proposals.[24] Miliband recognizes that a potential weakness of this more limited claim is the fact that capitalists usually colonize only the top command posts of government and administration. The colonization process is clearly unable to explain the operational unity of the entire state system and, therefore, one must be able to identify the mechanism that leads a number of relatively autonomous and divergent state subsystems to operate *as if* they were a single entity called *the* state.

Indeed, the loose connection of lower-level career administrators to the state elite is indicated by Miliband's description of them as servants *of* the state. In fact, these servants are frequently conceptualized as a separate professional-managerial class composed of lower- and middle-level career *state managers* (Ehrenreich and Ehrenreich 1977).[25] Miliband (1969, 119) observes that

> The general pattern must be taken to be one in which these men [i.e., state managers] do play an important part in the process of governmental decision-making, and therefore constitute a considerable force in the configuration of political power in their societies.

Likewise, a problem of systemic unity derives from the disparate organization of the contemporary state apparatus. To the extent that the state system is viewed as a web of decentered institutions, one must account for how the state elite and state managers are able to maintain some overarching interinstitutional cohesion that is "capitalist" in its content. Miliband has attempted to explain the coherence of the state system by suggesting that its operational unity is primarily ideological. He argues (ibid., 72, 75) that most state elites, including those who are not members of the capitalist class, "accept as beyond question the capitalist context in which they operate." Consequently, their views on public policy "are conditioned by, and pass through the prism of, their acceptance of and commitment to the existing economic system." In Miliband's account, the ideological commitments of state elites and state managers are of "absolutely fundamental importance in shaping their attitudes, policies and actions in regard to specific issues and problems with which they are confronted." The result of their underlying ideological unity is that "the politics of advanced capitalism have been about different conceptions of how to run the *same* economic and social system."

Miliband certainly recognizes that state elites and state managers in the various apparatuses, whether members of the capitalist class or not, "wish, without a doubt, to pursue many ends, personal as well as public." However, the underlying ideological unity of state elites and state managers means that "all other ends are conditioned by, and pass through the prism of, their acceptance of and commitment to the existing economic system" (ibid., 75). Thus, in an observation that seems to anticipate Claus Offe's (1975 and 1984, 126) "dependency principle," Miliband (1969, 75) observes that

> it is easy to understand why governments should wish to help business in every possible way... For if the national interest is in fact inextricably bound up with the fortunes of capitalist enterprise, apparent partiality towards it is not really partiality at all. On the contrary, in serving the interests of business and in helping capitalist enterprise to thrive, governments are really fulfilling their exalted role as guardians of the good of all.

Otherwise, as Miliband describes it, the modern state system in capitalist societies is a vast and sprawling network of political institutions loosely coordinated, if at all, through mechanisms providing a tenuous cohesion at best. Importantly, for Miliband, the diffuseness of the state system in capitalist societies also means that the conquest of state power is never an all or nothing proposition, because it is—in the Gramscian phrase—a war of fixed position, waged on many fronts, in many trenches, with shifting lines of battle, where victories and defeats occur side by side on the same day. The conquest of state power is never absolute; it is never uncontested; and it is never complete, because it is an ongoing and contingent *political* struggle.[26] Hence, Miliband's concept of the state requires an analysis and understanding of state power that always refers to particular historical circumstances and to institutional configurations that may vary widely from one capitalist society to another, and where over time class hegemony may shift in one direction or another within the same society. Indeed, Miliband (ibid., 77) is quite explicit in pointing out that state elites "have in fact been compelled over the years to act against *some* property rights, to erode *some* managerial prerogatives, to help redress *somewhat* the balance between capital and labour, between property and those who are subject to it."

Poulantzas's Theory of the State

Nicos Poulantzas was relatively unknown to Anglo-American scholars until he initiated the Miliband–Poulantzas debate with his review of *The State in Capitalist Society* in late 1969. When Poulantzas (1969, 67) informed readers that his critique of Miliband derived from epistemological positions presented more fully in his *Pouvoir politique et classes sociales* (1968), the debate itself stimulated a demand for Poulantzas's book, which was finally published in English in 1973.[27] In his outstanding intellectual biography of Poulantzas, Bob Jessop argues persuasively that this book was written during a phase of development when Poulantzas was "at his most structuralist" and consequently Jessop (1985, 14, 317) contends that "the resulting debate actually misrepresents the basic thrust of his [Poulantzas's] work" over time. However, at the time of the debate, Poulantzas's book was being read correctly as a hybrid Althusserian and Gramscian approach and, importantly, as Frances Fox Piven (1994, 24) observes, an objective historical consequence of the debate is that this type of structuralism tended to prevail after the Miliband–Poulantzas debate and thereafter "to dominate the intellectual fashion contest" that emerged from the debate. Thus, even if Jessop is correct in his claim that Poulantzas later moved significantly beyond this approach to the state, it is the Poulantzas of *Political Power and Social Classes* that introduced structuralism into Anglo-American Marxist theory and who defined the terms of the subsequent structuralist-instrumentalist debate (Clarke 1991, 35).

Social Class and Political Practice

In *Political Power and Social Classes,* Poulantzas (1978b, 1–33) claims that every mode of production can be understood theoretically in terms of the functional interrelations between its economic, political, and ideological levels.[28] Each level in a mode of production consists of *structures* that tend to reproduce and stabilize the mode of production and *class practices* that generate conflicts and contradictions within the mode of production (Poulantzas 1978b, 37, 86). A structure consists of one or more institutions that fulfill specific economic, political, or ideological functions necessary to sustain a particular mode of production. For instance, the economic structure of a capitalist society is constituted primarily by the social relations of production as defined in Marx's *Capital* (Althusser and Balibar 1977, 199–308). The political structures of a mode of production consist of the institutionalized power of the state (Poulantzas 1978b, 42). The ideological structures of a mode of production refer both to the subjective consciousness of individual social actors and to the collective thought systems that exist in a given society (Therborn 1980, 2; Poulantzas 1980, 28–34). A stable social formation is one in which the structures at each level function together as an integrated system to maintain and extend the dominant relations of production and, hence, the ability of a dominant class to appropriate surplus value from a subordinate laboring class.

However, Poulantzas emphasizes that the normal functioning of structures within the capitalist mode of production generates contradictory *class practices* that simultaneously destabilize the conditions of ruling-class domination. In *Political Power and Social Classes,* Poulantzas (1978b, 41) explains class practices as the effects of (1) structural dislocations generated by class struggle, and (2) the uneven development of structures between and within the levels of a social formation.[29] In direct contrast to what he calls the "historicist conception" of class practice, Poulantzas argues that "relations of production as a structure are not social classes . . . capital and wage-labour are not, of course, the empirical realities of 'capitalists' and 'labourers'" (ibid., 66). Instead, for Poulantzas, the relations of production

> consist of *specific forms of combination* of the agents of production and the means of production. This structure of relations of production "determines the places and functions occupied and adopted by the

agents of production, who are never anything more than the occupants of these places, in so far as they are supports of these functions." (Ibid.)

Thus, Poulantzas can never regard the main tasks of Marxist political theory as empirical or historical, because such analyses in his framework confuse the agents of production (i.e., groups of individuals) with the structural-functional relations that determine social class. Individuals "support" and "carry out" various functions within temporal history, but these functions are in no way dependent on particular individuals or groups of individuals. Hence, even before the publication of Miliband's *The State in Capitalist Society,* Poulantzas was dismissing the historicist conception of class practice as one that

> leads ultimately to the establishment of an ideological relation between individuals/agents-of-production ("men") and social classes; this relation is given a theoretical foundation in the status of the subject. Agents of production are perceived as agents/producers, as subjects which create structures; and social classes are perceived as the subjects of history. (Ibid., 62)

Poulantzas (ibid., 62, 67–68, 86) finds the historicist conception of class practice theoretically flawed because it "fails to recognize two essential facts: firstly, that the agents of production, for example the wage-earning labourer and the capitalist, as 'personifications' of Wage-Labour and Capital, are considered by Marx as the *supports* or *bearers* of an ensemble of structures; secondly, that social classes are never *theoretically* conceived by Marx as the genetic origin of structures." Consequently, Poulantzas contends that "*social class is a concept which shows the effects of the ensemble of structures, of the matrix of a mode of production or of a social formation on the agents which constitute its supports.*" Social classes are *structural effects* that mediate between structures (e.g., relations of production) and class practices (e.g., trade unionism). Indeed, according to Poulantzas, "social classes are conceivable only in terms of class practices" and it is these practices that determine agency, not vice versa.[30]

Importantly, Poulantzas (ibid., 86) views the identification of specific class practices as synonymous with the concept of "contradiction" because "class practices can be analysed only as conflicting practices in the field of class struggle . . . for example, the contradiction between those practices which aim at the realization of profit and those which aim at the increase of wages." In other words, it is impossible to understand the structural place of working-class practices that aim to increase wages without taking into consideration how such aims contradict capitalist class practices that aim to realize higher and higher profits. In this example, capitalist and proletarian class practices are each produced as the contradictory structural effect of relations of production on the agents of production (who merely carry out and support these practices within the capitalist system). Certainly, one can find explicit textual support for this claim in Marx's *Capital,* and such a reading is perfectly consistent with the theoretical status accorded to that work by Poulantzas and other structuralists.[31]

Yet, the importance of class practices in mediating between structure and history in Poulantzas's political theory raises some difficult and immanent epistemological issues. This is because Poulantzas (ibid., 41) equates "the political" with class practices, and thus he defines the specific object of politics as "the 'present moment' (as Lenin said), i.e., the *nodal point where the contradictions* of the various levels of a formation *are condensed* in the complex relations governed by over-determination and by their dislocation and uneven development." The epistemological difficulty for Poulantzas (ibid., 37) is that if the specific object of the political is the present moment, then "the problem of the political and politics is linked to the problem of history."

As noted earlier, Poulantzas argues that the "the problems of the general Marxist theory of the state and of the political class struggle" are addressed in a group of "political texts" by Marx, Engels, and Lenin that complement one's reading of *Capital.* Interestingly, the critical text forging an explicit theoretical nexus between structure and history is *The Communist Manifesto,* namely, the single most significant text that Poulantzas does *not* include on his list of "Marxian classics" in political theory. Yet, at a crucial point in the development of his argument, Poulantzas introduces two propositions from *The Communist Manifesto* to provide a theoretical nexus between politics and history: "(a) 'Every class struggle is a political struggle', and (b) 'The class struggle is the motive force of history'" (ibid.).

Poulantzas never mentions that passage on the state emphasized so heavily by Miliband, but he does recognize that is "possible to make a historicist reading" of *The Communist Manifesto.* In fact, to preempt such a reading, Poulantzas (ibid., 37–39) engages in a running polemic against "Marxist historicism" throughout *Political Power and Social Classes* and, after publication of *The State in Capitalist Society*, he immediately identified Miliband as an exemplar of this Marxist historicism. Significantly, Poulantzas never challenges Miliband's "first reading" of *The Communist Manifesto* as such, but instead questions *the effects* of such a reading on political practice as leading "to the ideological invariant voluntarism/economism and to the various forms of revisionism, reformism, spontaneism, etc." Yet, as if to compound the difficulty, Poulantzas, like Miliband, turns to Gramsci in addressing questions of the political only to find that Gramsci's views are "often tainted by the historicism of Croce and Labriola."

What Is the State?

The contradictory effects of class practices on the equilibrium of the capitalist system mean that potential crisis tendencies are always disrupting the functional stability of the capitalist mode of production. Thus, the basic structure of the capitalist mode of production generates contradictory class practices, dislocations, and crisis tendencies. It is this inexorable disruption of the capitalist system that necessitates a separate structure to specifically maintain, monitor, and restore its equilibrium as a system. Although Poulantzas (ibid., 45) modifies structuralism-functionalism by introducing class practices as a disequilibrating mechanism, nevertheless, he was clearly indebted to mainstream American functionalists and systems theorists insofar as he argues that the general function of the state in the capitalist mode of production is to serve as "*the regulating factor of its global equilibrium as a system.*"[32]

In particular, Poulantzas identifies three ensembles of class practices that require regulation by the state in order to maintain and restore the equilibrium of the capitalist system. First, he argues (ibid., 44–45), contrary to the mythology of neoclassical economic theory, that the economic level of the capitalist mode of production has never "formed a hermetically sealed level, capable of self-production and possessing its own 'laws' of internal functioning." Rather, the economic level of the capitalist mode of production is only *relatively* autonomous from the political and ideological levels, but given this relative autonomy, he concludes that structural "equilibrium is never *given* by the economic as such, but is maintained by the state." To this extent, the state fulfills a general maintenance function "*by constituting the factor of cohesion between the levels of a social formation.*"[33]

Consequently, Poulantzas (1980, 17) identifies a second ensemble of class practices, constituted by the fact that "*the political field of the State* (as well as the sphere of ideology) *has always, in different forms, been present in the constitution and reproduction of the relations of production.*" Capitalist relations of production do not appear ex nihilo in history, nor do they reproduce themselves on a day-to-day basis without struggle and resistance on the part of the subordinate classes whose labor is exploited by the capitalist class. Hence, in maintaining the cohesion of the levels of a social formation, Poulantzas (1978b, 52) observes that "the function of the state primarily concerns the economic level, and particularly the labour process, the productivity of labour."[34] This claims appears numerous times in *Political Power and Social Classes* and the claim is reiterated in both *Classes in Contemporary Capitalism* and *State, Power, Socialism.*[35] Despite the evident importance of this function, Poulantzas also notes that "this function of the state as organizer of the labour process is only one aspect of its economic function." The state also establishes and enforces the rules that organize capitalist exchanges (property and contract law, enforcement, punishment) and it functions to organize labor through its role of education, teaching, and so on. Finally, Poulantzas calls attention to an ensemble of class practices that occur "at the strictly political level" of the capitalist mode of production. He identifies the strictly political function of the state with "the maintenance of political order in political class conflict" (ibid., 53). By maintaining political order, by punishing disorder, and by monitoring political "subversion," that state represses revolution and thereby maintains conditions of exploitation under the neutral guise of "law and order."

The operational objectives of state policy are realized through three "modalities of the state function." The modalities of the state function identify the structural levels in which the *effects of state policies* are realized: (1) the technico-economic function at the economic level, (2) the political function at the level of class struggle, and (3) the ideological function at the cultural level. Regardless of the level at which the state's modalities are effected, however, Poulantzas (ibid., 55–53) contends that the state function is always oriented "with particular reference to the productivity of labor."

The modalities of the state function are always implemented through three functional subsystems of the state: the judicial subsystem, the ideological subsystem, and the political subsystem. Poulantzas (ibid., 53) argues that in capitalist societies the judicial subsystem is constituted as a set of rules that facilitate market exchanges by providing a "framework of cohesion in which commercial encounters can take place" (e.g., property and contract law, fair business practices). The state's ideological subsystem functions primarily through public educational institutions, while the strictly political subsystem consists of institutions engaged in "the maintenance of political order in political class conflict" (e.g., electoral laws, the party system, police).[36] The state's modalities each constitute *political* functions insofar as their operational objective is the maintenance and stabilization of a society in which the capitalist class is the dominant and exploitative class. As Poulantzas (ibid., 54) notes:

> the state's economic or ideological functions correspond to the political interests of the dominant class and constitute political functions, not simply in those cases where there is a direct and obvious relation between (a) the organization of labour and education and (b) the political domination of a class, but also where the object of these functions is the maintenance of the unity of the formation, inside which this class is the political dominant class. It is to the extent that the prime object of these functions is the maintenance of this unity that they [i.e., the functions and their modalities] correspond to the political interests of the dominant class.

It should be emphasized as a point of considerable theoretical significance that *structures* (i.e., the levels of the capitalist mode of production) are not reducible to the economic, political, or ideological *institutions* that compose them.[37] On this point, Gold, Lo, and Wright (1975a, 36n.) observe that for Poulantzas the concept of "structure does *not* refer to the concrete social institutions that make up a society, but rather to the systematic functional interrelationships among these institutions." Hence, Poulantzas's structural analysis always emphasized "the *functional relationship* of various institutions to the process of surplus-value production and appropriation" (ibid.),[38] whereas Miliband tends to emphasize the empirical organization, operation, and control of particular institutions.

What Is State Power?

Yet, the differences between Miliband and Poulantzas concerning the importance of institutions are much more than mere differences in emphasis or theoretical focus. Miliband and Poulantzas each articulate competing concepts of state power that are linked inextricably to their methodological differences. Whereas Miliband articulates an institutionalist conception of power, anchored by the methodological (Weberian) assumptions of power structure research, Poulantzas articulates a functionalist conception of power anchored by the methodological (Parsonian) assumptions of structural functionalism. Notably, and in direct contrast to Miliband, Poulantzas draws a sharp *analytic* distinction between the concepts of state power and the state apparatus (Therborn 1978, 148).

Poulantzas (1978b, 104) defines *state power* as the capacity of a social class to realize its objective interests through the state apparatus. Jessop (1982, 221) lends greater specificity to this idea by observing that within this framework, "state power is capitalist to the extent that it creates, maintains, or restores the conditions required for capital accumulation in a given situation and it is non-capitalist to the extent these conditions are not realised." In this respect, the objective *effects* of state policies on capital accumulation and the class structure are the main objective indicators of state power (ibid., 99).[39] On the other hand, the state apparatus is identified with two relations that are analytically (though not functionally) distinct from state power. Poulantzas (1978b, 116) defines the state apparatus as *(a)* "the place of the state in the ensemble of the structures of a social formation," that is, the state's functions, and *(b)* "the *personnel of the state*, the ranks of the administration, bureaucracy, army, etc." The state apparatus is thus a unity of the effects of state power (i.e., policies) *and* the network of institutions and personnel through which the state function is executed (Therborn 1978, 35, 151).[40]

The *functional* unity between state power and the state apparatus is emphasized by Poulantzas (1978b, 115 n. 24) with the observation "that structure *is not the simple principle of organization which is exterior to* the institution: the structure is present in an allusive and inverted form in the institution itself." For Poulantzas, the concept of the state apparatus intrinsically includes the functions executed through state institutions and by state personnel. Hence, in direct contrast to Miliband, he insists that "the institutions of the state, do not, strictly speaking, have any power. Institutions, considered from the point of view of power, can be related only to *social classes which hold power*" (ibid., 115).[41] State institutions are political arenas for the exercise of class power and exist as such only by virtue of their functional role in the capitalist mode of production.

The First Exchange: The Problem of Method (1969–70)

The Miliband–Poulantzas debate, narrowly conceived, consisted of three exchanges published in the *New Left Review* in 1969–70 (Miliband—Poulantzas), 1973 (Miliband), and 1976 (Poulantzas). The debate began with Poulantzas's critical review of Miliband's *The State in Capitalist Society,* and, from the outset, Poulantzas focused the debate on "the problem of method" in Marxist political theory. He prefaces his critique of Miliband with the observation that his theoretical comments "derive from epistemological positions presented" in *Pouvoir politique et classes sociales* (1969, 69). Thus, although the Miliband–Poulantzas debate has always been viewed as a contest between instrumentalist and structuralist theories of the state, it was actually more about methodology than about state theory.

Poulantzas's central criticism of Miliband's book was that "Miliband nowhere deals with the Marxist theory of the State as such" (ibid.), and this claim is only meaningful if one accepts the basic assumptions of an Althusserian or structuralist epistemology. Notably, Poulantzas praises Miliband for methodically attacking bourgeois conceptions of the state and political power by rigorously deploying a formidable array of empirical data to challenge the dogmatic assertions of pluralist democracy. He acknowledges that Miliband's empirical methodological approach had enabled him to "radically demolish" bourgeois ideologies of the state and to provide Marxists "with a positive knowledge that these ideologies have never been able to produce." For Poulantzas (ibid., 73), this means that Miliband's work functions as an ideology critique whose political value is its ideological effect in demystifying the claims of bourgeois social science.[42]

As an ideology critique that demystifies bourgeois conceptions of the state and political power, however, it does not elaborate a Marxist theory of the state. Ideology critique does not go far enough in challenging the dominance of bourgeois conceptions because, in Poulantzas's view, it is never sufficient to juxtapose empirical facts against theoretical concepts. The concepts themselves must be attacked at a philosophical and theoretical level with other "concepts situated in a different problematic." Instead of merely demystifying bourgeois ideology from within its own problematic, Poulantzas (ibid., 69) insists that it is necessary to *displace* that epistemological terrain and claims that "Miliband appears to omit this first step."[43] Poulantzas is not content with an analysis that empirically demystifies the concept of a plural elite, for example; he insists that one must reject the very concepts of bourgeois social science and replace them with "the scientific concepts of Marxist theory." This is because empirical facts only become "concrete" by having a new theoretical meaning conferred on them by their place within a radical theory constituted as an epistemological break with bourgeois social science.

Poulantzas insists that epistemology and theory construction must precede ideology critique for two reasons. First, ideology critique employs the theoretical concepts of an ideological adversary and, in using these concepts, Poulantzas is certain that "one legitimizes them and permits their persistence." Hence, even the limited objectives of an ideology critique are vitiated by a self-defeating exercise that strengthens one's adversary. Second, Poulantzas is concerned about the risk of being "unconsciously and surreptitiously contaminated by the very epistemological principles of the adversary." Although he *initially* agrees that Miliband's methodological procedures have not taken him too far down that path, he does caution that "Miliband sometimes allows himself to be unduly influenced by the methodological principles of the adversary" (ibid., 69), that is, bourgeois social scientists. Poulantzas identifies several specific instances where he believes that Miliband's methodology led him astray theoretically: (1) the problem of the subject, (2) the problem of state cohesion, (3) the problem of ideological apparatuses. If this series of "problematics" shaped the direction of Marxist political theory for the next decade, it is the Miliband–Poulantzas debate that defined the frontiers and boundaries of those explorations.

The Problem of the Subject I

Poulantzas (ibid., 70–71) defines the problem of the subject as "a problematic of *social actors,* of individuals as the origin of *social action.*" If individuals or groups of individuals are considered as social actors, then Poulantzas argues that theoretical research is diverted from "the study of the objective co-ordinates that determine the distribution of agents into social classes and the contradictions between these classes . . . to the search for *finalist* explanations founded on the *motivations of conduct* of the individual actors." He claims that Miliband's empirical and institutional analysis of states in capitalist societies "constantly gives the impression" that "social classes or 'groups' are in some way reducible to *inter-personal relations,* that the State is reducible to inter-personal relations of the members of the diverse 'groups' that constitute the State apparatus, and finally that the relation between social classes and the State is itself reducible to inter-personal relations of 'individuals' composing social groups and 'individuals' composing the State apparatus." Consequently, Poulantzas chastises Miliband for offering explanations of corporate behavior, the state elite, and state managers that are "founded on the *motivations of conduct* of the individual actors." Poulantzas contends that this method of analysis vitiates Miliband's ideology critique to the extent that he fails to comprehend "social classes and the State as *objective structures,* and their relations as an *objective system of regular connections,* a structure and a system whose agents, 'men', are in the words of Marx, 'bearers' of it." Otherwise, Poulantzas is concerned that "to transpose this problematic of the subject into Marxism is in the end to admit the epistemological principles of the adversary." Interestingly, in an earlier essay, also published in the *New Left Review,* Poulantzas (1967) argues that the problem of the subject is a theoretical error endemic to Anglo-American Marxism in general, and so in many ways his critique of Miliband merely serves to illuminate his assessment of much wider theoretical shortcomings within the Anglo-American left.

The Problem of State Cohesion I

According to Poulantzas, this same problem of the subject resurfaces in Miliband's treatment of the state bureaucracy, the army, regulatory agencies, and other personnel of the state system. The problem appears in the fact that Miliband places so much emphasis on the role of ideology in linking these agents to the capitalist class and the top state elite, because this explanatory mechanism suggests that the criterion for membership in a particular class is the shared motivations and subjective orientations of a group of individuals. Hence, Poulantzas (1969, 73) concludes that Miliband "seems to reduce the role of the State to the conduct and 'behavior' of the members of the State apparatus." Poulantzas (ibid., 71), of course, insists that Marx's criterion for the designation of class boundaries is "the objective place in production and the ownership of the means of production." Instead, he proposes (ibid., 73) that civil servants, military officers, regulators, and other state managers are "a specific *social category*—not a class. This means that, although the members of the State apparatus belong, by their class origin to different classes, they function according to a specific internal unity."[44] Thus, a social category's "internal unity derives from its actualization of the objective role of the State" (ibid., 74). Therefore, Poulantzas claims in a now legendary passage that

> the *direct* participation of members of the capitalist class in the State apparatus and in the government, even where it exists, is not the important side of the matter. The relation between the bourgeois class and the State is an *objective relation.* This means that if the *function* of the state in a determinate social formation and the *interests* of the dominant class in this formation coincide, it is by reason of the system itself: the direct participation of members of the ruling class in the state apparatus is not the *cause* but the *effect,* and moreover a chance and contingent one, of this objective coincidence. (Ibid., 73)[45]

Although Poulantzas insists that the state as a whole, as an objective system of power, is relatively autonomous from the dominant class, the state's *internal unity* requires that we not view its individual apparatuses and personnel as relatively autonomous. Rather, it is the general function of the state that gives cohesion and unity to the apparatuses and personnel and that makes it possible to refer both to *a* state and to the *capitalist* state. However, from Poulantzas's perspective, Miliband relies on factors "exterior" to the state itself, and therefore he lacks a theoretical capacity to *conceptualize the necessary unity and cohesion of the state.* In contrast, Poulantzas (ibid., 77) insists that "the State in the classic Marxist sense of the term, possesses a very rigorous internal unity which directly governs the relation between the diverse branches of the apparatus."[46]

The Problem of Ideological Apparatuses I

Nevertheless, given its prominence in Miliband's analysis, Poulantzas was not inclined to dismiss ideology altogether, but instead proposes to reconceptualize its production and distribution within a Marxist theory of the state. He was quite correct to point out that "the classic Marxist tradition of the theory of the State is principally concerned to show *the repressive role of the State,* in the strong sense of organized physical repression" (ibid., 76–77). On the other hand, ideology had been dismissed as epiphenominal (rather than constitutive) of social and political relations, mainly because ideology had been equated "with ideas, customs or morals without seeing that ideology can be embodied, in the strong sense, in *institutions:* institutions which then, by the very process of institutionalization, belong to the system of the State." Poulantzas proposes that the realm of ideology be brought inside the state by reconceptualizing the state as a dual matrix of apparatuses that perform either repressive functions or ideological functions.[47] Poulantzas defines the state ideological apparatuses to include churches, political parties, trade unions, schools and universities, the press, television, radio, and even the family.

In this manner, Poulantzas seeks to widen the potential range of revolutionary activities in capitalist society, since he maintains that "the principal objective of revolutionary action is *State power* and the necessary precondition of any socialist revolution is the destruction of the bourgeois State apparatus." As he observes: "according to Marxist-Leninist theory, a socialist revolution does not signify only a shift in *State power,* but it must equally '*break*', that is to say radically change, the State apparatus" and, hence, "the advent of socialist society cannot be achieved . . . whilst maintaining the State ideological apparatuses intact." However, he does issue a powerful warning to contemporary culture critics with his conclusion that "the 'destruction' of the ideological apparatuses has *its precondition* in the 'destruction' of the State repressive apparatus which maintains it" (ibid., 68). Consequently, he deems it an "illusory error" to believe that cultural revolution can occur without directly confronting the state repressive apparatus, or as he puts it, to consider "the 'destruction' of the university in capitalist societies, for instance" (ibid. 78) as a revolutionary activity. Culture is not what supports the repressive apparatus; it is the repressive apparatus that supports and promotes the dominant culture. In other words, revolutions occur on a political and not a cultural battlefield.

The Problem of Method

Miliband responded to Poulantzas's critique on most points, although he was convinced that many of Poulantzas's quibbles with his work were trivial and unwarranted. Miliband did not expend a great deal of energy replying to every minor criticism, but instead chose to address only those general points that seemed of particular importance to understanding the nature and role of the state in capitalist society. More important, the initial critique and rejoinder do not provide any basis for concluding that the two theorists' differences were merely matters of conceptual emphasis, degree, or mutual misunderstanding. Quite the contrary, the theoretical differences between them are real and significant, and this accounts partially at least for the fact that we still return to the debate.

Miliband readily acceded to Poulantzas's postulate that a precondition of any scientific approach to the concrete is to make explicit the epistemological principles of one's treatment of the concrete. The point, however, is that, from Miliband's perspective, he did "quite explicitly give an outline of the Marxist theory of the state" (1970a, 54). In defending this claim, Miliband refers us back to that famous passage in *The Communist Manifesto* only to reiterate his previous position that, once stated, it is only possible to elucidate that concept further in empirical terms. Thus, Miliband concludes from within his epistemological framework that Poulantzas, Louis Althusser, and their collaborators are "so profoundly concerned with the elaboration of an appropriate 'problematic' and with the avoidance of any contamination with opposed 'problematics', as to lose sight of the absolute necessity of empirical inquiry, and of the empirical demonstration of the falsity of these opposed and apologetic 'problematics'" (ibid., 55). As a wry gesture to the Poulantzasian interpretation of the Marxist classics, which emphasized the centrality of *Capital,* Miliband (ibid., 54–55) argues that, as a methodological text, *Capital* stresses "the importance of empirical validation (or invalidation)," while noting that Marx "spent many years of his life in precisely such an undertaking."

The Problem of the Subject II

Miliband also fundamentally rejects Poulantzas's indictment of his work as one contaminated by the problem of the subject. Quite the contrary, Miliband was convinced that Poulantzas greatly underestimated the extent to which he did take account of the objective relations that affect and shape the role of the state. Indeed, Miliband describes Poulantzas's methodology as "structural super-determinism" and concludes that it is Poulantzas's one-sidedness that makes it impossible for him to recognize Miliband's treatment of objective structural factors and that leads Poulantzas to go much too far in dismissing the nature of the state elite as irrelevant to an understanding of concrete differences between states and state policies in different capitalist societies. Instead,

Miliband (ibid., 57) takes Poulantzas to task for his *exclusive* stress on objective relations, which implies that "what the state does is in every particular and at all times is *wholly* determined by these 'objective relations': in other words, that the structural constraints of the system are so absolutely compelling as to turn those who run the state into the merest functionaries and executants of policies imposed upon them by 'the system.'"[48]

The Problem of State Cohesion II

Miliband's defense of the role of the state elite and his rejection of structural factors as absolutely determining allowed him to highlight another significant difference with Poulantzas. Whereas Poulantzas criticized Miliband for not being able to conceptualize state cohesion adequately, Miliband's very point was to emphasize the tenuous unity and tendencies toward disaggregation of the state apparatuses. Miliband's analysis is designed to demonstrate that "the state elite is involved in a far more complex relationship with 'the system' and with society as a whole than Poulantzas' scheme allows; and that at least to a certain but definite and important extent that relationship is shaped by the kind of factors" (ibid.) that Poulantzas dismisses as irrelevant—namely, ideology, individual motivations, the fragmentation and disunity of the state apparatuses. In other words, Miliband did not fail to conceptualize state cohesion adequately but was drawing the empirical conclusion that such unity does not exist for states in advanced capitalist societies.

The Problem of Ideological Apparatuses II

Finally, Miliband simply rejects outright Poulantzas's assertion about the neglect of ideology by Marxist political theory. First, Miliband points out that he devoted two chapters of *The State in Capitalist Society* to "the institutions which are the purveyors of ideology" and thus adopts exactly the method of analysis proposed by Poulantzas. Second, he rejects Poulantzas's suggestion that these institutions be conceptualized as part of the state apparatus. Precisely because ideological institutions are increasingly linked to and buttressed by the state, Miliband insists that it is important not to blur the fact that in bourgeois democracies they are not part of the state, but of a wider political or ideological system. Certainly, he agrees that ideological institutions *are* increasingly subject to a process of "statization" and he concedes that their statization "is likely to be enhanced by the fact that the state must, in the conditions of permanent crisis of advanced capitalism, assume ever greater responsibility for political indoctrination and mystification." Nevertheless, he draws the empirical conclusion that such a process has not gone far enough to permit the conceptualization of such institutions as part of the state, since most of them continue to "perform their ideological functions outside it" (ibid., 59).

The Second Exchange: The Problem of Method Again (1973)

Miliband continued his rejoinder in 1973 following the publication in English of Poulantzas's *Political Power and Social Classes*, which he viewed as "an opportunity to continue with the discussion" begun three years earlier. Miliband's essay again focused on the problem of method, although, as a review of Poulantzas's book, it shifted the emphasis from a defense of Miliband's own position to a critique of Poulantzasian and Althusserian structuralism. The availability of a sound English-language translation of Poulantzas's book confirmed Miliband's apprehension that the book is "obscurely written for any reader who has not become familiar through painful initiation with the particular linguistic code and mode of exposition of the Althusserian school to which Poulantzas relates" (1973, 83–84). Consequently, in his second rejoinder, Miliband frequently complains of Poulantzas's opaqueness and proposes that instead of describing his method as structural superdeterminism, it would be more appropriate to call it structuralist abstractionism. In fact, Miliband provides numerous examples of oxymoronic terminology, self-contradictory phraseology, and completely opaque scholasticism. A genre of structural abstractionism might make for great art, or even great literature, but Miliband did not think it made very good political theory.

First, although Miliband conceded that "poor exposition" is a secondary defect, he suggested that the abstractness of contemporary Marxist theory was paradoxical given its claim to be a science of working-class revolution. The most prominent Marxist theorists seem to compete with one another as to who can write at a level of abstraction so opaque that it is never likely to be accessible to anyone but a few highly educated and specialized professional academicians. In contrast, contemporary liberal and conservative political theorists routinely write "academic" works that are easily accessible to an educated lay audience and this in no way jeopardizes the intellectual integrity of the work. In this respect, if one is to judge the functional value of Marxist social science by its *objective effects* at the political level, Miliband (ibid., 84) suggests that the sooner the problem of excessive abstraction "is remedied, the more likely it is that a Marxist tradition of political analysis will now be encouraged to take root." At some point, the value and role of Marxist political theory must be judged against its effects on the political, that is, in promoting and facilitating socialism as opposed to its current preoccupation with establishing academic legitimacy within the dominant ideological institutions.

Second, as Miliband (ibid., 84–85) begins to recognize at this point, Poulantzas's main concern was not to provide a theory of the capitalist state (at least not as Miliband understands that concept), but "to provide a 'reading' of texts from Marx and Engels, and also from Lenin, on the state and politics." As Miliband notes, "such a 'reading', in the Althusserian sense, is, of course, not a presentation or a collation of texts; nor is it commentary on them or even an attempt at interpretation, though it is partly the latter." Instead, an Althusserian reading of the classic texts—which Miliband confesses makes him "a bit uneasy"—involves a complementation of the original texts. To his credit, Miliband did not follow the path of much contemporary literary/political theory by engaging Poulantzas and the structuralists in a debate over "methods of textual interpretation." Instead, he simply returns directly to the original texts as a basis for asking himself how well Poulantzas conducted his interpretive exercise and "whether the 'deciphering' has produced an accurate message." Miliband concludes on the basis of his own reading that "much of Poulantzas' 'reading' constitutes a serious misrepresentation of Marx and Engels and also of the actual reality he is attempting to portray." To put it bluntly, Miliband (ibid., 91) does not consider Poulantzas's reading of Marx to be very rigorous and, unfortunately, "care and scruple in textual quotation are not simply matters of scholarship: they also involve large political issues."

Miliband (ibid., 85) advances his own reading of Marx by noting that "the basic theme of the [Poulantzas's] book, its central problematic, is absolutely right." This theme, as Miliband understands it, is to reaffirm "that the political realm is not, in classical Marxism, the mere reflection of the economic realm, and that in relation to the state, the notion of the latter's 'relative autonomy' is central." However, in a significant and lengthy footnote that is generally ignored, Miliband (ibid., 85 n. 4) again returns to his original text to argue that Poulantzas's central theme is already fully contained in

> the most familiar of all the Marxist formulations on the state, that which is to be found in the *Communist Manifesto,* where Marx and Engels assert that "the modern State is but a committee for managing the common affairs of the whole bourgeoisie"... what they are saying is that "the modern state is but a committee for managing the *common* affairs of the *whole* bourgeoisie": the notion of common affairs assumes the existence of particular ones; and the notion of the whole bourgeoisie implies the existence of separate elements which make up that whole. This being the case, there is an obvious need for an institution of the kind they refer to, namely the state; and the state *cannot* meet this need without enjoying a certain degree of autonomy. In other words, the notion of autonomy is embedded in the definition itself, is an intrinsic part of it.

Thus, there is no need for a symptomatic reading of Marx and no reason to complement the Marxian classics, because the requisite theory and concepts are already sufficient to proceed with an analysis of the capitalist state. Moreover, for Miliband, the real problem with Poulantzasian structuralism is that it fails to achieve its stated purpose. Poulantzas claims to develop a theory of the capitalist state, and yet, Miliband (ibid., 84, 89) complains, "the book hardly contains any reference at all to an actual capitalist state anywhere," primarily because Poulantzas has "an absurdly exaggerated fear of empiricist contamination." From this perspective, Poulantzas's "'structural super-determinism' makes him *assume* what has to be *explained* about the relationship of the state to classes in the capitalist mode of production" and, hence, he sees no need for serious empirical or historical investigations. Thus, "the real trouble," as Miliband (ibid., 85) puts it, is that Poulantzas's *approach* to the questions raised in their first exchange is what "prevents him from providing a satisfactory answer to them." Thus, Miliband (ibid., 86) laments that "the world of 'structures' and 'levels' which he [Poulantzas] inhabits has so few points of contact with historical or contemporary reality that it cuts him off from any possibility of achieving what he describes as 'the political analysis of a concrete conjuncture.'"

The Problem of State Power

Miliband illustrates his methodological claim by contrasting their conceptions of state power. Poulantzas argues that state institutions, as such, do not have any power, but must be related only to social classes that hold power. Miliband (ibid., 87) observes, however, that if the state does not have any independent source of power, "this, *inter alia,* is to deprive the state of any kind of autonomy at all" and, for all practical matters, conceptualizes the state out of existence in everything but name only. Thus, aside from being a self-contradictory and self-defeating theoretical position, Miliband insists that one has to make a distinction between class power and state power, not only because it is necessary to conceptualize the state as relatively autonomous, but also because it is necessary to recognize that although state power may be the main and ultimate means of maintaining ruling-class domination, it is not the only form of class power, as Poulantzas's formulation implies. Miliband's point is that state power is not the only form, nor the only site, of ruling-class domination. This is another reason why Miliband again rejects Poulantzas's suggestion that institutions such as churches, the educational system, political parties, the press, radio, television, publishing, and the family should all be brought within the realm of state theory as components of a state ideological apparatus. Indeed, Miliband (ibid., 88 n. 16) scoffs at the suggestion as carrying "to caricatural forms the confusion between different forms of class domination and, to repeat, makes impossible a serious analysis of the relation of the state to society, and of state power to class power."

The Third Exchange: Stalemate (1976)

Poulantzas did not reply immediately to Miliband's scathing critique, but following the English-language publication of his *Fascism and Dictatorship* (1974), he decided that "the moment has come to continue the debate." In fact, Poulantzas's polemical strategy was to end the debate by shifting the terms from a direct confrontation over the problems of method and theory to an ideological divergence between contaminated Marxism and real Marxism. The third exchange essentially ended the debate—at least as a personal exchange between Miliband and Poulantzas—although by this time Poulantzas (1976, 63–64) recognized that "a good many others, in Europe, the United States, Latin America, and elsewhere, have joined in, in articles and books." By this time, Poulantzas was acutely aware that the differences between Miliband and himself were being conceptualized by other scholars, "especially in England and the United States, as a controversy between 'instrumentalism' and 'structuralism.'" He dismissed these terms "as an utterly mistaken way of situating the discussion." As a matter of fact, he complained (ibid., 76) that the only reason he decided to continue the debate was that "certain authors, especially in the United States, have perceived the debate between Miliband and myself as a supposed debate between instrumentalism and structuralism, thus posing a false dilemma." Consequently, Poulantzas hoped in one last salvo to clarify what he considered to be the "real" conflict as one between materialism and idealism or between Marxist social science and bourgeois ideology (i.e., contaminated Marxism).

The Problem of Method

Poulantzas curtly dismisses Miliband's comments on the difficulty of his terminology and on the lack of concrete analysis as evidence that their approaches are "situated on disparate[epistemological] terrains." He held firm to his Althusserian position that it is only possible to "carry on a far-reaching debate with the aid of a precise language, and . . . from within their respective problematics, to attach precise definitions to the concepts, terms or notions they are using." In his view, there was no point in continuing the debate further because Miliband's writings "are marked by the absence of any theoretical problematic" and allegedly it is the absence of an explicit problematic that accounts for Miliband's repeated criticisms of Poulantzas's work for its lack of concrete analysis. Hence, Poulantzas (ibid., 64–65) writes that "on the subject of Miliband's own work, I have nothing to add to what I wrote in my original review of his book." From his perspective, Miliband was not engaged in theory construction or in the production of new concepts capable of displacing his own epistemological position. Quite simply, Poulantzas and Miliband do not agree on how to read the Marxian classics, on what constitutes a concept, on what counts as a theory or as theory construction, or even on what counts as a concrete analysis, and most of these divergences are anchored in the fundamental assumptions of competing social-science methodologies.

Poulantzas is certainly aware of this fact and, for this reason, he explicitly rejects the ambitions of Anglo-American authors hoping to escape the dichotomy by finding a compromise between instrumentalism and structuralism or a synthesis of the two perspectives. Poulantzas understood from the beginning that the real debate was about the problem of method. More to the point, however, in his last essay of the debate, he seeks to conflate the categories of methodology and ideology to create a new dichotomy between materialism (Marxism) and idealism (bourgeois ideology).

Poulantzas begins to introduce this new distinction in his reply to Miliband's comments on "structural abstractionism." Poulantzas was evidently irritated by Miliband's reproach concerning the lack of concrete analyses or references to concrete historical and empirical facts in his writings. First, Poulantzas (ibid., 65) did not consider the reproach justified because he insisted that "constant and precise references to the state of the class struggle and to the historical transformations of the State are abundantly present in *Political Power.*" However, once he cites his discussions of the absolutist state, historical models of bourgeois revolution, and the forms of the capitalist state, it is clear that his notion of concrete analysis is a usage peculiar to structuralist epistemology and is certainly not what Miliband means by concrete analysis (e.g., a historical and empirical analysis of Thatcher policies in the 1980s).

Furthermore, Poulantzas (ibid.) emphasizes that the difference between him and Miliband over the meaning of the concrete goes back to their "respective approaches to 'concrete facts.'" For Poulantzas, as noted earlier, an isolated fact is an abstraction that only becomes concrete when it is given meaning "with the aid of a theoretical apparatus constantly employed throughout the length of the text." Thus, he concludes that without an explicit theoretical problematic, "one can pile up as many concrete analyses as one likes, they will prove nothing whatsoever." What Miliband calls a lack of concrete analysis, Poulantzas embraces as eschewing "the demagogy of the 'palpitating fact', of 'common sense', and the 'illusions of the evident.'" Indeed, Poulantzas (ibid., 67–68) returns to an old theme when he berates Miliband for succumbing to "the demagogy of common sense" and, for good measure, sideswipes "the dominant 'Anglo-Saxon culture' as a whole" as the source of this epistemological error. Poulantzas (ibid., 66–67) can scarcely conceal his disdain for "English readers" who, steeped in the demagogy of common sense and empiricism, are unable to grasp what he acknowledges was "sometimes needlessly difficult language." In the final analysis, he is only willing to concede that he shared "an over-rigid epistemological position" with Althusser at the time, but he defends it as one necessitated by the requirements of a concentrated "attack against empiricism and neo-positivism, whose condensates, in the Marxist tradition, are economism and historicism." Lest anyone think that such an admission carried with it some hope of a reconciliation or a synthesis, Poulantzas again reiterates that "I naturally maintain my essential difference with Miliband, one that is irreducible, theoretically."[49]

For Poulantzas, this irreducible theoretical break was the distinction between real materialist Marxism and contaminated Marxism. Although Miliband and other plain Marxists generally reject any description of their position as instrumentalism, it is still not widely acknowledged that Poulantzas also came to reject the structuralist label by 1976. Poulantzas was apparently stung by Miliband's references to his structural superdeterminism and structural abstractionism. However, in the last exchange, Poulantzas (ibid., 70) turns these concepts against Miliband by suggesting that such terms have been used historically to criticize Marxists for not granting "sufficient importance to the role of concrete individuals and creative persons; to human freedom and action; to free will and to Man's capacity for choice; to the 'project' as against 'necessity' (hence Miliband's term, 'super-determinism'); and so on and so forth." Poulantzas retaliates with the observation that Miliband's use of the term *structuralism* thus "falls within the humanist and historicist problematic, indeed within a traditional problematic of bourgeois subjectivist idealism such as has frequently influenced Marxism, namely the problematic of the subject." To the extent that Poulantzas always located Miliband's work within the problematic of the subject, this reference is a scarcely concealed effort to push Miliband completely off the terrain of Marxist political theory. In fact, Poulantzas ends the discussion with this rejoinder:

> I would like to state quite clearly that I have no intention of replying to this [charge of structuralism]. I consider that everything there is to say on this subject has already been said, and that all those who have not yet understood, or who have yet to be convinced . . . are certainly not going to be convinced by the few lines I could possibly add here on this subject. I shall, therefore, merely repeat that the term structuralism

> applied in this sense to *Political Power* is nothing more, in the final analysis, than a reiteration in modern terms of the kind of objections that bourgeois idealism has always opposed to Marxism of whatever stripe. (Ibid.)

Finally, Poulantzas concludes the debate by returning to the issue of whether one must draw a distinction between class power and state power. Poulantzas (ibid., 73) dismisses Miliband's argument that state institutions must be viewed as repositories of independent power (i.e., coercion) to have autonomy as nothing but a blatant "appeal to common sense." Rather than responding directly to the theoretical argument, Poulantzas again attempts to drive an ideological wedge between himself and Miliband by insisting that Miliband's conception of state power is "an old and persistent conception of bourgeois social science and politics." As if to make his point one last time, he dismisses the entirety of the debate with Miliband by concluding that after all is said and done, "all that remains is a polemical catch-phrase pure and simple, masking a factual and empirical critique" (ibid., 76).

Conclusion

In one sense, the Miliband–Poulantzas debate came to an abrupt and inconclusive end that left Marxist political theory divided between "instrumentalists" and "structuralists," even though Miliband and Poulantzas each, respectively, rejected these monikers. Hence, some scholars such as Leo Panitch (1995, 13), have suggested that "the theoretical and political significance of the famous debates between Miliband and Poulantzas should not be misunderstood as reflecting incompatible positions." On the other hand, the Miliband–Poulantzas debate left many Marxists with the uncomfortable reality of a still unresolved dichotomy at the core of Marxian political theory, and for many it brought an end to the idea that there is something called *the* Marxist theory of the state. Thus, the outcome of the debate is itself a matter of continuing interpretive dispute, engagement, and disagreement.

What is perhaps both unfortunate and inevitable is that so much of the Miliband–Poulantzas debate had nothing to do with "Marxism" as such, but revolved around methodological disputes that are not likely to be resolved and, more to the point, whose resolution is not likely to further the cause of socialism anyway (and that ought to be the point of Marxist political theory). The difficulty of relying on the Marxian classics to arbitrate between competing theories of the state is not just that the classical texts are "incomplete," but, as the debate itself highlighted, that they are often ambiguous and self-contradictory. Hence, the Marxian classics are compatible with a range of political theories depending partly on the selection of what counts as a classic political text (Das 1996). Thus, a range of theoretical positions is plausible and defensible from within the Marxian canon and, most important, the canon itself provides no clear basis for arbitrating among this range of positions.[50] This methodological problem at the core of Marxist political theory is why Marxist theorists, including Miliband and Poulantzas, must continually appeal to methodological and epistemological positions that, in principle, are not "Marxist" in any strict sense of the term in order to fill lacunae, arbitrate between competing or analytically incompatible texts, and provide strategies for the clarification of textual and conceptual ambiguities. Consequently, there may not be any overarching synthetic viewpoint from which to reconcile these competing positions within Marxism other than an uncomfortable methodological pluralism that puts the achievement of common political objectives above epistemological controversy.

Notes

The author acknowledges the exceptional contribution of Robert Mauro, a former research assistant, in completing this manuscript.

1. For example, Alford and Friedland (1985, 278) conclude that Poulantzas criticized Miliband "quite appropriately" for employing an "un-Marxist epistemology." Similarly, Wright (1978, 12–13) argues that "one of the central epistemological premises of Marxist theory is the distinction between the 'level of appearances' and the underlying social reality which produces those appearances. . . . Marxists, then, have generally stressed the importance of elaborating a theory of the underlying structures of social relations, of the contradictions embedded in those structures, of the ways in which those underlying structures generate the appearances which people encounter in everyday life." Consequently, Domhoff (1986–87, 295) observes that the debate degenerated into an infantile "dispute among Marxists concerning who was the most Marxist."

2. Jessop (1982, xiv) considers the Miliband–Poulantzas debate "sterile and misleading." Similarly, Holloway and Picciotto (1978).

3. On this point, my own position is in sharp contrast to Ollman (1993), who equates Marxist methodology with "dialectics."

4. Biographical information on Ralph Miliband is in Panitch (1994, 1995), Blackburn (1994), Piven (1994), and Kovel (1994).

5. For a self-review of Miliband's thirty years as coeditor of the *Socialist Register,* see Miliband (1994b).

6. See also Jessop (1991). Abercrombie, Turner, and Urry (1976) concur that Poulantzas's works "are amongst the most sophisticated and developed products of the Althusserian revolution in the reading of Marx."

7. Thus, Abercrombie, Turner, and Urry (1976, 512, 517) suggest that Poulantzas's "similarities with conventional functionalist arguments as found in sociology and political science" make his *Political Power and Social Classes* "a sort of Marxist equivalent of Talcott Parsons' *The Social System.*"

8. Although structural Marxists were evidently blind to this affinity, it was not lost on Easton (1990).

9. This idea first appears in Miliband (1965, 278), where he argues that Marx's "whole trend of thought on the subject of the state finds its most explicit expression in the famous formulation of the *Communist Manifesto:* 'The executive of the modern state is but a committee for managing the common affairs of the whole bourgeoisie.'"

10. Piven (1994, 25) recounts that "a mutual friend told me not long ago that Ralph had been deeply moved as a young man by the *Communist Manifesto.*" Similarly, Blackburn (1994, 22) observes that Miliband was aware that "the young socialist militant who first lent him a copy of the *Communist Manifesto*" perished in a Nazi extermination camp.

11. Elsewhere, Miliband (1977, 2) observes that "none of the greatest figures of classical Marxism, with the partial exception of Gramsci, ever attempted or for that matter felt the need to attempt the writing of a 'political treatise.'" See also Miliband (1970b, 309), where he reiterates that "*The State and Revolution* is rightly regarded as one of Lenin's most important works. In short, here, for intrinsic and circumstantial reasons, is indeed one of the 'sacred texts' of Marxist thought."

12. Poulantzas (1978b, 18) emphasizes that the raw materials of political theory are "the texts of the Marxist classics."

13. See Althusser and Balibar (1977).

14. Miliband (1965) references many of the works later cited by Poulantzas and, subsequently, by Theda Skocpol, as the textual basis for a "secondary view" of the state that considers exceptional historical circumstances of limited state autonomy. For Miliband, these texts—particularly Marx's *Eighteenth Brumaire of Louis Bonaparte* and Engels's *Origin of the Family, Private Property, and the State*—present qualifications to Marx's "primary view of the state."

15. The best examples are Étienne Balibar, "The Basic Concepts of Historical Materialism," in Althusser and Balibar, *Reading Capital,* pp. 199–308; Barry Hindess and Paul Q. Hirst, *Mode of Production and Social Formation* (London: Macmillan, 1977); Samir Amin, *Unequal Development* (New York: Monthly Review Press, 1976), pp. 13–26; Barry Hindess and Paul Q. Hirst, *Pre-Capitalist Modes of Production* (London: Routledge and Kegan Paul, 1975), pp. 1–12.

16. Strauss (1959, 56–77) draws a sharp distinction between the disciplines of "history" and "political philosophy," but the idea that political philosophy is concerned with reasoning about concepts in a timeless present is clearly not limited by the requirements that one accept a particular set of texts as the basis of one's interpretive canon. See also Strauss and Cropsey (1963). It may seem astounding to suggest that Strauss and Althusser share the same epistemological ground in political

philosophy, but Balibar (1994) documents that Althusser's references to different kinds and levels of knowledge, as well as his concept of an epistemological break, are fundamentally Platonist.

17. Miliband (1965, 278) was aware of this epistemological dichotomy early in the debate when he insisted that "what needs to be compared is not text with text, but text with historical or contemporary reality itself."

18. Note the similarity between Miliband's formulation and Sweezy (1942, 243), who asserts that the state is "an instrument in the hands of the ruling class for enforcing and guaranteeing the stability of the class structure itself."

19. Miliband is responding most notably to Dahl (1958, 463), who dismisses the ruling elite model as "a type of quasi-metaphysical theory.... The least we can demand of any ruling elite theory that purports to be more than a metaphysical or polemical doctrine is, first, that the burden of proof be on the proponents of the theory and not on its critics; and, second, that there be clear criteria according to which the theory could be disproved."

20. In contrast, Dahl (1958, 465) argues that "neither logically nor empirically does it follow that a group with a high degree of influence over one scope will necessarily have a high degree of influence over another scope within the same system."

21. In the same passage, Miliband (1969, 59) notes that capitalists "have never constituted, and do not constitute now, more than a relatively small minority of the state elite as a whole."

22. The passage cited is Kautsky (1910, 29). Miliband cites this passage nearly a decade prior to the widely acclaimed article by Block (1977).

23. For supporting evidence, see Riddlesperger and King (1989); Zweigenhaft (1975); Freitag (1975). For historical data, see Mintz (1975).

24. Importantly, however, Miliband (1969, 47) notes: "This does not mean that they [capitalists] have always known how best to safeguard their interests—classes, like individuals, make mistakes—though their record from this point of view, at least in advanced capitalist countries, is not, demonstrably, particularly bad."

25. Miliband (1983, 12) elsewhere points to this distinction by noting that the concept of the state "refers to certain people who are in charge of the executive power of the state—presidents, prime ministers, their cabinets, and their top civilian and military advisers."

26. Miliband (1969, 78) observes that state elites "have often been forced, mainly as a result of popular pressure, to take action against *certain* property rights and capitalist prerogatives." See Clarke (1991, 19).

27. Miliband (1970a, 55) observed that a translation of Poulantzas's book into English "is urgently needed."

28. Clarke (1977); Althusser and Balibar (1977, 201): "the concept of the 'mode of production' and the concepts immediately related to it thus appear as the first abstract concepts whose validity is not as such limited to a given period or type of society, but on which, on the contrary, the concrete knowledge of this period and type depends."

29. See also, respectively, Wright (1978) and Amin (1976).

30. Likewise, Poulantzas (1978b, 68 n. 16): "Classes always denote class *practices, and these practices are not structures.*"

31. For instance, Marx (1906, 15) states that "individuals are dealt with only inso-

far as they are the personifications of economic categories, embodiments of particular class relations and class interests."

32. Poulantzas (1978b, 48) insists that "a good deal of guidance on these questions is found in the Marxist classics," but in practice he cites Easton, Deutsch, Apter, Almond, and Coleman.

33. Poulantzas (ibid., 51) reiterates that "there is a global function of cohesion which is ascribed to it [the state] by its place" in the mode of production. Also see Bridges (1973).

34. Poulantzas (ibid., 53): "We must remember here the relation between the state (through the agency of the dominant class) and the general direction of the labour process, with particular reference to the productivity of labour."

35. For instance, Poulantzas (ibid., 28) insists that "the state's major contribution to reproducing the economic relations of a capitalist social formation is the effect of its policies on the reproduction of labor power and the means of labor."

36. For an example, see Mamut (1990) and Hirst (1979).

37. Poulantzas (1978b, 115 n. 24) defines an institution as "a system of norms or rules which is socially sanctioned.... On the other hand, the concept of structure covers the *organizing matrix* of institutions." However, on this point, he also notes "that structure *is not the simple principle of organization which is exterior to* the institution: the structure is present in an allusive and inverted form in the institution itself."

38. Cf. Wright (1978, 11n), who observes that "the point of the distinction is to emphasize that there are structural mechanisms which generate immediately encountered reality, and that a Marxist social theory should be grounded in a revelation of the dynamics of those structures, not simply in a generalization about the appearances themselves."

39. This definition assumes that the important conditions of capitalist accumulation are the productivity of labor, the security of private property, an efficient system of exchange and contract, and so on, as identified by Poulantzas.

40. Clark and Dear (1984, 45) observe that, "generally speaking, the term 'state apparatus' refers to the set of institutions and organizations through which state power is exercised."

41. Jessop (1982, 221) echoes this view with his observation that "the state is a set of institutions that cannot, *qua* institutional ensemble, exercise power." Indeed, he argues that a key methodological guideline in formulating a Marxist theory of the state is a "firm rejection of all attempts to distinguish between 'state power' and 'class power' (whether as descriptive concepts or principles of explanation)" (224). Similarly, Therborn (1978, 132) contends that "the state as such has no power; it is an institution where social power is concentrated and exercised."

42. Poulantzas (1969, 69) also concludes that "the procedure chosen by Miliband—a *direct* reply to bourgeois ideologies by the immediate examination of concrete fact—is also to my mind the source of the faults of his book."

43. In contrast, Wright (1978, 9) argues that in the United States, "to the extent that the debate [between bourgeois and Marxist social science] raged simply at the level of theory, non-Marxists found it relatively easy to dismiss our challenges."

44. This thesis was developed more extensively in Poulantzas (1973 and 1978a).

45. King (1986, 77) observes that in Poulantzas's formulation, "state bureaucrats

are constrained to act on behalf of capital because of the logic of the capitalist system, irrespective of their personal beliefs or affiliations."

46. Likewise, Poulantzas (1969, 75) insists that "the State apparatus forms an *objective system* of special 'branches' whose relation presents a *specific internal unity* and obeys, to a large extent, *its own logic.*"

47. Poulantzas (1973, 47) again suggests that "the state is composed of *several apparatuses:* broadly, the *repressive* apparatus and the *ideological apparatus,* the principal role of the former being repression, that of the latter being the elaboration and incubation of ideology. The ideological apparatuses include the churches, the educational system, the bourgeois and petty bourgeois political parties, the press, radio, television, publishing, etc. These apparatuses belong to the state system because of their objective function of elaborating and inculcating ideology."

48. Similarly, Abercrombie, Turner, and Urry (1976, 513) refer to Poulantzas's argument as "a form of omnipotent structuralism."

49. More specifically, Poulantzas was rejecting an effort by Laclau (1975).

50. For precisely this reason, Callinicos (1976, 7–9) argues that the Marxist tradition should not be identified "with a selection of texts," for this identification would "presuppose the existence of principles governing the selection and these principles would be by no means self-evident."

References

Abercrombie, Nicholas, Bryan Turner, and John Urry. 1976. "Class, State and Fascism: The Work of Nicos Poulantzas." *Political Studies* 24: 510–19.

Alford, Robert R., and Roger Friedland. 1985. *Powers of Theory: Capitalism, the State, and Democracy.* Cambridge: Cambridge University Press.

Allender, Paul. 1996. "A 'New' Socialist Party?" *Capital and Class* 59: 144–49.

Almond, Gabriel. 1988. "The Return to the State." *American Political Science Review* 82: 853–74.

Almond, Gabriel, and James S. Coleman. 1960. *The Politics of Developing Areas.* Princeton, N.J.: Princeton University Press.

Althusser, Louis. 1969. *For Marx.* New York: Pantheon Books.

———. 1993. *The Future Lasts Forever: A Memoir.* New York: New Press.

Althusser, Louis, and Étienne Balibar. 1977. *Reading Capital.* London: New Left Books.

Amin, Samir. 1976. *Unequal Development: An Essay on the Social Formations of Peripheral Capitalism.* New York: Monthly Review Press.

Apter, David. 1958. "A Comparative Method for the Study of Politics." *American Journal of Sociology* 64: 221–37.

Ashcraft, Richard. 1980. "Political Theory and the Problem of Ideology." *Journal of Politics:* 687–705.

Balibar, Étienne. 1994. "Althusser's Object." *Social Text* 39: 157–88.

Baran, Paul A., and Paul M. Sweezy. 1966. *Monopoly Capital: An Essay on the American Economic and Social Order.* New York: Monthly Review Press.

Barrow, Clyde W. 1993. *Critical Theories of the State: Marxist, Neo-Marxist, Post-Marxist.* Madison: University of Wisconsin Press.

Bernstein, Eduard. 1961. *Evolutionary Socialism.* New York: Schocken Books.

Blackburn, Robin. 1994. "Ralph Miliband, 1924–1994." *New Left Review* 206: 15–25.

Block, Fred. 1977. "The Ruling Class Does Not Rule: Notes on the Marxist Theory of the State." *Socialist Revolution* 7: 6–28.
Bridges, Amy Beth. 1973. "Nicos Poulantzas and the Marxist Theory of the State." *Politics and Society* 2: 161–90.
Callinicos, Alex. 1976. *Althusser's Marxism.* London: Pluto Press.
Carnoy, Martin. 1984. *The State and Political Theory.* Princeton, N.J.: Princeton University Press.
Clark, Gordon L., and Michael Dear. 1984. *State Apparatus: Structures of Language and Legitimacy.* Boston: Allen and Unwin.
Clarke, Simon. 1977. "Marxism, Sociology, and Poulantzas' Theory of the State." *Capital and Class* 2: 1–31.
———, ed. 1991. *The State Debate.* New York: St. Martin's Press.
Comninel, George C. 1987. "Review of *Nicos Poulantzas: Marxist Theory and Political Strategy,* by Bob Jessop," *American Political Science Review* 81: 616–17.
Dahl, Robert A. 1956. *A Preface to Democratic Theory.* Chicago: University of Chicago Press.
———. 1958. "A Critique of the Ruling Elite Model." *American Political Science Review* 52: 463–69.
———. 1959. *Social Science Research on Business: Product and Potential.* New York: Columbia University Press.
Das, Raju J. 1996. "State Theories: A Critical Analysis." *Science and Society* 60: 27–57.
Domhoff, G. William. 1978. *The Powers That Be: Processes of Ruling Class Domination in America.* New York: Vintage Books.
———. 1986–87. "Corporate-Liberal Theory and the Social Security Act: A Chapter in the Sociology of Knowledge." *Politics and Society* 15: 295–330.
Easton, David. 1953. *The Political System: An Inquiry into the State of Political Science.* New York: Alfred A. Knopf.
———. 1965. *A Systems Analysis of Political Life.* Chicago: University of Chicago Press.
———. 1981. "The Political System Besieged by the State." *Political Theory* 9: 303–25.
———. 1990. *The Analysis of Political Structure.* New York: Routledge and Kegan Paul.
Edwards, Richard C., Michael Reich, and Thomas E. Weisskopf, eds. 1978. *The Capitalist System.* 2d ed. Englewood Cliffs, N.J.: Prentice Hall.
Ehrenreich, Barbara, and John Ehrenreich. 1977. "The Professional Managerial Class." *Radical America* 11: 7–31.
Evans, Peter B., Dietrich Rueschemeyer, and Theda Skocpol, eds. 1985. *Bringing the State Back In: Contemporary and Historical Perspectives.* Cambridge: Cambridge University Press.
Freitag, Peter. 1975. "The Cabinet and Big Business." *Social Problems* 23: 137–52.
Galbraith, John Kenneth. 1952. *American Capitalism: The Concept of Countervailing Power.* Boston: Houghton Mifflin.
Gold, David A., Clarence Y. H. Lo, and Erik Olin Wright. 1975a. "Recent Developments in Marxist Theories of the Capitalist State, Part I." *Monthly Review* 27: 29–43.
———. 1975b. "Recent Developments in Marxist Theories of the Capitalist State, Part II." *Monthly Review* 27: 36–51.
Hindess, Barry, and Paul Q. Hirst. 1975. *Pre-Capitalist Modes of Production.* London: Routledge and Kegan Paul.

———. 1977. *Mode of Production and Social Formation.* London: Macmillan.
Hirsch, Arthur. 1981. *The French New Left: An Intellectual History from Sartre to Gorz.* Boston: South End Press.
Hirst, Paul Q. 1979. *On Law and Ideology.* London: Macmillan.
Holloway, John, and Sol Picciotto. 1978. "Introduction: Towards a Material Theory of the State." In John Holloway and Sol Picciotto, *State and Capital: A Marxist Debate.* Austin: University of Texas Press. 1–31.
Jessop, Bob. 1977. "Recent Theories of the Capitalist State." *Cambridge Journal of Economics* 1: 353–72.
———. *The Capitalist State.* New York: New York University Press.
———. 1985. *Nicos Poulantzas: Marxist Theory and Political Strategy.* New York: St. Martin's Press.
———. 1991. "On the Originality, Legacy, and Actuality of Nicos Poulantzas." *Studies in Political Economy* 34: 75–107.
Kautsky, Karl. 1910. *The Social Revolution.* Chicago: Charles H. Kerr.
King, Roger. 1986. *The State in Modern Society.* Chatham, N.J.: Chatham House Publishers.
Kovel, Joel. 1994. "Remembering Ralph Miliband." *Monthly Review:* 51–58.
Laclau, Ernesto. 1975. "The Specificity of the Political: The Poulantzas–Miliband Debate." *Economy and Society* 5: 87–110.
Lukács, Georg. 1971. *History and Class Consciousness: Studies in Marxist Dialectics.* Cambridge: MIT Press.
Mamut, L. S. 1990. "Questions of Law in Marx's *Capital.*" In Bob Jessop, ed., *Karl Marx's Social and Political Thought: Critical Assessments.* London: Routledge, Chapman, and Hall. 95–105.
Marx, Karl. 1906. *Capital.* Vol. 1. New York: Modern Library.
Mason, Edward S. 1964. *Economic Concentration and the Monopoly Problem.* New York: Atheneum.
Means, Gardiner C. 1939. *The Structure of the American Economy.* Washington, D.C.: U.S. Government Printing Office.
Miliband, Ralph. 1965. "Marx and the State." In Ralph Miliband and John Saville, eds., *Socialist Register.* New York: Monthly Review Press. 278–95.
———. 1969. *The State in Capitalist Society.* New York: Basic Books.
———. 1970a. "The Capitalist State: Reply to Poulantzas." *New Left Review* 59: 53–60.
———. 1970b. "Lenin's *The State and Revolution.*" In Ralph Miliband and John Saville, eds., *Socialist Register.* London: Merlin Press. 309–19.
———. 1973. "Poulantzas and the Capitalist State." *New Left Review* 82: 83–92.
———. 1977. *Marxism and Politics.* New York: Oxford University Press.
———. 1983. "State Power and Class Interests." *New Left Review* 138: 37–68.
———. 1993. "Harold Laski: An Exemplary Public Intellectual." *New Left Review* 200: 75–81.
———. 1994a. *Socialism for a Skeptical Age.* London: Polity Press.
———. 1994b. "Thirty Years of the Socialist Register." In Ralph Miliband and Leo Panitch, eds., *Socialist Register.* London: Merlin Press. 1–19.
Mintz, Beth. 1975. "The President's Cabinet, 1897–1972: A Contribution to the Power Structure Debate." *Insurgent Sociologist* 5: 131–48.

———. 1989. "United States of America." In Tom Bottomore and Robert J. Brym, eds., *The Capitalist Class: An International Study.* New York: New York University Press. 207–36.

Offe, Claus. 1975. "The Theory of the Capitalist State and the Problem of Policy Formation." In Leon Lindberg, ed., *Stress and Contradiction in Modern Capitalism.* Lexington, Mass.: D. C. Heath. 125–44.

———. 1984. *Contradictions of the Welfare State.* Cambridge: MIT Press.

Ollman, Bertell. 1982. *The Left Academy: Marxist Scholarship on American Campuses.* New York: McGraw-Hill.

———. 1993. *Dialectical Investigations.* New York: Routledge, Chapman, and Hall.

Panitch, Leo. 1994. "Socialist Scholar." *Nation* (June 13): 821–22.

———. 1995. "Ralph Miliband, Socialist Intellectual, 1924–1994." In Leo Panitch, ed. *Socialist Register.* London: Merlin Press. 1–21.

Parsons, Talcott. 1951. *The Social System.* Glencoe, Ill.: Free Press.

Piven, Frances Fox. 1994. "Reflections on Ralph Miliband." *New Left Review* 206: 23–26.

Poster, Mark. 1975. *Existential Marxism in Postwar France: From Sartre to Althusser.* Princeton, N.J.: Princeton University Press.

Poulantzas, Nicos. 1967. "Marxist Political Theory in Great Britain." *New Left Review* 43: 57–74.

———. 1968. *Pouvoir politique et classes sociales.* Paris: Maspero.

———. 1969. "The Problem of the Capitalist State." *New Left Review* 58: 67–78.

———. 1973. "On Social Classes." *New Left Review* 78: 27–54.

———. 1974. *Fascism and Dictatorship: The Third International and the Problem of Fascism.* Trans. Judith White. London: New Left Books.

———. 1976. "The Capitalist State: A Reply to Miliband and Laclau." *New Left Review* 95: 63–83.

———. 1978a. *Classes in Contemporary Capitalism.* London: Verso Books.

———. 1978b. *Political Power and Social Classes.* London: Verso Books.

———. 1980. *State, Power, Socialism.* London: Verso Books.

Riddlesperger, James W., Jr., and James D. King. 1989. "Elitism and Presidential Appointments." *Social Science Quarterly* 70: 902–10.

Ross, George. 1994. "Ralph Miliband." *PS: Political Science and Politics* 27: 572.

Saville, John. 1995. "Parliamentary Socialism Revisted." In Leo Panitch, ed., *Socialist Register.* London, Merlin Press. 225–38.

Singer, Daniel. 1970. *Prelude to Revolution: France in May 1968.* London: Jonathan Cape.

Strauss, Leo. 1959. *What Is Political Philosophy? and Other Studies.* Glencoe, Ill.: Free Press.

Strauss, Leo, and Joseph Cropsey, eds. 1963. *History of Political Philosophy.* Chicago: Rand McNally.

Sweezy, Paul. 1942. *The Theory of Capitalist Development: Principles of Marxian Political Economy.* New York: Monthly Review Press.

Therborn, Göran. 1976. *Science, Class, and Society.* London: New Left Books.

———. *What Does the Ruling Class Do When It Rules? On the Formation of Sociology and Historical Materialism.* London: New Left Books.

———. 1980. *The Ideology of Power and the Power of Ideology.* London: Verso.

———. 1987. "Review of *Nicos Poulantzas: Marxist Theory and Political Strategy*, by Bob Jessop." *American Journal of Sociology* 92: 1230–31.

Touraine, Alain. 1971. *The May Movement.* New York: Random House.

Truman, David. 1951. *The Governmental Process.* Westport, Conn.: Greenwood Press.

Useem, Michael. 1984. *The Inner Circle: Large Corporations and the Rise of Business Political Activity in the U.S. and U.K.* Oxford: Oxford University Press.

Wright, Erik Olin. 1978. *Class, Crisis, and the State.* London: New Left Books.

Young, Nigel. 1977. *An Infantile Disorder? The Crisis and Decline of the New Left.* Boulder, Colo.: Westview Press.

Zeitlin, Maurice. 1974. "Corporate Ownership and Control: The Large Corporation and the Capitalist Class." *American Journal of Sociology* 79: 1073–1119.

Zweigenhaft, Richard. 1975. "Who Represents America?" *Insurgent Sociologist* (spring): 119–30.

CHAPTER TWO

The State and Contemporary Political Theory

Lessons from Marx

Adriano Nervo Codato and Renato Monseff Perissinotto

The goal of this essay is to present a reading of the Marxist theory of the state that is more complex than the version produced by recent "neo-institutionalist" critiques. With Marx's historical works (*Revolution and Counter-Revolution* [1848], *Class Struggles in France, 1848 to 1850* [1850], and *The Eighteenth Brumaire of Louis Bonaparte* [1852]) as our point of departure, we attempt to show that his conception of the state takes its internal institutional dynamics into account without forfeiting the perspective of class analysis. In this manner, when Marx introduces the *institutional aspects* of the capitalist state apparatus into his historical analysis, he develops a conception of the state that is both more sophisticated than the "instrumentalist" perspective of some Marxists and some critics of Marxism and less formalist than institutionalist interpretations.

The General Theory of the State in Marx and Engels

Too well known to be taken up again here is the fact that Marx, as part of his intellectual project, intended to devote himself to a more systematic treatment of the state—as his letters to Ferdinand Lassalle (February 22, 1858), to Fredrick Engels (April 2, 1858), and to Joseph Weydemeyer (February 1, 1859), written even before the publication of *A Contribution to the Critique of Political Economy* in Berlin, attest. Yet this was a task he was never able to complete. Similarly, his study of "capital" (and, within it, the chapter on "social classes") remained incomplete. Nonetheless, it can be argued that a generic conception of the state can be found in Marx and Engels's work that can provide the "guiding principle," as

Marx himself claimed ("Preface," 1859), for political analysis. This conception consists, in a nutshell, of the notion of the *class character* of the state. Marxist political theory therefore implies the categorical rejection of the vision in which the state is seen as an agent of "society as a whole" and of "national interests."[1]

This is, in short, the essence of all Marxist conceptions of the state, as summarized with notable clarity in the well-known formula from *The Communist Manifesto:* "The executive of the modern state is but a committee for managing the common affairs of the whole bourgeoisie (Marx and Engels 1848 [1969])."[2] Engels expressed the same idea in an equally famous passage: "The central link in civilized society is the state, which in all typical periods is without exception the state of the ruling class, and in all cases continues to be essentially a machine for holding down the oppressed, exploited class" (Engels 1884 [1969]).

Yet, although the assertion of the class character of the state apparatus is a necessary condition for the analysis of the state system, when one goes on to look at its *internal configuration,* its *levels of decision making,* and the functions fulfilled by its diverse *centers of power,* whether as decision makers or as political organizers of the interests of dominant classes and class fractions, this determination is highly insufficient. The *state apparatus,* Poulantzas reminds us, "is not reducible to *state power.*" "The State really does exhibit a peculiar material framework that can by no means be reduced to mere political domination" (Poulantzas 1978, 14). In this sense, the mediating role that the state plays through its administrative and routine bureaucratic activities acquires a decisive importance with regard to its *class character.* In an analogous way, this latter problem does not refer exclusively to the "effects of state policies—which involve analytically distinct, though empirically closely related questions of state power—but to their form and intrinsic content" (Therborn 1978, 39).

The most defining characteristic in the development of contemporary Marxist political theory has been the absence of questions referring to the processes of internal organization of the state apparatus. Even Poulantzas, who sought to comprehend "the specific system of organization and internal workings of the capitalist state apparatus" through the concept of "bureaucratism" primarily explored the *ideological effects* of this system on the *practices* carried out by the state (bureaucracy) (Poulantzas 1968, 153–93).

According to common critiques, the reasons for such systematic omission should be sought precisely in the confusion that the Marxist tradition has promoted through its stubborn conflation of *state power* and *class power*, reducing the state apparatus to an instrument controlled by dominant interests. It is almost as if the identification of the state's *class character* had freed Marxists from the analysis of the concrete forms through which it unfolds (that is, the way the state *works*). At best, Marxists have devoted attention to the meaning (in class terms) of *state policies* (i.e., the social sectors that benefit from particular decisions, generally economic), but not the modes of *internal organization of the state apparatus* and their repercussions on decision-making processes.

This critique comes in two versions. The first one emphasizes the effects of this restrictive notion of politics and the state on the theory of political regimes; the second draws attention to the difficulties of a theory of the state in Marx and later Marxisms. We will take a closer look at each one of them.

The "Institutionalist" Criticism to Marx's Theory of the State

Beginning in the mid-1960s, most notably in Italy, the literature belonging to the "revisionist" strand emphasized the incipient nature of Marxist *political* theory.[3] According to Norberto Bobbio, the fact that Marx never wrote the book he had planned to on the state (which could be conceived of as merely circumstantial) in fact confirms the biased treatment that the problem received at the hands of this theoretical tradition. The state was frequently conceived of as "instrumental" (in terms of class domination) or as a mere "reflection" (of the structures determined by the economic "base"). This is exactly where we can find Marxism's main difficulties in dealing with the two most recurring problems of traditions of political thought: the problem of "forms of government" and its correlate—which polarized the theoretical agenda of political science at the end of the twentieth century—the problem of "political institutions."

In its essence, the argument can be presented in the following manner: in insisting on the *class nature of state power*, classical Marxists did not theorize the different modes in which power is exercised. Because they were always concerned with "who" exercises political domination and not with "how" it is exercised, in a class-divided and stratified society, government—*any government* under whatever form (whether "democratic" or "dictatorial")—was always conceived of as oriented toward fulfilling the general interests of the ruling class, regardless of its form, as can be gleaned from the following passage:

> Marx and Engels (and in their following, a revolutionary leader such as Lenin), convinced as they were that the political sphere is a sphere of force (and in this sense they were perfectly right), always set up for themselves the problem of the historical argument of this force, as particularly expressed from time to time in the ruling class, rather than inquiring into the *various modes* through which such force can be exercised (which is the problem of institutions). (Bobbio 1979, 28-emphasis added)[4]

This leads to a theory of the state that, according to Norberto Bobbio, is essentially partial and incomplete. This is both a theoretical and a political problem. The backwardness, the lacunae, and the contradictions of Marxist political theory, in this sense, impinged on the development of a more articulate reflection regarding the organizational form of the socialist state—and the "dictatorship of the proletariat"—with its specific institutions.

This critique was reinforced and built up by contemporary literature in political science, whose main current today—neo-institutionalism—predicates a "return to the state" and rejects purely societal explanations for historical processes. Such an approach maintains that Marx's vision of the state (and of bureaucracy) was impoverished and schematic, and that there is not, in his work, a more careful treatment of the problem that goes beyond the mere *confirmation* of the class character of processes of political domination.[5] In consequence, the state, from Marx's perspective, can never be studied as "an independent actor," to use Skocpol's expression, that is, as an autonomous variable or an explanatory factor of social and political phenomena in its own right. From this perspective, there cannot really be a theory of the state. Even the most recent works on the capitalist state, in spite of some undeniable progress with regard to the recognition of the "relative autonomy of the political," have not overcome what we could refer to as this "genetic" difficulty of Marxist political theory.[6] For example, Fred Block, one of the representatives of this perspective, argued that the concept of the "relative autonomy" of the state was not more than a renewal, albeit a more sophisticated one, of the stubborn Marxist reductionism that identifies state power and class power (Block 1987a, 83). This makes it impossible to understand both "state" and "society" from a relational perspective that would give the proper weight to each one in a sociological explanation that thus leads to a more "complex" view.

This essay does not intend to take inventory of the classic and contemporary contributions in the Marxist camp in order to contrast them to neo-institutionalist critiques. Our goal is much more modest: to respond to such interpretations, contrasting them to a less superficial and more careful reading from certain selected passages from Marx's "historical works." From our point of view, the political analyses that Marx develops in *Revolution and Counter-Revolution, Class Struggles in France, 1848 to 1850,* and *The Eighteenth Brumaire of Louis Bonaparte* successfully bring together two distinct levels of analysis.

At a more general and abstract level, Marx's point of departure for understanding the French and German states is in fact their *reproductive* functions. In this sense, the autonomy that these "institutions" acquire in particular historical situations does not make them an "autonomous" or "detached" social force. From the "reproductive" point of view, the state is the "political form" of bourgeois society and "state power" is identified with class power. Its reproductive role vis-à-vis the social order—a fundamental criterion in defining the state's class character—becomes evident in the following passage, in which the effects of the autonomy of the Bonapartist state for the broader reproduction of French industrial capitalism are evaluated:

> It [the empire] was acclaimed throughout the world as the savior of society. Under its sway, bourgeois society, freed from political cares, attained a development unexpected even by itself. Its industry and commerce expanded to colossal dimensions; financial swindling celebrated cosmopolitan orgies; the misery of the masses was set off by a shameless display of gorgeous, meretricious and debased luxury. The state power, apparently soaring high above society, was the very hotbed of all its corruptions. (Marx 1871)

Nonetheless, at the level of analysis of political conjuncture, where analyses of the struggles of groups, factions, and class fractions are carried out, the state can be perceived as an "institution" endowed with its own "institutional resources," resources that bestow on it the ability to "take initiatives" and "make decisions." In concrete political struggle, political groups and social classes perceive the state as a powerful institution that is capable of defining the distribution of diverse resources within society. Because of this, struggles occur over the direct *control* or exercise of *influence* from afar over the different branches of the state apparatus. *At this level of analysis,* it is possible to think of the state, on the one hand, and class, on the other, as distinct and autonomous realities. Therefore, we are able to think of "state power" as different from "class power" and of a *conflict-based relationship between the two.* Thus we can find in Marx's texts themselves—and this is the basis of our argument—certain clues that enable us to think of the state "as an institution," to use the term that is so much in vogue today.[7]

The State as Institution in Marx's Historical Works

Marx's political analyses always preserved the decisive difference between the state *apparatus* and state *power.* It was precisely the attention that he devoted to the former that enabled him to emphasize two other correlated differences: between the *dominant* economic class (or class fraction) and the class (or fraction or group) that *governed* politically, and between *state* and *government.* This latter problem can be better understood by considering the opposition that the author established between social classes' *real* and *nominal* power. In fact, a particular class (or class fraction) can hold the helm of the state in its hands—that is, the "government" per se—without being the *ruling class,* and vice versa. Moreover, this is a topic that has been of utmost importance to a whole tradition within Marxism, as represented, for example, by Gramsci.

In the works we analyze here, the distinction between *real* and *nominal* power fulfills the role of emphasizing the importance of the *institutional* dimension of the state in political struggle. As we intend to demonstrate, the "political predominance" of a given class or class fraction at a particular historical conjuncture depends to a large extent on its ability to *control* or *influence* the branch of the state apparatus that holds *real power.* This power has a hold over a quantity of institutional resources (budget, administration, repression) that endow the branch within which they are concentrated with "decision-making power" and hands the "administrative reins" over to the class that is installed therein. Marx's historical analyses reveal, among other quite suggestive elements, that there is intense struggle between ruling classes and class fractions over the *control* of these apparatuses. In this sense, the political struggles that took place in Germany in 1848 and in France in the 1848–51 period show, contrary to the neo-institutionalist argument, a relational conception of the pair "state"/"dominant classes," a conception that could only develop to the extent that Marx understood the "state" as a reality separate from social classes.

Where in Marx can this problem be found? In a series of four articles published at the end of 1848 in the *Neue Rheinische Zeitung*, Marx analyzes the reasons for the failure of the antifeudal revolution and the founding of a specifically bourgeois political domain in Germany (Marx 1987). To get back to the central question: why is it that the German 1848 does not repeat the English 1648 or the French 1789? The events that occurred between March and December show that, whether under Camphausen or the Hansemann ministry, and even though the German bourgeoisie may have been "nominally in control" at "the helm of the Prussian state" (owing to its hesitations and the backward steps taken before the democratic demands of the "people" and to its ability to assume only its "most *narrow*, immediate interests"), the "feudal counter-revolutionaries" as represented by the "old bureaucracy" and the "old army," loyal to the Crown, ended up taking over "all important positions" of the state apparatus, thus guaranteeing the restoration of the ancien regime.[8]

> The Prussian bourgeoisie was *nominally* in control and did not for a moment doubt that the powers of the old state had placed themselves unreservedly at its disposal and had become offshoots of its own omnipotence. Not only in the cabinet but throughout the monarchy the bourgeoisie was intoxicated with this delusion. (Ibid.)

How was this able to happen? Or, more precisely: what is the source of this illusion? It is the belief that because the Prussian bourgeoisie was at the "helm of the state" (government office; at the head of the government cabinets), it also held *real power* in its hands. This strategic mistake was what led this class to engage in "*Suppression of every political move of the proletariat* and of all social strata whose interests do not completely coincide with the interests of the class which believes itself to be standing at the helm of state" (ibid.). Thus, this movement led to the *strengthening* of the old repressive institutions: "the old Prussian police force, the judiciary, the bureaucracy and the army, who, since they receive their *pay* from the bourgeoisie, also *serve* the bourgeoisie, as Hansemann thought" (ibid.). It was precisely this *institutional base* that allowed the old social forces to organize the feudal counter-revolution.

Let us take a look at this same problem—the lack of overlap between real power and formal power—from another point of view. How is this expressed in the realm of the state apparatus? At the heart of the state apparatus there are only some branches that, in detriment of others, hold "effective power" or, more properly speaking, real decision-making power—what Marx has called, in *The Class Struggle in France*, the (capacity for) "initiative in the government." In concrete terms, political power is concentrated in specific nuclei of the state apparatus; these, in turn, can be occupied directly (or controlled or influenced) by different social classes; in this case, the relative power of each of them is determined by its proximity to or distance from the most important *center of decision making*. This can be gleaned from the following passage:

> Marche, a worker, dictated the decree by which the newly formed Provisional Government pledged itself to guarantee the workers a livelihood by means of labor, to provide work for all citizens, etc. And when a few days later it forgot its promises and seemed to have lost sight of the proletariat, a mass of 20,000 workers marched on the Hôtel de Ville with the cry: *Organize labor! Form a special Ministry of labor!* Reluctantly and after long debate, the Provisional Government nominated a permanent special commission charged with *lending* means of improving the lot of the working classes! This commission consisted of delegates from the corporations [guilds] of Paris artisans and was presided over by Louis Blanc and Albert. The Luxembourg Palace was assigned to it as its meeting place. In this way the representatives of the working class were banished from the seat of the Provisional Government, the bourgeois part of which retained ***the real state power and the reins of administration*** exclusively in its hands; and *side by side* with the ministries of finance, trade, and public works, *side by side* with the Bank and the Bourse, there arose a *socialist synagogue* whose high priests, Louis Blanc and Albert, had the task of discovering the promised land, of preaching the new gospel, and of providing work for the Paris proletariat. ***Unlike any profane state power, they had no budget, no executive authority at their disposal.*** They were supposed to break the pillars of bourgeois society by dashing their heads against them. While the Luxembourg sought the philosopher's stone, in the Hôtel de Ville they minted the current coinage. (Marx 1964, 42–43; boldface emphasis added)[9]

Thus, this indicates that the State (or, more precisely, the "institutional system of state apparatuses") is a complex compound with *higher (ruling) levels*—what Marx also refers to as "decisive posts," where in fact the "reins of administration" are held—*and subordinate levels* (with "no executive authority," as we have seen).[10] The task of Marxist political analysis is, precisely, to identify those apparatuses where "real power" is concentrated. What could be called the center(s) of real power are, in this context, the indispensable site where class hegemony is exercised. Therefore, it should be emphasized that real power emanates directly from a series of *institutional resources*—administration, budget, executive power—concentrated in a specific branch of the state apparatus, through which the social class that controls it is endowed with a superior position in political struggle. The contrast between the Luxembourg Palace and the Hôtel de Ville speaks eloquently in this regard.

In turn, the way in which the bureaucratic structure of the state and political hegemony are articulated can be better understood by following Marx's analyses of French politics during the period that precedes the December 1851 coup. The February revolution, which undermined the financial aristocracy's exclusive dominion that had been consecrated by the July Monarchy, had the major task of consummating bourgeois rule, "by allowing . . . all the propertied classes to enter the orbit of political power" (ibid., 40).[11] This critical compromise was to be definitively broken at the beginning of November 1849 with Minister Barrot-Falloux's dismissal and Minister d'Hautpoul's ascent. What was the real meaning of this change in government? In sum, the restoration of the financial aristocracy through its control over a decision-making center.

According to Marx himself, the new cabinet's finance minister was Achille Fould. "Fould as Finance Minister signifies the official surrender of France's national wealth to the Bourse, *the management of the state's property by the Bourse and in the interests of the Bourse.* With the nomination of Fould, the finance aristocracy announced its restoration in the *Moniteur.* . . . In place of the names of the saints [the bourgeois republic] put the bourgeois proper names of the dominant class interests. . . . *With Fould, the initiative in the government returned to the finance aristocracy*" (ibid.; emphasis added).

Now, as we can see, this fundamental shift in the heart of the power-holding bloc occurred through the recovery of the finance ministry and the maintenance of this apparatus insofar as it represented the seat of effective power. All the political struggles of this subperiod, which spans from June 13, 1849, to March 10, 1850, can be summarized in this episode of (re)conquest of "executive power":

> The Barrot-Falloux Ministry was the first and last *parliamentary ministry* that Bonaparte brought into being. Its dismissal forms, accordingly, a decisive turning point. With it the party of Order lost, never to reconquer it, an ***indispensable position*** for the maintenance of the parliamentary regime, ***the lever of executive power.*** It is immediately obvious that in a country like France, where ***the executive power commands*** an army of officials numbering more than half a million individuals and therefore constantly maintains an immense mass of interests and livelihoods in the most absolute dependence; where the state enmeshes, controls, regulates, superintends, and tutors civil society from its most comprehensive manifestations of life down to its most insignificant stirrings, from its most general modes of being to the private existence of individuals; where ***through the most extraordinary centralization*** this parasitic body acquires a ubiquity, an omniscience, a capacity for accelerated mobility, and an elasticity which finds a counterpart only in the helpless dependence, the loose shapelessness of the actual body politic—it is obvious that in such a country ***the National Assembly forfeits all real influence when it loses command of the ministerial posts.*** (Marx 1963, 61–62; boldface emphasis added)

The financial aristocracy travels the opposite route of the Party of Order. It struggled to regain its political influence—undermined by the 1848 revolution—throughout the Republican period. This influence was recovered through the (re)conquest of the finance ministry and of the maintenance of this apparatus specifically as the site where effective power was concentrated. When Bonaparte dismissed Minister Odilon Barrot and replaced him with Achille Fould, he was in fact allowing the financial aristocracy to recover the privileged position it held within the state apparatus under Louis Philippe.

Looking at these elements, we are able to establish two fundamental criteria that, when combined with others, enable us to describe and explain the concrete configuration taken on by the state system: in the first place, it reflects the variation in the correlation of forces between the "executive branches" that make up the state apparatus in accordance with their real participation in the decision-making process (as exemplified by Marx's contrast between the "Luxembourg Palace" and the

"Hôtel de Ville"); in the second place, the relationship of competition and predominance between the executive and the legislative (the "National Assembly") in the tortuous process of defining governmental policies must be considered. Taken together, these factors should be able to indicate, with a reasonable margin of certainty, the site where effective power is located within the state apparatus.

In short, at the political juncture Marx analyzed, the "political supremacy" of a particular class fraction results from the *control* or *influence* that this class (or its representatives) are able to exercise over the apparatus in which *real power* is concentrated. Thus, it seems difficult to maintain that Marx underestimates the importance of the state "as an institution" that contributes to the precise configuration taken on by the relations of force in a political scenario within a given historical situation. To maintain such a position, one must ignore all of the passages cited earlier. What we can perceive are the various groups and social classes in conflict over the control of institutional resources monopolized by the state apparatus or, more specifically, by some of its branches. If the state were an institution of lesser importance, how could Marx characterize it as the major "object of desire" of social classes in struggle? The state, in Marx's "historical works," constitutes the principal target of political struggle precisely because it concentrates an enormous amount of "decision-making power" and a significant ability to allocate resources.[12]

Conclusion: The Limits of "Neo-institutionalism"

Neo-institutionalists have accused the Marxist theory of the state of committing the serious mistake of underestimating the state as an institution. This mistake is seen as the inevitable consequence of the Marxist emphasis on the class character of the state apparatus, which, in turn, would make it impossible, from this theoretical perspective, to elaborate a theory of the state per se.

We have tried to demonstrate that the analyses in Marx's "historical works" place value on the state as an institution separate from the ruling classes and class fractions, endowed with resources of its own and, especially in the French case, possessing considerable ability to take initiative and make decisions. It is this *institutional* dimension of the state that motivates social groups and classes, to conquer a privileged position within it. The French political scenario, from 1848 to 1851, was the stage of a struggle between antagonistic social classes, on the one hand, and ruling classes and class fractions, on the other, over the conquest, increase, or consolidation of their respective political influence on state institutions. This is, without doubt, a vision in which "state" and "class" constitute autonomous poles of a single relationship. At the same time, because we do not want to turn Marx into an "institutionalist" *avant la lettre*, it is necessary to emphasize that his analyses, and studies done by Marxist theorists in general, go beyond the "immediate" dimension of specific political struggles and the institutional aspect of the state apparatus.

To recognize the autonomy of the state, its institutional reality, its logic, and the specific interests of its "state agents" should not, according to Marx and the Marxists, stop us from asking what kind of social relations the actions of the "autonomous state" reproduce. It has been precisely through this concept of "state power" that Marxists have tried to respond to this question. As Nicos Poulantzas emphasized:

> The various social institutions, in particular the institution of the state, do not, strictly speaking, have any power. Institutions, considered from the point of view of power, can be related only to *social classes which hold power.* As it is exercised, this power of the social classes is organized in specific institutions which are *power centres:* in this context the state is *the centre of the exercise of political power.* (Poulantzas 1973, 115)[13]

The problem of "state power" is theoretically distinct from the problem of the "state apparatus." Insofar as the latter refers to the institutional dimension, the former seeks to identify which social relations are guaranteed through the public policies that the state promotes. Thus, the social class whose privileged position in the productive structure of a given society is maintained through state actions can be considered the class that holds power.

If we disregard the risk of an exacerbated *functionalism* that can spring from this theoretical position—that is, from *assuming* that the state is functional for the ruling classes' long-term interests—it is undeniable that it represents progress in relation to the neo-institutionalist conception. The identification of the "specificities" of the state apparatus and the bureaucratic origin of particular measures is just a first step in the analysis of the relationship between "state" and "society." Evidence of disputes between the state and ruling classes is not enough to warrant any conclusions before inquiring into the results that such conflicts have in terms of the social relations that structure a given social formation. It is true that Marxist insistence on the question of "state power" may very often lead to underestimating the political conflicts between the state and social classes that are of a more situational nature, which tend to be qualified as "superficial," "short-term," or referring to mere "immediate interests." Nonetheless, it is important to recognize that the Marxist position is a guarantee against the opposite "sin," which would be to interpret these conflicts as irrefutable evidence that the state is not a class state.

Another problem that the neo-institutionalists point out, just as important as the first, is the highly general and abstract character of neo-Marxist theories of the capitalist state. From this point of view, the theoretical discussions initiated by Nicos Poulantzas have only produced ahistorical, and therefore nonoperational, formulations. Thus, according to the neo-institutionalists, if, on the one hand, the state must be understood *theoretically* as a fully autonomous institution, theoretical explanations must at the same time avoid excessive generalization. It is only through historical research that the *real degree of autonomy* of any concrete state can be revealed, and it is only through this type of research that such autonomy can be "measured" (cf. Barrow 1993, 125–45; Skocpol, 1985). The state can be autonomous to a greater or lesser degree, totally autonomous or totally subordinate to the ruling classes, depending on concrete historical situations. As Skocpol argues (1985, 14):

> "state autonomy" is not a fixed structural feature of any governmental system. It can come and go.... Thus, although cross-national research can indicate in general terms whether a governmental system has "stronger" or "weaker" tendencies toward autonomous state action, the full potential of this concept can be realized only in truly historical studies that are sensitive to structural variations and conjunctural changes within polities.

In our opinion, such a position leads to two problems. The first, and perhaps least compromising, resides in the lack of originality in the affirmation that the state's "degree of autonomy" vis-à-vis the ruling classes is a historical matter and that for this reason it cannot be derived from a general theory of the capitalist state. We believe that the Marxian analyses we have cited reveal exactly the historical variation in the relationship between the state and the economically dominant classes. Both in Germany and in France, the relationship between the two fluctuates according to the dynamics of political struggle, in which diverse class fractions, social groups, and the state bureaucracy participate. In the French case, as we have seen, before Bonaparte's coup there was also a fraction of the bourgeoisie that held *real power* directly. The 1851 coup, in any event, was the fruit of a political process that led to a new situation in which the state's degree of autonomy grew considerably. Poulantzas himself, accused of excessive general theoretical abstraction, always emphasized the historical dimension of the state's degree of relative autonomy with regard to the political struggles of ruling classes and class fractions. The same can be said of Max Weber's work on the modern state, which in fact can be considered the matrix of the premises of neo-institutionalist theory, as Skocpol herself recognizes (ibid., 7).[14]

A more serious problem can be found in the fact that the concept of autonomy that is used by the neo-institutionalists, and Theda Skocpol in particular, leads to an excessively formalist conception of the state, in spite of all of the "historicizing" theoretical discourse that these authors put forth. As Clyde Barrow has noted, the emphasis on the state's "institutional capacity" and on the historical dimension of this capacity has led to a "strong state"/"weak state" antinomy, that is, a scale of measurement in which the state's autonomy varies according to specific historical situations. Only the concrete relationship between "state agents" and social forces in any given society can determine whether the state in that society is "strong" or "weak." In this manner, we would not arrive at a theory of the state, as the neo-institutionalists argue, but at a mere triviality according to which strong states—that is, those that are endowed with significant institutional resources—are more capable of acting autonomously against the interests of the ruling class, given their institutional capacity to do so. Conversely, weak states have lesser chances to act against the interests of the ruling class, even when this is the will of the state elite, given their lesser institutional capacity (Barrow 1993, 132).[15]

This purely "quantitative" view of the question of state autonomy is a tributary of J. P. Nettl's seminal article (Nettl 1968), cited several times in the book by Evans, Rueschemeyer, and Skocpol, which in the end amounts to a purely functional account of the state, as the author himself admits. Nettl first presents a schema of essential traits that characterize a state (internal and external sovereignty, autonomy, sociocultural roots) and then goes on to assert that his concept provides a measurement of *stateness* (or, in another formulation of his, the "saliency of the state") for a given society. Because this is a "quantitative variable," the best way to measure would be through functional analysis. Thereby, societies characterized by centralized administration directed by the state, state sovereignty that has been institutionalized in detriment of other nonstate organizations, in which the state has autonomy (in other words, capacity to take initiatives), and consequently, the ability to implement its objectives, can be seen as societies with high levels of stateness; on the contrary, societies in which these attributes are weak or absent can be seen as possessing a low level of stateness. Ultimately, the main concern of the approach suggested by neo-institutionalists is the (conceptual) definition and (empirical) measurement of the stateness of a given society. For this purpose, certain functional attributes have been posited as defining the state, and their empirical presence, as more or less intense, serves as a yardstick for qualifying a state as weak or strong.[16]

The preference for the functional analysis of this quantitative variable is justified, according to Nettl, because in this way a generic definition of the state can be produced, without including certain structural characteristics that, as historical and therefore variable, can be identified through empirical research.[17] In our opinion, this quantitative vision of the autonomy of the state, which aims to leave the structural specificities of the state to historical analysis, becomes highly abstract and formalist to the extent that it ignores the existing correspondence between particular political structures and particular types of relations of production.

As a result, this theoretical perspective is not able to structurally differentiate different states, that is, to perceive that strong or weak states, in spite of this quantitative similarity, can be structurally distinct to the extent that they correspond to different social relations. The institutionalist approach would lead us to identify the French society of the absolutist monarchy as a society with a high degree of *stateness,* and to say the same regarding French society of the postrevolutionary period, because both states were capable of exercising all of the prototypical functions.[18] Yet this position disregards the fact that these are two different types of state, with different organizational structures and that fulfill their functions in qualitatively different ways, with their own ideologies and mechanisms for establishing legitimacy, corresponding to two historically distinct types of society. For this reason, the materialist thesis of the correspondence between the relations of production and the forms taken on by the state, as Marx synthesized in his Preface to *A Contribu-*

tion to the Critique of Political Economy, seems extremely important to us. Without this possibility, we would be left at a very generic and formal level in which we would only be able to determine if society x or y entertains greater or lesser *stateness*, but would be unable to explain *why* the states under consideration take on the form that they do or operate in one way rather than another.

Marxism, in taking into account the inescapable links between political structure and relations of production in a particular society, thus supplies us with a theory of the state that is at once general and historical. This is in fact Nicos Poulantzas's project in *Political Power and Social Classes*. As is known, this author has a clearly functional perspective insofar as he defines any and every state as a "factor of cohesion in a given social formation." At the same time, and following Marx's indication, he sees this function as exercised differently by qualitatively different states, that is, states that are differentially structured. Thus, in a functional sense we could say that capitalist states and the states of slave societies are equivalent. Nonetheless, they are extremely different from the structural point of view and in the way in which they carry out their function, because they belong to qualitatively different societies. In this sense, the "generality" of the theory of the capitalist state in Poulantzas is much less abstract than the vision of the state elaborated by the institutionalists, for it includes only one historical type of state structure. Thus, when we speak of a "capitalist state," we are speaking of something very specific, of a historically particular type of state; on the other hand, when we speak of a "strong state," we are referring to *any* state that incorporates the attributes that Nettl and Skocpol have identified. Thus, neo-institutionalism, in rejecting the connection between the state and relations of production, produces a purely quantitative and highly abstract "theory" that, in spite of its historical discourse, can be indiscriminately applied to all types of state, without giving due value to their structural differences.

Notes

This is a modified version of the paper presented at the seminar "The Concept of State in Modern and Contemporary Philosophy," organized by the Department of Philosophy of the Federal University of Paraná (Brazil), April 17 and 20, 2000. It has been translated from Portuguese by Miriam Adelman.

1. One of the most fundamental theoretical conquests of modern political theory was the assertion of the class character of processes of political domination by classical Marxists. See, in this regard, Macpherson 1985, chapter 5.

2. This is also Ralph Miliband's (1983a) interpretation with regard to the core of Marxian (and Marxist) conception of the state.

3. On the "underdevelopment" of Marxist intellectual production within the domain of political and economic theory from the 1930s on, and the prevalence of aesthetic and cultural studies, see Anderson 1976.

4. See also Bobbio 1983 (21–35) and 1980 (153). Actually, this problem was first emphasized by Aron (1960).

5. As Robert Goodin (1996, 1) has observed, "neo-institutionalism" includes a variety of theoretical currents in a wide variety of fields of knowledge (economics, sociology, history, political science). However, all of them share the more general thesis according to which political institutions should be seen as *autonomous explanatory variables*, endowed with a logic of their own, and not as the result of social forces in conflict. Evidently, this article does not intend to dialogue with all of these theoretical currents, but only with those that choose Marxism as their main interlocutor. Here we have specifically in mind Theda Skocpol's well-known article (Skocpol 1985, 3–43). See also Block 1987a and 1987b; Miliband 1983b; and March and Olsen 1989, 1–19.

6. The concept of the "relative autonomy" of the capitalist state was theoretically elaborated by Nicos Poulantzas in his book *Pouvoir politique et classes sociales*. This was a seminal work that propelled Marxist and Marxist-inspired authors to take up the study of the state again. This was the concern of authors such as Joaquim Hirsch, Claus Offe, Elmar Altvater, and Ralph Miliband, among others, who in their works theoretically conjoined the notions of the "class nature" of the state apparatus and the "relative autonomy" of this apparatus vis-à-vis the ruling classes. The neo-institutionalist perspective is an attempt to go beyond the limits of the "societary" analysis of the state carried out by neo-Marxists. In this regard, the title of Fred Block's (1987a) article is significant: "Beyond Relative Autonomy: State Leaders as Historical Subjects." For a summary of neo-institutionalist critiques of Marxism, see Barrow (1993, 125–45).

7. The distinction between the two levels of analysis that are present in Marx's political theory is obviously not original. Nicos Poulantzas was the first to systematize this as he perceived it in Marx (see Poulantzas 1968). His argument emphasizes the general or *systemic* function of the state as a "factor of social cohesion" (or reproducer of class relations) and the main or *historic* characteristic of the capitalist state in class struggle: its "relative autonomy" with regard to ruling classes and fractions. However, Poulantzas was primarily concerned with the *first level of analysis*, in other words, with theorizing on the class character of the state starting from its reproductive function within capitalist relations of production. We would like to insist, based on Marx's own work, on the importance of the institutional aspects of the state for understanding its conflict-based relationship with ruling classes and fractions and its political consequences. See also Draper (1977, 319).

8. All the expressions within quotation marks belong to Marx (1848).

9. The sentences in italics were highlighted by Marx; the sentences in bold italics are our emphasis.

10. "Thus in the approaching mêlée between bourgeoisie and proletariat, all the advantages, *all the decisive posts,* all the middle strata of society were in the hands of the bourgeoisie, at the same time as the waves of the February Revolution rose high over the whole Continent, and each new post brought a new bulletin of revolution, now from Italy, now from Germany, now from the remotest parts of southeastern Europe, and maintained the general ecstasy of the people, giving it constant testimony of a victory that it had already forfeited" (Marx 1964, 70).

11. "It was not the French bourgeoisie that ruled under Louis Philippe, but *one faction* of it: bankers, stock-exchange kings, railway kings, owners of coal and iron mines and forests, a part of the landed proprietors associated with them—the so-called *financial aristocracy.* It sat on the throne, it dictated laws in the Chambers, it distributed public offices, from cabinet portfolios to tobacco bureau posts" (ibid., 33–34).

12. The following can also be deduced: The fact that the French ruling classes and class fractions were successful (or unsuccessful) in exercising direct or indirect *control* over the "center of real power" in the state apparatus—which could constitute a certain "instrumentalism"—is a historical fact and not the result of a theoretical vice; it is the result of historical research and not a theoretical conjecture.

13. See also Therborn 1978.

14. On Nicos Poulantzas, see 1968, 1976, 72.

15. On Skocpol's position, see also 1979.

16. According to Skocpol, these attributes are complete integrity and stable administrative and military control over a territory, the existence of a body of loyal and qualified staff, and economic resources that are abundant enough to guarantee the efficacy of state action. See Skocpol 1985.

17. "The overall conceptual identification of the state with law, with bureaucracy, or with government merely reimposes an artificial . . . notion of state by grouping structures that are better particularized and that are part of the state in some empirical situations but not in many others where some or all of these structures exist and function without any valid notion or phenomenon of state at all" (Nettl 1968, 563).

18. This is just the type of formalism that Marx did not allow himself. In his view, just as the absolutist monarchy served the interests of the emerging bourgeois society but had to be swept away by the "gigantic broom" of the French Revolution to make way for a new political structure more adequate to that society, "the working class cannot simply lay hold of the ready-made state machinery, and wield it for its own purposes" (Marx 1871). From this perspective, we can certainly assert that the absolutist monarchy, the postrevolutionary French state, and a possible socialist state are "strong states." However, to limit ourselves to this evaluation would be to belittle the specificities of these state structures and their relationship to the different societies in which they operate.

References

Anderson, Perry. 1976. *Considerations on Western Marxism.* London: New Left Books.

Aron, Raymond. 1960. "Les sociologues et les institutions représentatives." *Archives Européennes de Sociologie* 1(2): 142–57.

Barrow, Clyde W. 1993. *Critical Theories of the State.* Madison: University of Wisconsin Press.
Block, Fred. 1987a. "Beyond Relative Autonomy: State Managers as Historical Subjects." In *Revising State Theory: Essays in Politics and Postindustrialism.* Philadelphia: Temple University Press. 81–99.
———. 1987b. "The Ruling Class Does Not Rule: Notes on a Marxist Theory of the State." In *Revising State Theory: Essays in Politics and Postindustrialism.* Philadelphia: Temple University Press. 51–68.
Bobbio, Norberto. 1979. "Existe uma doutrina marxista do Estado?" In *O marxismo e o Estado.* Rio de Janeiro: Graal. 13–31.
———. 1980. *A teoria das formas de governo na história do pensamento político.* Brasília: Editora da UnB.
———. 1983. "Democracia socialista?" In *Qual socialismo? Debate sobre uma alternativa.* 2d ed. Rio de Janeiro: Paz e Terra.
Draper, Hal. 1977. *Karl Marx's Theory of Revolution: State and Bureaucracy.* New York and London: Monthly Review Press.
Engels, Frederick. 1884 (1969). *The Origin of the Family, Private Property, and the State.* In *Marx/Engels Selected Works.* Moscow: Progress Publishers, vol. 3, chap. 9, "Barbarism and Civilization." Online version: Marx/Engels Internet Archive (http://www.marxists.org/archive/marx/works/1884-fam/index.htm).
Goodin, Robert. 1996. "Institutions and Their Design." In Robert E. Goodin, ed., *The Theory of Institutional Design.* Cambridge: Cambridge University Press. 1–53.
Macpherson, C. B. 1985. *The Rise and Fall of Economic Justice and Other Essays.* Oxford: Oxford University Press.
March, James G., and Johan P. Olsen. 1989. *Rediscovering Institutions: The Organizational Basis of Politics.* New York: Free Press.
Marx, Karl. 1848. *Revolution and Counter-Revolution.* Articles from the *Neue Rheinische Zeitung* (December 10, 15, 16, and 31, 1848). Online version: Marx/Engels Internet Archive (http://www.marxists.org/archive/marx/works/1840/neue-rz/index.htm).
———. 1859. "Preface to a Contribution to the *Critique of Political Economy.*" In *Marx/Engels Selected Works.* Online version: Marx/Engels Internet Archive (http://www.marxists.org/archive/marx/works/1850/pol-econ/preface.htm).
———. 1964. *Class Struggles in France, 1848 to 1850.* New York: International Publishers. Online version: Marx/Engels Internet Archive (http://www.marxists.org/archive/marx/works/1850-csf/csf.htm#S1).
———. 1963. *The Eighteenth Brumaire of Louis Bonaparte.* New York: International Publishers. Online version: Marx/Engels Internet Archive (http://www.marxists.org/archive/marx/works/1852–18b/index.htm).
Marx, Karl. 1871. *The Civil War in France.* Online version: Marx/Engels Internet Archive *(http://www.marxists.org/archive/marx/works/1864iwma/1871-cwf/cwf03.htm).*
———. 1987. *The Communist Manifesto.* Chicago: Gateway Editions.
Miliband, Ralph. 1983a. "State." In Tom Bottomore, ed., *A Dictionary of Marxist Thought.* Oxford: Basil Blackwell.
———. 1983b. "State Power and Class Interests." In *Class Power and State Power.* London: Verso/New Left Books. 63–78.
Nettl, J. P. 1968. "The State as a Conceptual Variable." *World Politics* 20: 559–92.

Poulantzas, Nicos. 1973. *Political Power and Social Classes.* London: New Left Books.
———. 1976. "The Capitalist State: A Reply to Miliband and Laclau." *New Left Review* 95: 63–83.
———. 1978. *State, Power, Socialism.* London: Verso Books.
———. 1985. *O Estado, o poder, o socialismo.* 2d ed. Rio de Janeiro: Graal.
Skocpol, Theda. 1979. *States and Social Revolutions.* Cambridge: Cambridge University Press.
———. 1985. "Bringing the State Back In: Strategies of Analysis in Current Research." In Peter B. Evans, Dietrich Rueschemeyer, and Theda Skocpol, *Bringing the State Back In: Contemporary and Historical Perspectives.* Cambridge: Cambridge University Press. 3–37.
Therborn, Göran. 1978. *What Does the Ruling Class Do When It Rules?* London: New Left Books.

CHAPTER THREE

Bringing Poulantzas Back In

Paul Thomas

In my 1994 *Alien Politics: Marxist State Theory Retrieved,* I advanced the view—a view I stand by to this day—that Nicos Poulantzas's theory developed over the all too brief span of his career in such a way that we can almost read in his successive writings the history of twentieth-century Marxist state theory in miniature, or *in petto.* Initially, Poulantzas advanced an explicitly Leninist strategy according to which the working-class movement was to be mobilized in a counterstate organization external to the capitalist state. The movement was of course to be subject to the leadership of a revolutionary vanguard political party. The capitalist state itself was at first regarded by Poulantzas every bit as much as by Lenin as the unambiguous and unequivocal institutional expression of bourgeois political domination. What follows from these characterizations of revolutionary organization and of the capitalist state is the categorical impossibility of working-class utilization of the capitalist state even—or especially—in its liberal, parliamentary or "representative" form. The state must rather be summarily "smashed" as a—or the—precondition of the exercise of proletarian political power.

Poulantzas's thinking at the stage of development represented by *Political Power and Social Classes,* to put the same point another way, was explicitly hostile to Gramsci, among other "Western Marxist" thinkers. Poulantzas, in 1968, believed that the working class cannot attain hegemony before it has seized power and transformed the structure of the state—a position that, of course, had been the official, orthodox Communist Party line against Gramsci all along. What is significant here is the way in which Poulantzas quickly, adroitly, and in principle moved beyond this hidebound *point d'appui.* He experienced what I tried, in *Alien Politics,* to characterize as his very own Brumaire, the Greek colonels' coup d'état of 1967, followed in short order by his own epiphany, *la jolie fête de mai* of Paris in 1968. As a result of these experiences, Poulantzas began seriously to consider not so much "states" per se but regimes—which Marxism, with its obsession(s) with "the" state, had for far too long overlooked. The Greek dictatorship was mischaracterized by others as fascist, whereas to Poulantzas the practical, programmatic question at the time of the Greek coup was how best to prevent it from consolidating its mass base in the manner of real fascist regimes. In this way, the study of Greece and Portugal in the late 1960s and beyond led Poulantzas back to the study of Italy, Germany, and Spain in the 1930s, along with the fateful and invidious strategy of the Comintern toward such regimes. In criticizing the tragic errors of the Comintern, Poulantzas concluded that a successful revolution, or even the successful defense of working-class gains within capitalist society as currently constituted, required the primacy of political class struggle over economic class struggle, the consistent pursuit of a mass line, and an ongoing commitment to proletarian internationalism. At first glance, these broadly Leninist positions do not seem very different from the then official positions of the French Communist Party (PCF): even the other elements of Poulantzas's agenda—the development of workers' councils as the site of mass struggle, the development of a united front of the working class at the rank-and-file level, and the development of a popular front with the poorer peasantry and the petite bourgeoisie—are scarcely without pedigree and may even have had an already shopworn air about them.

Yet Poulantzas, to his credit, was careful to inflect or weight these elements in a way very different from, and finally irreducible to, the regnant party orthodoxy; and he concluded from this very inflection or weighting that the errors of Comintern leadership during the 1930s were still in evidence (in a kind of sedimentary form) in the 1960s. Orthodox theories of state monopoly capitalism (Stamocap) and the antimonopoly alliance can certainly stand as examples of this unwanted residual staying power. More to the point, what further reinforced Poulantzas's status as a maverick within or outside Communist orthodoxy was his principled denial of the continuing validity of the Leninist "dual power" strategy of building up a counterstate outside the capitalist state, a denial advanced on the grounds that the "dual power" strategy, finally, had done nobody any good in Greece or Portugal, and that, in any case, the capitalist state had, by the late 1960s or early 1970s, undergone significant, and presumably irreversible, changes since Lenin's time. Lenin's legacy had, not to mince words, outlived whatever usefulness it may once have had, closer to the turn of the twentieth century.

The modern state, this is to say, is, according to Poulantzas, in no way what Gramsci had termed a *veilleur de nuit*, a "night-watchman" state. Nor indeed can it be considered a mere organ of open, unveiled political repression. Like it or not, the state since the heyday of classical political economy has expanded in scope and scale in such a way that it now permeates and penetrates—or can in principle permeate and penetrate—every crevice of social life, every nook and cranny of "civil society." On top of this engorgement, what is more, there is within the state apparatus a specific condensation of class contradictions, a condensation of the kind that makes possible class struggle within the official state apparatus as well as—not instead of, but as well as—class struggle at a distance from this same apparatus. The military dictatorships Poulantzas examined in the 1970s collapsed in the course of time because of internal contradictions within their respective "power blocs," contradictions that in the event were intensified through popular struggles at some distance from the core of the state; the failure of revolutionary mass parties to coordinate and centralize such popular struggles under working-class hegemony was the main reason why the dictatorships, when they did finally collapse, were replaced not by democratic socialist regimes—or nondemocratic ones, as seemed likely for a heady period in the case of Portugal—but by bourgeois democratic ones. (This very scenario, it bears mentioning in passing, also seems broadly to fit the later transitions from military dictatorships to civilian regimes in Brazil, Argentina, and other Latin American countries: for this and other reasons, one is given to suspect that its usefulness is not yet at an end.) The important theoretical point here is that no "power bloc," being based on a "social formation" that in turn is irreducible to the more encrusted, traditional Marxist notion of a "mode of production," is going to be unitary or monolithic by definition or fiat, but is, to the contrary, by its very nature going to be a "contradictory unity" that is likely to be a much more open and flexible political site of contestation than Lenin's understanding of the state ever proved, in practice, to have become.

What this means, inter alia, is that the state is not a mere instrument to be captured by the working class or its shock troops in a heroic frontal assault, or through the quintessentially Leninist (or Maoist) tactics of encirclement or infiltration. The hard fact of the matter is that different states have different institutional forms that circumscribe changes in the balance of forces and enable the bourgeoisie to recuperate state power—should the working class fail to establish the institutional preconditions for the exercise of its own class power. This way of putting the matter can be made to sound—and, of course, was made to sound—Leninist. But in reality the Leninist wheel had at this point turned full circle, for Poulantzas's thinking by the time he wrote *State, Power, Socialism* (1978) is much more Gramscian than orthodox Leninist. In this book, which sadly stands as his testament, Poulantzas tells us that class struggle should aim not at capturing the state apparatus from without, but rather at transforming it from within. In insisting on this point, Poulantzas, I like to think, is taking literally (and unusually seriously) Marx's principled insistence that "the working class cannot simply take hold of the existing (capitalist) state machinery and wield it for its own purposes" (Marx 1962, 516), and is reading this insistence in what is a distinctively non-Leninist (or, at the very least, post-Leninist) manner. More specifically, a successful democratic transition to socialism, according to Poulantzas, would have to be more flexible than the axiomatic and legendary Leninist coup d'état; it would have to be three-pronged, and not single-minded or concentrated (*décontracté,* one might say) in the Leninist sense. It would instead have to involve at one and the same time coordination of action within the state, action to transform the state, and action at a distance from the state.

State, Power, Socialism was above all, to my mind, an overwhelmingly prescient volume. It was no mere settling of accounts with a misguided, if well-intentioned, past (some of it Poulantzas's own past). In its pages, to begin with, Poulantzas indicates his growing concern with the problems of what was then called "actually existing socialism" in Central and Eastern Europe, problems he thought a left-Eurocommunist standpoint might have been able to alleviate. (I am by no means convinced he was wrong about this, but could not at this remove prove his conclusion was anything other than wishful thinking. This is a question whose answer we shall never know, sadly enough, for the left-Eurocommunist perspective was eclipsed by other, to my mind less salutary, viewpoints, and never came to prevail or even to find significant voice. We may all of us be the poorer for this, in the end.) More projectively (as matters turned out), Poulantzas also indicated in *State, Power, Socialism* his concern with the erosion of democratic sentiment and spirit *within* the emergent "authoritarian statist" system of bourgeois political domination. And this concern, I would want to insist, was prescient indeed, expressed as it was in advance of the era of Reagan and Thatcher, who surely intensified the authoritarian tendencies that were (and still are) at issue.

Poulantzas, again, was no less prescient in pinpointing, in advance, one is tempted to say, the problems posed by the troubled relationship between class struggle and nonclass movements on the left. Both these presentiments pointed in the same, premonitory direction: that of the need to preserve and extend the institutions and values of representative democracy alongside, though not at the expense of, direct rank-and-file democracy in the transition to socialism. To do away with parliamentary democracy because its institutions and values were, at the end of the day, "bourgeois" would be to throw out the baby with the bathwater. Without a parliamentary, representative forum within which issues could be raised, ventilated, discussed, and decided upon, there would and could be no guarantee that the emergent organs of direct, rank-and-file democracy would not be crushed by a self-appointed vanguard party (the historical precedents for such crushings are, in our post-Tiananmen era, all too hideously obvious). It follows that the liberties of a plural party system are not, and should not be regarded as being, anything but a Lenin-defined smoke screen concealing the maneuverings of a predatory bourgeoisie seen as the personification of capital (even if in practice they can become little more than this). Liberties are, to the contrary, in principle, the measure, or at least the hint, of something real and valuable. To take them as ends in themselves, or as forces capable of developing their own momentum, would be a serious first-order mistake. But to dismiss them out of hand, on the spurious grounds that they are purely "bourgeois," purely "formal," thus meaningless and a distraction, snare, or delusion, would be no less mistaken and myopic. Very much in the spirit of Marx's original formulation of "political" as opposed to "human" emancipation (in "On the Jewish Question"), Poulantzas is concerned not to excoriate or dismiss parliamentarism out of hand, nor to take at face value the claims advanced unashamedly on its behalf by parliamentarians, but to treat it as what it is—as unfinished business, as the mark or hint of a fuller, more substantiated democracy that awaits its realization, and as something that may well have preconditions that, taken in and of themselves, are far from ideal.

Just as Marx had needed the experience of Bonapartism and its antithesis, the Paris Commune, to sharpen his understanding of "the political form, at last discovered, beneath which to work out the economic emancipation of labor" (Marx 1962a, 521–22), and just as Gramsci, in his turn, had to undergo the rigors of theoretical work in a fascist jail, so Poulantzas was stimulated in turn to complete his trajectory from Leninist vanguardism to a distinctively left-Eurocommunist position under the impulse and impetus provided by his very own analyses of contemporary authoritarian regimes. These regimes, Poulantzas came to believe, demonstrate the brittleness, frailty, and fragility of what are, to all appearances, strong states; they also led him to understand, as we should all understand, that state power is best understood not as a derivative epiphenomenon of something categorically different and (somehow) more fundamental in civil society. State power is to be understood rather as the condensation of, or form taken by, class struggles, which are themselves going to vary from time to time and from place to place. The state can be a—or even *the*—factor of cohesion and equilibrium of a social formation: it can equally easily be the nodal point of that social formation's contradictions. It all depends on what kind of social formation we are talking about. The left's failure to adequately oppose authoritarianism, to extend Poulantzas's argument, goes along with, and is inherently connected with, its failure to understand what a democratic alternative to authoritarianism might finally comport. It is too often overlooked in the available literature that for Marx, Gramsci, and Poulantzas, authoritarian forms of government were often much more present as a threat and much more immediate as a stimulus than were nonauthoritarian ones. And who, in the end, is to say that they will not persist as a similar kind of threat and a stimulus in the new millennium?

It is, of course, not surprising that I saw fit to praise Poulantzas as fulsomely as I did in *Alien Politics,* a book in which I did my level best to settle my own accounts with an instrumentalist ruling-class theory of the state, the very theory of the state Poulantzas himself had in his sights at a much earlier date. Indeed, it came as no small relief to me to discover at first hand that the center of gravity at the conference I was invited to attend in the spring of 1997, ostensibly on Poulantzas *and* Miliband (and held at the Graduate Center of the City University of New York, Miliband's home base toward the end of his career), visibly shifted away from the Miliband–Poulantzas debate of yore in the direction of a serious, critical engagement with Poulantzas's legacy per se. (This shift is reflected in the character of the present volume.) It may be that Miliband's impassioned and principled, but in my view ultimately unsuccessful, defense of an instrumentalist, ruling-class theory of the state was its very swan song, though this cannot be my concern here.

What can and should be my concern is the provision of a more detailed, more nuanced, more prospective evaluation of Poulantzas's legacy as it has come down to us and, if I am not mistaken, as it points ahead, even (or especially) today. The proceedings of the 1997 conference had the effect, in truth, of making me humbly aware of how strategically, how summarily, I had treated Poulantzas in *Alien Politics.* Rethinking his contribution in the light of these proceedings, I find myself struck all over again by the originality and prescience of the state theory he left us.

To characterize this originality and prescience at all adequately, I must briefly recapitulate the main lineaments of his arguments about the modern state. He sought to explain why national-popular, representative, democratic government is the normal form of political domination in capitalist societies. In particular, he sought to explain how the state functions as a means of political class domination even though class as such is specifically absent from its institutional and ideological organization, and to explain what this paradox, in turn, implies for political struggles in capitalist societies. (Poulantzas was always concerned with problems of revolutionary strategy; his big point against Foucault is that power and knowledge coincide and intersect primarily *at the level of the state,* and that it is their very coincidence at this level that makes possible political resistance.) Poulantzas insists on what he calls the "institutional materiality" of the state, a materiality in which political class domination is embedded. What this means is that the state is actively involved in constituting and maintaining the capitalist division of labor and capitalist relations of production, as well as in organizing hegemonic unity within the power bloc and managing the material bases of consent. (His big point against Althusser is, accordingly, that the state is on no account to be reduced to its ideological and repressive state apparatuses.)

More specifically, the state, according to Poulantzas, constitutes "the factor of cohesion between the different levels of a social formation" (1973, 45); "the political field of the state . . . has always, in different forms, been present in the configuration and reproduction of the relations of production" (1978, 17). This means, in part, that the state draws up and enforces the rules that govern exchange (property law, contract law, etc.), and that it functions to discipline the labor force via its ideological apparatuses (especially the educational system).

Because "the maintenance of political order in political class conflict" (Poulantzas 1973, 53) is a province of state action and state power, and because state power itself consists in considerable measure in the capacity of a dominant social class to realize its objective, political interests through the state's apparatuses, there is an ensemble of class practices that occur "at the strictly political level" (ibid., 104). What this means is that, in examining the protocols of the capitalist state, we must adopt a dual optic, the economic alongside (though not at the expense of) the political. On the one hand, the levels at which the effects of state policies are realized are threefold: the directly economic (the state's enabling contribution to the accumulation process); the political (the state's superintendence and management at the level of class struggle); and the ideological (or the cultural-educational level). Regardless of which level a given capitalist state may be operating at in a given instance, the state's function within this optic is always geared "with particular reference to the productivity of labor" (ibid., 50, 53), and through this to the accumulation of capital—which is to say that the capitalist state is a *capitalist* state.

On the other hand, the state as such has subsystems that are all its own: the juridical (which regulates market exchanges and individuates workers or citizens, if need be, as plaintiffs and defendants); the ideological (especially the superintendance of educational institutions); and the political (maintenance of order, electoral law, superintendance of the party system, the police, the armed forces, the prison system). Each of these, whatever else it may be, is also ultimately political, because each is geared to the maintenance and dominance of the capitalist class (ibid., 54); which is to say that the capitalist state is a capitalist *state.*

The fundamental role of the capitalist state so defined is to ensure the reproduction and the political cohesion of capitalist societies. With regard to the latter function (as Bob Jessop points out in his essay in this volume), although the state is but one among several institutionally separated ensembles within the social formation, it alone is uniquely charged with overall responsibility for maintaining the cohesion of the class-divided social formation of which it is nevertheless a constituent part. Everything points to the same conclusion (though this "conclusion" is, for Poulantzas, a hypothesis on which to build further): that the state should not be regarded either as an instrument or object, or as a subject endowed with an autonomous will all of its own. Instead, the state should be regarded as a site enjoying a relationship of relative autonomy from society. But "relative autonomy" itself is going to have different levels, different meanings, and different modalities at different stages of capitalist development. For one thing, the capitalist state, by its very nature, is going to intervene in the workings of civil society—Poulantzas is adamant, and rightly so, that all capitalist states have done this, and still do—but its intervention, though constant, is not for this or any other reason invariant or uniform from instance to instance. The meaning, bearing, and scope of the state's intervention(s) will vary from social formation to social formation, as will, for that matter, the structural limits on the state's very capacity to intervene.

The state, that is to say, is (to reiterate) not a thing, a material object, nor yet an "instrument" or a "subject." It is a structure called upon to fulfill a fundamental role within capitalist society, that of helping to reproduce capitalist relations of production and domination. At the same time, the capitalist state is the major means for maintaining the cohesion of the social formation on all levels, including the national or territorial level. Both functions require and necessitate constant state intervention: the state is, in other words, constantly called upon to facilitate and undergird the process of accumulation, and to separate and individuate the citizenry within a legally structured, institutionalized, and ideologically homogeneous society (this is the "isolation effect," which Poulantzas, for all I know, might have derived from Jean-Paul Sartre's far from unrelated concept of "seriality," as well as from his own background as a law student). In all these ways, the state is the "condensation" of the various levels and types of class contradictions in a given society. This means not that the state is easy to classify and characterize, but, to the contrary, that there is a density to the state and to what the state does, an opacity that can make it difficult to "place" and define. Yet the basic point remains:

> relative autonomy is inscribed in the very structure of the capitalist state by the relative "separation" of the political and the economic that is specific to capitalism; it is in no way a function of the state or "political instance" as such, but rather derives from the separation and dispossession of the direct producers from ownership of the means of production that characterizes capitalism. In this respect, this relative autonomy is simply the necessary condition for the role of the capitalist state in class representation and in the political organization of hegemony. (Poulantzas 1978, 98)

All this needs to be assessed with some care. If "relative autonomy" so understood is in some sense a given, "structural" characteristic of the capitalist state, this in and of itself tells us very little, save at the level of preliminary definition (or, if you will, of "concept formation"). Relative autonomy takes different forms, and these forms themselves are subject to modification or transformation according to the imperatives of capitalist accumulation, which themselves are anything but regular or invariant. If the form of relative autonomy changes, as is likely, there will be a corresponding shift not just in the character, but also in the functions, of the state.

This is to say that the institutional and ideological transformations to which the state—any state—is subject must be interpreted historically, not just definitionally. And to do this one must perforce be able to take the long view, much as Poulantzas himself (almost uncannily) proved able to do, particularly in his last book, a book so startlingly ahead of its time that those among us who read it hot on the heels of its appearance were unprepared for it and (I dare say) hard put to it to understand its full import and directionality.

To take but one example of Poulantzas's extraordinary prescience, he was able to itemize and characterize authoritarian statism as a project implicit in then current bourgeois (and nonbourgeois) state forms in advance of what the rest of us had to live through and endure, the rigors of the Reagan–Thatcher years. Similarly, Poulantzas was able to speak the language of "globalization" even before the term *globalization* enjoyed much currency. He could tell us where we were (and still are) tending, by virtue of the original vocabulary of concepts he was able to bring to bear on a series of developments he was right to select as pointing the way forward (if not exactly the way ahead): the modification of

Fordism as a type of production; the abandonment of Keynesian macroeconomic techniques for "fine-tuning" the economy; the decline of social democracy—twenty years before Tony Blair's New Labour!—and the welfare state; the increased global reach of capitalism and information technology; the rise, then dominance, of the neoconservative ideologies of the radical right. Others were to notice these unwelcome developments (how could they not have recognized their unwanted arrival?), but their recognition was apt to be haphazard and disconnected. Poulantzas alone, we can see in retrospect, could join the dots. He had elaborated the theoretical apparatus that made such a synthesis possible, as well as desirable.

The upshot? The increasing mobility and fluidity of capital, the increasing reach and spread of information technologies, must entail that accumulation and exploitation, the very linchpins of capitalism, will themselves become increasingly supple and pliable. Accumulation and exploitation these days, as Poulantzas foresaw, are no longer wedded to particular territories; they are eminently exportable. And yet, writing as I am in the state of California, what could be more obvious than the fact that, in the wake of what Guillermo Gómez Peña calls "Naftastroika," while productive capacity and finance capital are free to move across national boundaries, people are being rendered much less free to cross *la frontera* in their wake? This signals a mismatch between the economic and the political, a mismatch that is the product of capitalist states, much as Poulantzas might have predicted. As he insisted in 1975, "every process of internationalization is effected under the dominance of the capital of a definite country" (Poulantzas 1975, 73).

In order to get some purchase on what Bob Jessop at our conference called "Globaloney," or on Poulantzas's insistence that the process of globalization will not, in the end, diminish so much as reconfigure the role of the capitalist state, I can only, in conclusion, indicate in a rough-and-ready way some of the themes expanded upon far more thoroughly in Constantine Tsoukalas's contribution to this volume, in the belief that, although Poulantzas may not have provided us with a key to unlock every door, he was nevertheless the most farsighted and (dare I say?) prophetic Marxist state theorist of the second half of the twentieth century. Poulantzas bequeathed us the wherewithal to think ahead, which is now our task. Ahead to what? The barest bare-bones summary will have, provisionally, to suffice. To begin with, globalization implies limits on the accumulative autonomy of dominant fractions of capital within national boundaries. Because domestic capital is permeated from without, it will reproduce within national boundaries what are external interimperialist contradictions. This will call forth neither the "national" nor the "comprador" fractions of the bourgeoisie of yore, who, in the nature of things, are going to get marginalized, but the "domestic bourgeoisie," who are bound up with globalization; "import substitution" is no longer a viable option, but a dead letter. National capital can no longer be protected; indeed, there is no longer any purely domestic structure that must be protected. Domestic deregulation in this sense follows from international deregulation. Conversely, and here is a Poulantzasian point of real dialectical magnitude, contradictions among fractions of capital within national boundaries will themselves get increasingly "internationalized." This in turn imposes new limits on the autonomy of state structures and on the power blocs they represent, at a time when the power of the national state in the face of internationalization depends, crucially, on the unity and cohesion of the power bloc undergirding and represented by the state. Disinvestment and "capital flow" are no longer even threats that need to be leveled for overtly political reasons. Chronic structural unemployment is at the same time no longer solvable by Keynesian means, means that are no longer on any conceivable political agenda. Social costs are no longer negotiable, and a withered, denatured trade-union movement is usually not even available (now that it has been denied access and made to count for very little) to make the case for negotiation anyway. So much for the once-vaunted "corporatism," which today is strictly a nonstarter. Any redistribution will now be at the behest of the supposed "imperatives" of the (internationalized but no less supposed) "free market" itself. Does this leave states with nothing to do? Under Poulantzas's influence, I hardly think so. It is the state—what else?—that has to superintend and regulate "deregulation," and this can be hard work, hard work that nobody else is going to want to do. If the Reagan–Thatcher years taught us anything, they taught us that states can be very dirigiste, very regulatory indeed as they seek to deregulate. The state will be called on to pick up the pieces, whether or not it proves able to do so; the working class and the underclass will, after all, remain territorially tied and bounded, for how could it be otherwise? Any way you cut it, the accumulation of international capital bids fair to be just as dependent on state intervention as any earlier form of accumulation. This may not be an optimistic prognosis. But don't say that Poulantzas—of all people—didn't warn you.

References

Marx, Karl. 1962a. *The Civil War in France.* In Karl Marx and Frederick Engels, *Selected Works in Two Volumes.* Moscow: Foreign Languages Publishing House.

———. 1962b. *The Critique of the Gotha Programme.* In Karl Marx and Frederick Engels, *Selected Works in Two Volumes.* Moscow: Foreign Languages Publishing House.

Poulantzas, Nicos. 1973. *Political Power and Social Classes.* London: New Left Books.

———. 1975. *Classes in Contemporary Capitalism.* London: New Left Books.

———. 1978. *State, Power, Socialism.* London: Verso Books.

Thomas, Paul. 1994. *Alien Politics: Marxist State Theory Retrieved.* New York: Routledge.

II

The Contemporary Relevance of Miliband and Poulantzas

CHAPTER FOUR

The Impoverishment of State Theory

Leo Panitch

Once upon a time, the capitalist state did not exist. I am not speaking of the period before the middle of the millennium that has just come to a close, the era before the transition from feudalism to capitalism. I am speaking not of five hundred years ago but of less than fifty years ago, the late 1950s and early 1960s; and when I say that the capitalist state did not exist, what I really mean to say is that it did not exist as a term within mainstream political discourse, even as this discourse was reflected in the concepts and theories of the discipline of political science. In the early 1960s, the term *capitalism* itself was rarely used in polite company. It was considered acceptable within the university classroom, even a mark of some intelligence, to point out that capitalism had once existed; it was even considered a plausible argument that back in the era of the robber barons there had actually existed a capitalist ruling class in North America. But that was all "once upon a time." We lived in a mixed economy with a pluralist political system. The term *state* itself was considered either vulgarly radical or tediously arcane as applied to the institutions of government in relation to society, and was rarely employed except to refer to the nation-state in the international political system.

Students of a critical bent in the early and mid-1960s strained against this discourse. Just as we did not let the words *ceteris paribus* go unchallenged in our introductory economic courses (that is, we refused to accept that other things actually were equal), so we wrote essays challenging pluralism in political science, insisting, as Schattshneider already had way back in the 1940s, that the pluralist choir sang with a distinctly upper-class accent. But the exercise we were engaged in was negation. Even C. Wright Mills's *The Power Elite* (1956) and John Porter's *The Vertical Mosaic* (1965) and John Kenneth Galbraith's *New Industrial State* (1967) were mainly appreciated for the evidence they compiled and the tools they lent for tearing down the conceptual prison of mainstream social science. It was only with the emergence of the Marxist theory of the state in the late 1960s and early 1970s that we finally felt ourselves moving from a repetitive and increasingly tedious (because it was so easy) exercise of tearing down pluralism to actually participating in building up a new, far more sophisticated way of studying politics. We sensed, on reading Miliband (1969), Poulantzas (1968), and O'Connor (1973), that we were no longer confined to being just critics, constantly merely negating the old; we sensed that it might be possible to engage ourselves in developing an alternative and better theory, fashioning new conceptual tools for the purpose. It was a highly exhilarating feeling.

It needs to be stressed today that we did not at all see ourselves as falling back on a prefabricated Marxism; the new theory of the state had Marxist roots but it was founded on the notion that nothing like an elaborated and coherent theory of the capitalist state (in contrast with the complex array of concepts and tendential laws that constituted Marxian economics and historical materialism) had been fashioned either by Marx himself or by his successors—up to and including Gramsci. And the new theory was concerned to displace the narrowly ideological official Marxism of the Communist parties.

The recognition that the attempt to develop a Marxist theory of the state was a serious social-scientific exercise yielded a certain toleration of the new theory in academic political-science circles; indeed, it even became rather fashionable. In the 1950s and into the 1960s, political-science theory had been derivative of leading sociologists, but now it was sociologists who were drawing on political scientists such as Miliband, Poulantzas, and their disciples. It appeared that what Gramsci had written a half century earlier was finally being confirmed:

> If political science means science of the State, and the State is the entire complex of practical activities with which the ruling class not only justifies and maintains its dominance, but manages to win the active consent of those over whom it rules, then it is obvious that all the

> essential questions of sociology are nothing other than the questions of political science. (1971, 244)

All this meant that graduate students in political science and sociology who identified themselves with the new state theory were not often barred for that reason from academic employment or publication (provided, at least, they sanitized Miliband and Poulantzas as "neo-Marxists"); sometimes it actually was a guarantee of visibility, which is usually what is meant in academic life by "success."

My own edited book on the state (Panitch 1977), which applied the concepts of O'Connor, Miliband, and Poulantzas to Canada, became a standard text in Canadian politics courses. That any book with the hardly heart-stopping title *The Canadian State* (let alone a Marxist one—the subtitle was *Political Economy and Political Power*) should quickly become an academic best-seller was unheard of. For Miliband's *State in Capitalist Society* to have been favorably reviewed in the *American Political Science Review* was startling enough; but when the review of *The Canadian State* in the country's mainstream public administration journal insisted that "not to read it is to exclude oneself from much of the intellectual action and passion of our time," it appeared that the Marxist theory of the state was reaching places other brands could not.

Few of us were, I think, under any illusions about what this actually meant politically. Those who took up the new theory of the state recognized that imminent social transformation was not on the agenda for the advanced capitalist states, that it would likely not fall to our generation, despite May 1968, to build a new world. (I wonder now whether we learned this from reading Miliband and Poulantzas, or whether we were inclined to read them seriously because we already recognized this and thus saw little odds in joining the vanguard Trotskyist or Maoist parties.) Of course, we took very seriously the importance for long-term strategy of developing a new political science, but most of us knew that all the talk of strategy was empty so long as it remained within the halls of academe. As I put it in the preface to *The Canadian State:*

> One must of course cautiously avoid the illusion that by virtue of its strengths alone a Marxist theory of the state will gain prominence. The rise and fall of theories is not merely the product of intellectual competition with the most fruitful coming out on top. The acceptance of any particular theory and its conceptual elements rests on some

> consensus among intellectuals with regard to the importance of the "significant problems" it identifies. On the identification of those problems, questions of interest as well as objectivity, ideological hegemony as well as academic freedom, will inevitably play their part. Most important of all will be the question of whether the generation of Marxist theory will itself continue to be divorced from the working class in Canada. For without a working class helping to identify the "significant problems" by its own actions, and taking up cultural as well as political and economic struggle by re-examining its history and developing a theory and practice for future change, Marxist theory will lack a social base, which is finally the *sine qua non* for the sustenance of any body of ideas. (Panitch 1977, x)

I do not think I realized when that was written just how little time we had, how contingent the further development of the Marxist theory of the state would be on immediately favorable political conditions. How quickly, in retrospect, it all passed. By the beginning of the 1980s, a strong reaction to the new Marxist state theory set in and it soon became quite unfashionable. This is, of course, one of the dangers of academic fashion. The advances made in Marxist state theory were swept away as part of the general post-Marxist, poststructuralist, postmodernist trend, marked especially by the displacement (via Foucault and Derrida) of the academic "focus of attention from the state and class struggle to the micro-physics of power and the problems of identity formation" (Jessop 1991, 91). But this is only one part of the story. Within political science and political sociology, one of the legacies of the new Marxist theory was actually that the state was firmly reestablished as part of the conceptual lexicon for the study of contemporary politics. In this respect, we might say that reaction against the new Marxist theory did not entail a shift of attention away from the state; on the contrary, research increasingly become determinedly and self-descriptively "state-centered."

There was a remarkable paradox in this development. The state autonomy perspective that emerged in the 1980s involved the theoretical assertion of the institutional autonomy of the state at the very time when the structural power of capital and the strategic and ideological reach of capitalist classes has become perhaps never more nakedly visible. The Marxist theory of the state had emerged to challenge the pretensions of social-democratic reformism, epitomized in claims such as those advanced in Anthony Crosland's *The Future of Socialism* (1956) that business had lost its commanding position inside the state in the context of an irreversible shift of power from the business to the laboring classes.

The development of the concept of relative autonomy was precisely about providing the tools of analysis to understand the distinct limits of the state's independence from capital, and one might have thought that the crisis of the social-democratic/New Deal regime in the face of the contradictions it gave rise to by the 1970s would have been taken as confirming and sustaining this approach to the study of the state. But the challenge to that regime posed by the new "free-market" right instead produced two contrary tendencies. First, there was an insistence against Marxist state theory that, where deeply institutionally embedded, the social-democratic regime would be able to withstand both the New Right and the mass unemployment that everywhere (including in Sweden and Germany) has accompanied the reemergence of severe crises tendencies within capitalism. Second, there was an insistence against the free-market theorists themselves that state intervention in the economy is not necessarily inefficient, inflationary, and so on. This has often entailed accepting the New Right's categories of analysis—states and markets, public and private—but inverting the values of each category.

The result has been a remarkable impoverishment of state theory. This is not the place to undertake anything like a comprehensive survey, but a critical examination of the "new paradigm," in the form advanced by even as radical a thinker as Fred Block, may help to clarify the nature of the problem. Block graces the "new paradigm" with the label of "market reconstruction" because it "emphasizes the degree of choice available in structuring markets and the possibility of reconstructing markets to achieve greater efficiency, greater equality, or other ends" (Block 1994, 697). Block made his own original contribution to the Marxist state theory literature in the 1970s, but he now lumps both liberalism and Marxism together into one "old paradigm." The "old paradigm" was allegedly structured in terms of a continuum of left and right prejudices ranging from distrust of the state on the right to distrust of the market on the left, but what was common to all positions on this spectrum—and which justifies, for Block, Marxism's and liberalism's representation in terms of a common "paradigm"—was the incorrect treatment of "modernity" as a process of opening up more and more activities to market forces. The alleged originality of the "new paradigm" lies in its recognition that states and markets, though structured in different ways, have always been dependent on one another.

What is primarily notable about this type of argument is how historically vague are the conceptual categories of state and market. It is almost as though—in attempting to confound the neoclassical economic view of free markets—one is drawn into responding to them in their own categories of analysis, and thus we find even as sophisticated a thinker as Block slipping into a discourse that empties the categories of state and market of historical and comparative specificity. This is readily revealed in the absurdity of the notion that Marxism somehow "trusted" the state (classical Marxism plainly did not do so, and although many twentieth-century Communists certainly trusted the Soviet state, they hardly did the capitalist state). But it is also revealed in the very abstractness and generality of the concept of markets. The alleged great insight of the "new paradigm"—that it is incorrect to see states as having more and more opened up societies to market forces—is based on the claim that modern history has seen as many markets closed down as opened up. The evidence offered in this respect is the Protestant church's banning of the selling of indulgences to the highest bidder, the ending of the international market in slaves, the restriction of child labor, the elimination of the sale of political offices. But this trivializes what is involved in capitalism's general commodification of social life (including the commodification of labor power and the development of the capitalist labor market).

Block tries to sustain his argument by asserting that the discontinuity between feudal and capitalist social relations has been exaggerated. He weakly offers as evidence a fictional family capitalist who, in trying to defy the local norms governing the treatment of his employees, would soon find his sources of credit and markets dry up in a community that regards him as a "deviant entrepreneur." And he claims that the corporate CEO within capitalism is as much restricted in his economic activity as the feudal lord and Soviet manager. Such gross categories of analysis must yield a sloppy historical sociology, as is revealed in the banal claim that in "feudal, capitalist and socialist property systems, the basic rights of employees and employers are established through state action" (Block 1994, 701). What goes missing here, of course (revealed in the ahistorical transposition of the terms *employer* and *employee* back into feudalism), is the necessary discrimination between the class nature of one social order as opposed to another.

What also goes missing, as a result of adopting states and markets rather than social relations of class and class power as the basic units of analysis, is any pattern of determination regarding state action. The Marxist theory of the state was not only challenging pluralist and social-democratic claims that the modern state had freed itself from the dynamics of capitalist accumulation, but was precisely trying to enrich the tools of class analysis so as to understand the (varying) patterns of determination of capitalist state structure and action. In contrast, "the point of the market reconstruction perspective," as Block puts it, is to stress "the extensive capacities of governments" and their "considerable scope to decide whether they want more price stability or economic growth." This is not only a vastly narrower perspective; even as such it is an impoverished one, for Block offers little guidance regarding the conjunctural and structural conditions—the variations and limits of such policy autonomy—in different states or in any given state at different periods or in different conjunctures. Nor does he systematically confront general claims about policy autonomy to what he in the end admits is "the effect of the explosive growth of international financial transactions" in terms of the "powerful pressures on states to 'deregulate' those transactions" (ibid., 704).

Block's book on the American state (1995) focuses on the veto power that financial markets have over elected governments. But he largely presents this "financial dictatorship" as standing *external* to the state, and fails to draw much attention to what he knows better than most, given his own important contribution in the 1970s to the study of financial power as political power in the postwar era: the long-standing and deep structural, personal, and ideological linkages between the Treasury and the Federal Reserve and financial capital. His new mode of analysis unfortunately does not encourage an investigation of the modalities of class power *within* the state apparatuses and the role these apparatuses play in sustaining and reinforcing the economic and social power of financial capital. Thus, while advancing radical policies of capital and exchange controls clearly designed to reduce the power of financial capital, he fails to focus on the key question of how such policies could conceivably be carried through by the Treasury and Federal Reserve (or the German Bundesbank or the British Treasury or the Canadian Department of Finance) as they are presently constituted.

It is, indeed, in the critical arena of what has come to be known as "globalization," which these powerful state institutions have played such a large role in sponsoring, that the impoverishment of state theory may be most readily recognized and lamented. This is especially evident in Paul Hirst and Grahame Thompson's much-heralded *Globalization in Question* (1996). The book has the virtue of understanding that one "key effect of the concept of globalization has been to paralyse radical reforming national strategies" and to insist that the processes associated with globalization were "at least in part policy driven" by states themselves. But although their concern to avoid the hysteria and defeatism associated with the term *globalization* is admirable, their claim that globalization is only "conjunctural" and that there is "nothing unprecedented about the levels of integration experienced at present" cannot be sustained. Even less acceptable is the claim that it is only "the political will that is lacking at present to gain extra leverage over undesirable and unjust aspects of international and domestic economic activity" (15–17). It is precisely this kind of trajectory from Althusserian superstructural determinism—for which Hirst was himself so famously criticized by E. P. Thompson in *The Poverty of Theory* (1978)—to sheer liberal/social-democratic voluntarism that most clearly defines what I have called the impoverishment of state theory.

Hirst and Thompson define states as "communities of fate which tie together actors who share certain common interests in the success or failure of the national economies" (146). This is not on the surface very different from Jessop's definition of the state as that "distinct ensemble of institutions and organizations whose socially accepted function is to define and enforce collectively binding decisions on the members of a society in the name of their common interest or general will" (Jessop 1990, 341). But Jessop explicitly locates his definition within a conceptualization of hegemonic class domination and in this light problematizes the contradictions and strategic dilemmas entailed in the state's performance of this function. Because Hirst and Thompson do not do this, it is difficult to know whether to take their definition seriously in analytic terms (as opposed to mere idealism or wishful thinking) insofar as it is completely silent on the key issues of socioeconomic inequality and power—and the conflicts of interest that have their roots therein. Their claim that "markets need to be embedded in social relations" and that "political authority remains central in assuring that markets are appropriately institutionalized and that the non-market conditions of economic success are present" is empty of content in relation to the actual social relations in question.

It is scarcely surprising, in the face of this kind of theoretical evasion, that what was promised at the beginning of the book as a "radical reformist" strategy for the state turns out to amount to nothing more than a return to corporatist intermediation—the state's function is to bring about a "distributional coalition" and an "orchestration of social consensus" to the end of "promoting competitive manufacturing performance" (146). Of course, it now turns out that there is more than political will involved in achieving even this modest goal. The chances of the United States or the United Kingdom emulating the alleged successes of Germany and Japan in this respect are reckoned as slim. The reasons for this, however, only have to do with respective "political processes and interest group cultures." Shades of Easton and Almond; capitalist class strategies and the balance of class forces do not get a look in. It seems we are back, theoretically speaking, in the 1950s. The varying way states are constituted to reinforce capitalist class power is out of sight. Such is the conceptual impoverishment of state theory today.

It should be pointed out, moreover, that Hirst and Thompson's initial promise that political will could also readily address the "unjust aspects" of international economic activity turns out to have been empty. We discover not only that their optimism regarding the governance of the international economy was much exaggerated, but that what they meant by the possibility of such governance had little to do with justice. Arrangements among the leading advanced capitalists states, we are told,

> can assure some minimal level of international economic governance, at least to the benefit of the major industrial nations. Such governance cannot alter the extreme inequalities between those nations and the rest, in terms of trade investment, income and wealth. Unfortunately that is not the problem raised by the concept of globalization. The issue is not whether the world's economy is governable towards ambitious goals like promoting social justice, equality between countries and greater democratic control for the bulk of the world's population, but whether it is governable at all. (189)

In other words, Hirst and Thompson's promise that all we needed was political will to provide leverage against the "undesirable and unjust aspects" of globalization not only turns out to have been so much hot air, but also they are prepared—"unfortunately"—to limit their strategic concerns to the problems raised by conventional conceptualizations of globalization.

In my own work on globalization and the state (Panitch 1994, 1996) I have also contested the widespread notion that capital has "bypassed" or "escaped" or "diminished" the power of the state. I have argued that this notion reflects a perspective that not only exaggerates the actual institutional autonomy of states from capital in the Keynesian/Bretton Woods era, but also fails to see that globalization is a process that takes place under the aegis of states and is in many ways authored by states. But it will not advance our understanding very much if we merely assert the continuing importance of states amid globalization, while failing to explore the determining patterns of state action in our era. To properly make sense of globalization, we cannot do without many of the tools of analysis of Marxist state theory.

By the early 1980s, with the rise of the Thatcher–Reagan regime, governments and bureaucrats proudly enveloped themselves in an ideology that proclaimed the necessity of the state subordination to the requirements of capital accumulation and markets and even to the norms and opinions of capitalists themselves. Through the course of the decade, moreover, as social-democratic regimes (including even Sweden's) found their freedom to maneuver restrained by the new limits to capitalist growth and a renewed ideological militancy on the part of capitalists, they soon abandoned all pretext that the mixed economy had not all along been a capitalist one and that the welfare state had not always been dependent on and necessarily contained within the limits of capital accumulation. What this suggests is that, far from abandoning the kind of research on ideological links between state and capital that Miliband pioneered, we should have extended, enriched, and multiplied our investigations of ruling class–state "partnerships" (as Miliband termed them) in our time. Whatever the merits of theorizations that want to go beyond research on the ties between business and state elites to deeper structural factors, we can hardly ignore the significance of such linkages when they bulk as large as they do today.

Robert Reich's account of life inside the Clinton administration, *Locked in the Cabinet,* contains a humorous passage (1998, 82–83) in which Reich, after describing a lunch with Alan Greenspan at the Federal Reserve, reveals to his readers what he really had wanted (but did not have the courage) to ask Greenspan, and how he believes Greenspan would have replied had he been completely honest:

Q: What's your purpose in life?
A: To stamp out inflation.

Q: Even if that means high unemployment.
A: You bet.

Q: Even if it requires slow growth and stagnant wages?
A: Right you are.

Q: Even if it means drastic cuts in federal programs that help working people and the poor?
A: Absolutely, if that's what it takes to balance the budget and remove all temptation to inflate away the government debt.

Q: But why? A little inflation never hurt anybody.
A: You're wrong. It hurts bond traders and lenders.

Q: But why place their interests over everybody else's interest in good jobs?
A. Because I'm a capitalist and capitalism is driven by the filthy rich. They make their money off bonds. Your constituents are just plain filthy. They have to work for a living.

Q: You're the nation's central banker. You should be accountable to all Americans.
A: But I'm not and neither is the Fed...

Q. Well you can take your crummy lunch and cram it, you robber-baron pimp.
A: Go suck on a pickle, you Bolshevik dwarf.

But what if Clinton had made Reich head of the Federal Reserve rather than Greenspan? Would that not have solved the problem? Don't start by imagining the reaction on Wall Street. Think first of all of the reaction inside the Federal Reserve itself. Reich knows this—that is why he has Greenspan say that not only is *he* primarily accountable to capitalists, but *so is the Fed.*

As Clyde Barrow (1993, 30) made clear in his useful book on state theory, even Miliband did not confine himself to the way in which capitalist class–state personnel linkages produced a common ideology but explicitly tried to ground this ideology in relation to the practices of what he termed the "complex of institutions" that constitute the state, or what Poulantzas termed the "hierarchy of state apparatuses." And the time we now live in is one in which explicit theorizations and investigations of the increasingly close *structural* relationship between state and capital are more than ever required. Poulantzas was not wrong when he said: "The (capitalist) state, in the long run, can only correspond to the political interests of the dominant class or classes" (Poulantzas 1976, 72). (And he knew that he and Miliband were in agreement on this: because Miliband was "not some incorrigible Fabian, he of course knows this already.") The general *capitalist* definition of the nature of the state does not mean, however, that there are not variations among states in terms of their relative autonomy, and it was precisely this that needed to be empirically studied in each case:

> the degree, the extent, the forms, etc.... of the relative autonomy of the state can only be examined... with reference to a given capitalist state, and to the precise *conjuncture* of the class struggle (the specific configuration of the power bloc, the degree of hegemony within this bloc, the relations between the bourgeoisie and its different fractions on the working classes and supporting classes on the other, etc.). (Ibid.)

Poulantzas also insisted, of course, on the need to recognize and study the "pertinent effects" of working-class economism and reformism in any given conjuncture. But his overall strategic conclusion (one that Miliband shared) has proved entirely correct: that is, that economistic/reformist policies were ineffectual, not only in the sense that "this policy could not lead to socialism," but also in the sense that the reforms were always reversible. We are living in a period when social democracy's "pertinent effects," as crystallized in institutional form and cultural values, have been undone in good part even in Sweden. As for those like Hirst and Thompson who now take Japan or Germany as their models, they not only ignore the negative aspects of these state-capitalist partnerships models in comparison with the old Swedish model, they also ignore the extent to which Japan's and Germany's own institutional arrangements are increasingly being destabilized.

The study of the capitalist state today still must meet three requisites (see Panitch 1977, 5–9). It is necessary, first of all, to delineate the institutions of the state in terms of their "structural selectivity" vis-à-vis the field of political struggle. Second, it is necessary to maintain a constant stream of empirical research on the specific linkages between state institutions and class actors in terms of ideology, personnel, relations of dependence and influence, and so on. Finally, it is always necessary to situate the first two in relation to the state's functions of promoting capital accumulation and the legitimating capitalist domination of the social order. As I have suggested elsewhere (Panitch 1994, 1996), what especially needs to be investigated in the context of globalization is whether the important shifts in the hierarchy of state apparatuses really are those, as Cox (1987) suggests, that bring to the fore those institutions, like central banks, most directly linked to the international "caretakers of the global economy," such as the IMF and the World Bank; or whether a more general process is at work, determined more from within the state itself, whereby even those agencies without such direct international links, but that nevertheless directly facilitate capital accumulation and articulate a "competitiveness" ideology, are the ones that gain status, while those that fostered social welfare and articulated a class-harmony orientation lose status. Ministries of labor, health, and welfare are perhaps not so much being subordinated as themselves being restructured. We need to investigate whether that loss of status is considerable, or even permanent; and this will partly depend on the transformations these latter agencies are going through in terms of being made, or making themselves, more attuned to the exigencies of global competitiveness and fiscal restraint.

Students who go back to Miliband and Poulantzas today for guidance as regards this agenda would do well to pay less attention to the polemic between them (and the many caricatural commentaries on it) over "instrumentalism" versus "structuralism." They would also do well not to take too seriously the epistemologically ill-informed and rather hysterical charges of functionalism against Marxist state theory that came to be heard in the 1980s. To understand how certain institutions or policies evolve through the push and pull of policy debate and class struggle (what Poulantzas called "the unstable equilibrium of compromises") in such a way as to sustain or at least conform with capitalist social relations is not at all about ascribing perfect strategic foresight to subjects. Nor does it entail the notion that everything that happens is unidimensionally reproductive of the system. On the contrary, the very notion of contradiction within Marxism invites the theory of the state to be especially sensitive to the dysfunctional tendencies that emerge through the very process of systemic development and reproduction (Hobsbawm 1972).

The era of globalization we are living through is replete with such contradictions. We have witnessed a significant *decrease* since the early 1980s in politicians' and bureaucrats' relative autonomy from capitalist ideology: the state's goals—and the discourse it employed to advance these goals—became more explicitly those of business itself. The legitimation problem this might have been thought to entail in a democracy was somewhat offset by the fact that at the same time there was an apparent increase in the state's relative autonomy from specific capitalist interests. That is, as states became more and more responsible for the extension and reproduction of the world capitalist order, they appeared less directly tied to the specific interests of indigenous capitalists: national industrial subsidies and tariff protection were exchanged for deregulation and regressive taxation; the macroeconomic policies were inflected toward each state's readings of the situation of the global economy and its responsibility to it. States presented themselves as promoting free markets, competition, capitalism, rather than promoting specific capitalist interests.

But this could only go so far because states remained anchored in their social formations. Reflecting the growing dominance of financial capital within each social formation, responsibility to the world economy was read through responsibility to Wall Street and the City of London and Bay Street. At the same time, governments could not avoid, especially in the context of the competitive world order they had helped to author, acting as "promoters" of their respective capitalists. (On the business–government trade junkets that are so common today, it is difficult to distinguish between the politician and the promoter, the statesman and the "shill.") For many governments, such promotion extends to foreign-owned corporations located within a given state's borders, but in any case the dominant multinational corporations, while operating on a global scale, themselves remain firmly based in the world's most powerful states (Ruigrok and von Tulder 1995). To advance their own multinational corporations, states bend, challenge, or even threaten to break the rules of international commercial treaties they only recently signed on to; and individual capitalists—without access to general industrial subsidies any longer—pay off politicians and parties to ensure that their governments will act as promoters for these capitalists and will try to bend the rules of trade and investment in their favor (see Tsoukalas, in this volume).

The contradictions abound. They are increasingly reflected not only in blatant instances of corruption and favoritism, but in the ever greater challenge that states face in managing an unstable world financial order. They have also been reflected in the growing incidence of strikes in the advanced capitalist world and in IMF riots in the "third world," as well as in a marked change in working-class awareness. A *New York Times* poll in 1996 found that 55 percent of Americans defined themselves as working class, while only 36 percent defined themselves as middle class, a major reversal of the traditional American pattern; and no less than 60 percent of those who had experienced a layoff in their family attributed "a lot of the blame for the loss of jobs on the economic system in this country" (*New York Times,* March 5, 1996). In Britain, the proportion of people believing there is a "class struggle" reached 81 percent by the mid-1990s, up from 60 percent in the 1960s (*Economist,* September 27, 1997). All this may well be taken to signal that the era of global neoliberalism—despite the accommodation of politicians such as Clinton and Blair, and their respective parties, to it—cannot last forever.

The impoverishment of state theory arose in the context of a defensive reaction against neoliberalism, whose ideological assault on the state employed the crude concepts of free-market neoclassical economics. One way to cling to New Deal/welfare-state reforms seemed to be to assert that state regulations were necessary for efficient markets, contributing to making capitalism less irrational—or at least more rationally competitive. Such an argument, it must have been expected, would obtain a greater public hearing than the Marxist theory of the state could. But what was lost by way of depth of analysis was not in fact compensated for in terms of actual political effect. Conventional social-democratic party politicians, as well as liberal ones, who it was hoped would listen, proved as poor listeners as ever. Meanwhile, a generation of students have been robbed of the tools they really need to understand the state in our era.

The anxiety to obtain a greater public hearing is not to be dismissed. The point of radical theory, after all, *is* to effect real political change. But there are no shortcuts. The central purpose of the new Marxist theory of the state was to arrive at a clearer understanding of the way in which the institutions of the state needed to be restructured and the networks of relations between state and class altered in the face of the crises of social-democratic and New Deal regimes, and to build this understanding into popular projects for radical egalitarian change. It was understood that this would entail fundamentally changing the old social-democratic or Communist parties, or, more likely, building new ones concerned with and capable of not just entering the state, but transforming its structures, linkages with civil society, and relations with other states. This is an even more pressing task in the era of globalization. Undertaking that task will mean many things, but one of them will have to be overcoming the impoverishment of state theory.

References

Barrow, Clyde. 1993. *Critical Theories of the State.* Madison: University of Wisconsin Press.

Block, Fred. 1994. "The Roles of the State in the Economy." In Neil J. Smelser and Richard Swedborg, eds., *The Handbook of Economic Sociology.* Princeton, N.J.: Princeton University Press. 691–710.

———. 1995. *The Vampire State and Other Myths and Fallacies about the U.S. Economy.* New York: New Press.

Cox, Robert. 1987. *Production, Power and World Order: Social Forces in the Making of History.* New York: Columbia University Press.

Crosland, Anthony. 1956. *The Future of Socialism.* London: Jonathan Cape.

Galbraith, John Kenneth. 1967. *The New Industrial State.* Boston: Houghton Mifflin.

Gramsci, Antonio. 1971. *Selections from the Prison Notebooks.* Ed. Quintin Hoare and Geoffrey Nowell Smith. London: Lawrence and Wishart.

Hirst, Paul, and Grahame Thompson. 1996. *Globalization in Question: The International Economy and the Possibilities of Governance.* Cambridge: Polity Press.

Hobsbawm, Eric. 1972. "Karl Marx's Contribution to Historiography." In Robin Blackburn, ed., *Ideology in Social Science.* London: Fontana.

Jessop Bob. 1990. *State Theory: Putting Capitalist States in Their Place.* Cambridge: Polity Press.

———. 1991. "On the Originality, Legacy, and Actuality of Nicos Poulantzas." *Studies in Political Economy* 34 (spring): 75–107.

Miliband, Ralph. 1969. *The State in Capitalist Society.* New York: Basic Books.

Mills, C. Wright. 1956. *The Power Elite.* New York: Oxford University Press.

O'Connor, James. 1973. *The Fiscal Crisis of the State.* New York: St. Martin's Press.

Panitch, Leo. 1994. "Globalization and the State." In *Socialist Register 1994.* London: Merlin Press. 60–93.

———. 1996. "Rethinking the Role of the State." In James Mittelman, ed., *Globalization: Critical Reflections.* Boulder, Colo.: Lynn Rienner. 83–113.

———, ed. 1977. *The Canadian State: Political Economy and Political Power.* Toronto: University of Toronto Press.

Porter, John. 1965. *The Vertical Mosaic: An Analysis of Social Class and Power in Canada.* Toronto: University of Toronto Press.

Poulantzas, Nicos. 1968. *Pouvoir politique et classes sociales.* Paris: Maspero.

———. Nicos. 1976. "The Capitalist State: A Reply to Miliband and Laclau." *New Left Review* 95 (January/February): 63–83.

Reich, Robert. 1998. *Locked in The Cabinet.* New York: Vintage Books.

Ruigrok, Winfried, and Rob van Tulder. 1995. *The Logic of International Restructuring.* London: Routledge.

Thompson, E. P. 1978. *The Poverty of Theory.* London: Merlin Press.

CHAPTER FIVE

The Stateless Theory

Poulantzas's Challenge to Postmodernism

Andreas Kalyvas

> If we confine ourselves to waiting, we will not get the "great day" at all, but rather the tanks in the small hours of the morning.
>
> —NICOS POULANTZAS

Nicos Poulantzas's pathbreaking and seminal analysis of the nature of the capitalist state was provoked by a very specific political conjuncture and by a predominant intellectual current that had obliterated the state as a valid object of theoretical investigation. Against liberal pluralistic-functionalist approaches as well as orthodox, economistic versions of Marxism, which Poulantzas regarded as the two main causes for the disappearance of the state from academic studies, he sought to refocus the attention of mainstream political science (and of the left) on the capitalist state (Poulantzas 1978, 263–74). More than two decades after his untimely death in the fall of 1979, we are surprisingly confronted with a situation that is not at all that different from that of Poulantzas. Although perhaps for other reasons, there is no doubt that today as then, the state seems once again to have retreated from the realm of social sciences.

There are, I think, among others, two important causes that have contributed to the current dissolution of the state. The first is the overemphasis on globalization, the crisis of national sovereignty, and the alleged failure of the nation-state to fulfill its conventional role as an autonomous actor over a bounded territory. The vogue of globalization in academic circles has greatly hampered the study of the state. Second, the rise of postmodern and poststructuralist discourses and the concomitant stress on the multiplicity of microtechnologies of power and their diffuse character have substantially undermined the image of the state as a pivotal and sovereign power center and as the main location of political domination. Hence, globalization and postmodernism together have relativized the state, reducing it either to an impotent and irrelevant international agent or to an inconsequential and derivative domestic social institution. It has now become a commonplace to argue that the state no longer enjoys the monopoly of power and of legitimate physical force over a territory and that, consequently, it cannot be considered a central terrain for the reproduction of capitalist-liberal hegemony or a privileged site of class struggle. This means, at least for the left, that now the main subjects worthy of attention, are, on the one hand, expanding world markets, the globalization of capital, and patterns of international labor mobility, and, on the other hand, local identities, multiple differences and particularities, ethnic minorities, new social movements, and their struggles for symbolic recognition.

This shift in interest from a bounded political domination either to the deterritorialization and transnational circulation of capital and labor or to the multiplicity of microcenters of power relations that cannot be located in one particular instance of the social domain has one major implication: if the state is not important for the reproduction of capitalism and the consolidation of class divisions and inequalities, then neither is it significant as a political target, and therefore it rightly should be neglected as a strategic priority of the left. The priorities are in the process of shifting from a supposedly narrow and futile (nation-) state-centered approach to a broader and more promising (international) market-centered perspective. Instead of concentrating on the mechanisms, institutions, apparatuses, and relations that compose and transverse the organizational materiality of the modern state and the manifold ways they interact with the capitalist mode of production, the existing class structure, and the hegemony of the power bloc, the contemporary left prefers to devote its energies to engaging in a detailed critical analysis and denunciation of international organizations or to promoting the global promulgation of human rights.

I do not intend to discuss the problems that globalization and its theoretical versions have posed for the left. I leave this topic to other contributors of this volume. Instead, I will focus on the unfinished critical dialogue between Poulantzas and postmodernism regarding the contemporary state. This dialogue has three parts, each of which corresponds to the three sections of this essay. The first section provides a quick, and for this reason rather lacunary, presentation of the two most representative postmodern theories of the state. In the second section, I will argue that precisely because Poulantzas avoided the excesses of poststructuralism—while integrating many of its contributions—his work provides powerful tools for articulating a systematic critique and for overcoming many of its limitations.[1] Finally, in the third section I will explore how Poulantzas's theory might provide a more convincing analysis of the current political situation by relocating the study of the state at the center of the ongoing discussions in radical political theory. More particularly, I will argue that what Poulantzas so perceptively called "authoritarian statism" has taken a new, more alarming form, that of "liberal authoritarian legalism," which refers to the new face of the victorious capitalist-liberal state in this postwelfare age. As I will argue, the contemporary state and its juridical armor constitute a crucial organizational terrain for the continuing cohesion of the ruling power bloc, the securing of liberal-bourgeois hegemony, and the repression of different segments of the working class (the new poor, the unemployed, the illegal immigrants, the part-time workers, the unskilled and semiskilled workforce, etc.). I will conclude by suggesting ways of reconceiving an egalitarian-democratic strategy of political transformation.

This essay is informed by the conviction that although Poulantzas's work hardly appears in current discussions of the different versions of political postmodernism (cf. Heller and Fehér 1988; White 1991; Connolly 1991, 1993), it did considerably influence it by anticipating many of its central themes and concepts. It also continues to live, in a hidden, subterranean form, in the various forms of poststructuralism and in the writings of authors who identify themselves as post-Marxists (cf. Laclau and Mouffe 1990; Vadée 1998; and Carvel 1998). With the notable exception of Bob Jessop, no one has really examined the ways in which Poulantzas anticipated many of the best-known themes of poststructuralism (Jessop 1985, 318–20; 1990, 229–47).

I will not directly tackle this issue here, even though it is a subject that calls for serious examination.[2] Suffice it to say, however, that I agree with Ellen Meiksins Wood's characterization of Poulantzas as a "forerunner" of post-Marxism. Her argument that all major themes of post-Marxism "are present in embryo in the work of Nicos Poulantzas" although "he certainly never went so far," informs the central argument of the present discussion (Wood 1998, 25).

Postmodernism and the State

Michel Foucault shook up the conceptual and theoretical foundations of Marxism by arguing that the juridical and repressive model of power related to the image of an omnipotent, centralized state-sovereign was becoming an anachronism in the modern world. It was a historical phenomenon confined to the classical age and superseded by the emergence of new, more pervasive forms and modalities of power, during the eighteenth century. One of Foucault's main targets was the classical liberal view, according to which the state is the central repository of power. This liberal view endowed the state with the sinister potentiality of submitting the entire society to its control. Meanwhile, society, in the form of civil society, was perceived by liberalism as a power-free realm, where social (economic) interactions are spontaneously and unintentionally self-regulated, tending thus naturally toward balance and equilibrium. State power, as a neutral institution external to social relations, was instituted, with all the necessary legal and constitutional precautions, to intervene in those rather rare and exceptional cases of crime, transgression, conflicts, and anomie that could threaten the "system of natural liberty" (Smith 1981, 687). The central state, which emerged out of the religious civil wars by acquiring the monopoly of legitimate violence over a particular territory, speaking through the word of the law, was the only instance of concentrated power capable of restoring the social order, securing peace, protecting private property, and incarnating the public interest.

Unlike other political and economic theories of its time, liberalism contained a powerful normative dimension about the emancipatory character of civil society as the only sphere where individual liberties are realized and esteemed. Modern civil society shatters traditional hierarchies, exclusions, privileges, and relations of personal dependency that had predominated in feudal times. Rather than change and suppress human nature and human rights to accord with an abstract moral code, a closed and inflexible system of social hierarchy, or a specific ethical worldview, civil society accepts the propensities of humankind and is attentive and respectful of their character. Thus, for classical liberals, civil society and markets give full expression to individual (economic) liberties (Foucault 1980, 88, 93, 95; 1990, 83–86).

Foucault rejected this dualistic framework that divided the social into two opposed and mutually exclusive spheres: the state versus civil society, a power-ridden versus a power-free realm. He also fiercely attacked the juridical model of power in its social contract version, which was based on the presupposition that power is an amount contractually regulated and transferable, which authorizes the sovereign to exercise a repressive power but always through and within a legally defined area of competence, so that the ruler(s) can always remain accountable to citizens. This definition of power was intrinsically associated with the liberal belief that power can be made visible, localized, restricted, contained, and supervised within strictly defined legal norms whose boundaries are clearly delimited by the constitutional rights of a pre-given subject, endowed with natural and inviolable entitlements.

Obviously, Marxism did not ascribe to this liberal theory of power. It is well known that it provided one of the first and most powerful critiques of civil society, the liberal rule of law, and the associated chimera that the state is the only repository of political power, operating within the realms of a well-defined legality (cf. Babb 1951; Kelsen 1955; and Collins 1982). Nevertheless, Marxism shared with liberalism the idea that the state was a system of organized and legalized coercion and therefore to speak of the state was to speak of political power and repression. Contrary to liberalism, however, Marxism understood the state in terms of class and economic power. Thus, rather than viewing the state as a neutral, extrasocial institution of domination representing and maintaining the common good (the state as subject) Marxism conceptualized it in terms of class interest and the private ownership of the means of production (the state as object). The state, according to this interpretation, was the instrument that the bourgeoisie used to dominate and repress its class opponents, and particularly the working class. As Marx and Engels put it, the capitalist state is nothing else "but a committee for managing the common affairs of the whole bourgeoisie"—the "dictatorship of the bourgeoisie" (Marx and Engels 1978, 475). Thus, although the state was theorized in terms of the topographical metaphor of an epiphenomenon, a reflection of the deeper and more real sphere of the economy, it was recognized as a crucial instrument of class oppression.

For this reason, within the history of Marxism, and especially around the turn of the twentieth century, the state became a privileged political target that could advance the objectives of the organized working class. Because it represented the central mechanism of political power, once conquered, it could easily be turned against the bourgeoisie. The "dictatorship of the proletariat" signified the proletarian appropriation of the political power of the state and its use for the elimination of its class enemies. Therefore, the state had first to be conquered and second, after a transitional period, to wither away. For, much like liberalism, Marxism too believed in the idea, projected in this case in a utopian, postcapitalist future, of a stateless, power-free society composed of autonomous and equal producers, a future in which political power and the state, defined restrictively as "the organized power of one class for oppressing the other," would be eradicated once and for all (ibid., 490).

Foucault was correct, then, in criticizing this limited conception of power as something negative and exclusively repressive imposed on the social body from an external location (Foucault 1980, 88–89). Although he acknowledged that Marxism advocated a more sophisticated theory of power that did not confine it solely to the state but located it also within the economic structures of the material reproduction of society—the "factory regime" (Marx 1990, 719, 449–50, 549, 672)[3]—Foucault nonetheless objected to the limiting of power to the circumscribed realm of the economy and its mere reflection in the political and juridical sphere in the form of legal state power (cf. Foucault 1991b). Ultimately, for Foucault, Marxism as well as liberalism gravely misunderstood the new forms of power relations emerging in the interstices of the seventeenth and eighteenth centuries out of the remnants of the classical age and the demise of the absolutist, monarchical state.

Against these dominant theoretical constructions, Foucault provocatively argued that disciplinary power, the power associated with modernity, is not a quantity or a substance that someone—usually the sovereign or the dominant class—can hold, use, or exchange (Foucault 1979, 26–27; 1990, 94). Nor is it located at one particular instance of the social (i.e., the economic or the political), but rather permeates the entire social body and is immanent in any social relations.[4] Power does not have a transcendental power-free "outside." It saturates the entire social field. Therefore, power relations should not be perceived as coming from the top, but instead as emanating from the bottom. Finally, power is not only repressive and negative, manifesting itself through a prohibiting law and a centralized command. It is mainly positive and productive, operating through multiple, plural, and complex networks of disciplines, techniques, discourses, and practices, which, rather than coercing and punishing bodies from the outside, create new subjectivities, produce new individualities, and give rise to normalizing effects. According to Foucault, what is distinctive about the modern disciplinary regime is the way in which coercion by physical or symbolic (i.e., internalized and veiled, thus ideological) violence incarnated in the state (repressive and ideological state apparatuses, in Althusser's terms) has been largely replaced by the subtler force of the microphysics of power operating in peripheral and minor institutional settings, such as prisons, schools, hospitals, armies, and mental institutions. Likewise, he stressed the way public, majestic, and theatrical displays of the juridical model of power have been displaced by the imperceptible, arcane, and hidden deployment of new techniques based on a detailed and immanent knowledge of their targets.

In this strategic paradigm where the social field is portrayed as a fluid and unstable constellation consisting of a constant and endless war of all against all, an inexorable struggle, the state loses all its past privileges and becomes one contingent site of power among so many others (Foucault 1980, 90–91, 114–15; Honneth 1991). In other words, it loses its specificity, autonomy, and superiority. The state is dissolved into the social. Modern power relations inundate and overflow the strict confines of the state. This transformation of power in the modern age had, for Foucault, some major implications. One of them, as he programmatically put it, was that we should no longer direct our research "towards the juridical edifice of sovereignty, the State apparatus and the ideologies that accompany them, but towards forms of subjection and the inflections and utilisations of their localised systems, and towards strategic apparatuses. We must eschew the model of Leviathan in the study of power. We must escape from the limited field of juridical sovereignty and State institutions, and instead base our analysis of power on the study of the techniques and tactics of domination" (Foucault 1980, 102).

Foucault's recommendation that it is time to abandon the study of the state and start looking at other social networks and institutional constellations of power was eagerly emulated. Accepting the assessment that the state did not possess the totality of power in modern capitalist societies and that the roots of the modern disciplinary, "carceral" society lay somewhere outside the state, intellectuals and militants of the left became gradually disillusioned with the traditional idea that radical political transformations should engage the state apparatus. Meanwhile, the capitalist state saw itself absolved of all its crimes that the left had accused it of during the heated days of the 1960s and early 1970s. All of the accusations of a fascist, authoritarian, semitotalitarian capitalist-bourgeois state suddenly disappeared. This change of discourse and of political analysis offered the Western state a unique historical opportunity to reinvent and rebuild its liberal, classless, and neutral facade and to reemerge stronger from its ashes.

This postmodern assault on the state initiated by Foucault was brought into its completion only recently. In a controversial and influential article published in 1991, Timothy Mitchell set out to further develop Foucault's approach of the state. Mitchell's effort was significant in that it represented the first attempt to articulate a conclusive and systematic revision of state theories directly and exclusively based on methodological premises borrowed from poststructuralism and deconstructionism. Mitchell's theory of the state is a provocative elaboration, extension, and in fact radicalization of Foucault. Specifically, Mitchell appropriates from Foucault his major insight of the productive and all-pervasive character of power relations and disciplines.[5] But by introducing Martin Heidegger's notion of "enframing" he moves beyond Foucault, arguing that the state not only is internal to a wider strategic field of power relations, as Foucault had already asserted, but that it is also their effect. Having been one site of power among others for Foucault, the state is now reduced to a mere effect of power relations, to a metaphysical illusion, to a simple "metaphor" (Mitchell 1988, 34–63; 1990, 571).

Mitchell shifts the focus of attention from the individual to the state. He appropriates what Foucault had described as the process of individualization and normalization, according to which the individual is constructed on a set of dichotomies, such as mad/sane, sick/healthy, normal/abnormal. But whereas Foucault analyzed these dichotomies—which are not real, factual dichotomies, but constructed/cultural ones—in relationship to the emergence of new subjectivities and with regard to the creation of the image of a bipolar individual identity, Mitchell analyzes them with respect to the state. These modern practices, discourses, and microphysics of power, according to this amended argument, do not only produce new subjectivities; they also produce the effect of the state as an autonomous entity, separated from society, with clear and well-defined spheres of competence, an immanent rationality, a specific reason of state, and a particular bureaucratic apparatus (Mitchell 1990, 546).

These characteristics that make the state appear as a concrete institutional entity in everyday political life are parts of an illusionary effect. There is no such entity as "the state." There is simply a metaphor, an image produced by a multiplicity of dispersed and fragmented networks of power relations and discourses.[6] What Foucault had claimed for the formation of the modern subject, Mitchell now claims for the state. Disciplinary power, through the mediation of various tactics and techniques, transforms a number of separated and diffuse sites of power relations (prisons, police, hospitals, family, schools, armies) into a unitary, coherent, single, and superior institutional subject: a suprasubject that looks like an independent, supreme power center endowed with a distinct rationality and with its own separate interests, capable of coherent, collective action (Mitchell 1991, 93). This representation and personification of the state as a higher subjective agency gives the wrong impression that there is a real, concrete entity, whereas in fact there are only a number of scattered and unrelated sites of power relations. For Mitchell, therefore, the state is not an actual, real structure or a concrete institutional ensemble, but rather "a powerful, metaphysical effect of practices that make such structures appear to exist" (ibid., 94). The state is nothing but an "appearance of structure" (ibid., 91). From the decentering and "death" of the subject, Mitchell moves on to announce the decentering and "death" of the state and to execute the final act in the postmodern "deconstruction" of the state.

The strength of Mitchell's thesis does not lie in the argument that the state is the outcome of previous power relations and disciplines. Foucault, after all, had argued that "the state is superstructural in relation to a whole series of power networks. . . . True, these networks stand in a conditioning-conditioned relationship to a kind of 'meta-power' [i.e., the state] which is structured essentially around a certain number of great prohibition functions; but this meta-power with its prohibitions can only take hold and secure its footing where it is rooted in a whole series of multiple and indefinite power relations that supply the necessary basis for the great negative forms of power" (Foucault 1980, 122). Nor does the novelty lie in Mitchell's challenge to the idea of the state as a unitary actor-subject, the locus of political power, and the site of sovereignty. Such was Foucault's challenge. Rather, the intriguing aspect of Mitchell's analysis is owing to the definition of the state "as-an-effect" of the "enframing" process, a metaphysical abstract construction that appears to be separated from society, lying above power relations. This analysis presupposes not only that diffused disciplines produce and transverse the state, but that they also create a powerful illusion: the deception of the state as a superior concrete, unitary, and material institution. This illusion is the result of the "enframing" function of the disciplinary model of power, which creates an imaginary structure or a subjective (collective or individual) agency that it reifies and hypostatizes in the powerful form-illusion of an actual real structure, standing apart and above the factual multiplicity of power relations. The process of enframing does not create new material structures; it produces the appearance of a structure, the misconception that there is an essence and a substance ("the state," "the cogito," etc.), the deceptive perception that there is a structure, though there is none. As Mitchell puts it characteristically, "through the techniques of enframing, power will now appear as something essentially law-like. It will seem to be external to practice, as the fixed law that prescribes a code against which changing practices are then measured. This transformation occurs, moreover, at precisely the point when power in fact becomes most internal, most integral, and continuously at work within social and economic practices" (Mitchell 1990, 571).

Mitchell is able to extend Foucault's argument by replacing the ontological question of the previous, traditional approaches that had focused on the question of "Who or what is the state?" with the genealogical-historical question of "How and why does the state appear as a free-standing agent?" The intent of the question is not to provide a new definition of what the state is (an ontological question), but "to explain how it has been possible to produce this practical ghost-like effect. What... has made possible the apparent autonomy of the state as a free-standing entity" (Mitchell 1991, 91), which is a genealogical question. Mitchell answers this question with the concept of "enframing," which he defines as "a variety of modern practices that seem to resolve the world's shifting complexity into two simple and distinct dimensions. Such practices... give rise to the effect of a purely material world opposed to and given order by what now appears as a free-standing, non-material realm of meaning" (Mitchell 1990, 566). "Such techniques [i.e., disciplinary forms of power]," Mitchell goes on to argue, "have given rise to the peculiar, apparently binary world we inhabit, where reality seems to take the two-dimensional form of individual versus apparatus, practice versus institution, social life and its structure versus the state" (Mitchell 1991, 94).

It should be noted at this point that there is an important difference between Foucault and Mitchell. Although Foucault relativized the state as being one site of power among others, he never questioned its actual material existence. As he made clear, "I do not want to say that the state isn't important; what I want to say is that relations of power, and hence the analysis that must be made of them, necessarily extend beyond the limits of the State ... because the State, for all the omnipotence of its apparatuses, is far from being able to occupy the whole field of actual power relations" (Foucault 1980, 122). It would be mistaken, therefore, to go so far as to argue that Foucault completely ignored the state, as Honneth suggests. For Honneth, the state seems to play no role at all and to be virtually absent from Foucault's writings (Honneth 1991, 159–60). Mitchell, on the other hand, directly questions the material, institutional, and organizational existence of the state. He views the state as an effect of power relations, a discursive construction, which conceals the completely fragmented and dispersed reality of modern disciplines behind the powerful metaphysical illusion of a concrete, objective apparatus.

Thus, rather than searching for "the state" in the form of a site, an object, or an agent, Mitchell advises us to look at the way modern techniques and discursive processes have given rise to this seemingly omnipotent abstraction. By doing so, he takes the postmodern dissolution of the state a step further to its logical culmination. In this stronger version, the state is completely erased from social and political reality; it becomes simply the outcome of a discourse. Reading Mitchell, one has the impression that modern capitalist societies, though obviously stateless, live under an enormous, mass illusion: the illusion of the state.

Returning to Poulantzas's Critique

Poulantzas's theoretical and conceptual framework provides a fertile resource and a promising starting point for examining the limitations, contradictions, and alarming political implications of postmodernism for the left—especially with respect to political domination, class hegemony, alternative strategies of radical-democratic transformation, and real effective democracy. Equally important, Poulantzas's selective confrontation with Foucault anticipated many of the subsequent critiques of Foucault's work during the 1980s.[7] Thus, Poulantzas's astute observations about the underestimation of the state, the eradication of the economic, the relinquishing of class categories, and the absolutization of power became the main themes among Foucault's later critics.

To begin with, there is no doubt that Poulantzas was one of the first commentators on Foucault to note the metaphysical elements of his theory of power (Poulantzas 1979, 7–8).[8] Foucault, by seeking to conceptualize power independently of the material and social bases of modern capitalist society and by severing the ties between the formation and exercise of power from social classes, class interests, and class struggles, "essentialized," "hypostatized," and "absolutized" power relations. He turned them into a "mysterious and almost metaphysical diagram," reminiscent of "the purest spiritualist tradition" (Poulantzas 1978, 150, 69, 149). At the core of Foucault's arguments, Poulantzas saw a reification of the outcome of historical and social processes, which now were traced back to a foundational origin. Although it was not conceptualized in terms of a conscious act of a creative subject, this origin nonetheless implied the existence of a first cause, an unmoved mover, and an ultimate foundation beyond which there was nothing else. Thus, Foucault, as Poulantzas rightly observed, essentialized power relations in the form of regimes, networks, disciplines, and discourses, over against parts, thus replacing abstract liberal individualism with an equally abstract hyperholism. Where liberalism predicated the individual as the initial, elementary nucleus of the social and the basis of collective power, Foucault presumed power relations to be the real and ultimate basis of the social field and the individual "one of the prime effects of power" (Foucault 1980, 98). Thus, Foucault executed an outstanding reversal of the methodological and epistemological premises of liberalism by turning upside down the two poles of the equation (the individual monad versus power relations), without, however, superseding its two constitutive terms.[9]

In addition to this critique, Poulantzas noticed that once the question of the origins of these new disciplines and techniques was raised, Foucault's framework appeared in a totally different light. Obviously, for Foucault the modern concept of power could neither be imposed from above, by the state, nor conceived and carried out by a social class or group. Rather, it must have developed gradually, unintentionally, and spontaneously, in local piecemeal fashion in what he called "disciplinary institutions." Within these institutional niches, disciplinary power perfected a variety of functions for the fabrication, subjugation, and normalization of individuals as epistemic objects and targets of power without expressing an overarching design or representing the interest of particular social groups. It was only later, according to Foucault, in a subsequent historical stage, that these scattered techniques were exported from the confines of their institutional environments and appropriated by the state, which integrated them within its sphere of global political domination (Foucault 1979, 213–15).

It is here that we can locate an additional aspect of Poulantzas's critique. Once we put aside Foucault's radical statements about the newness of the disciplinary model of power and we instead focus on his more prosaic historical narrative, another, more conventional, image emerges, which has at its center the state, the bourgeoisie, and capitalism. Indeed, as Poulantzas correctly saw, all of Foucault's examples of the sites of new power relations were in fact an integral part of the strategic field of the capitalist-liberal state: prisons, national armies, public education, and public health. They emerged during the historical process of national state formation and the centralization of political power in a bounded institutional and territorial unity occupied by the bourgeoisie (Poulantzas 1978, 93–120). Actually Foucault acknowledged this historical development by conceding that the new disciplines were "co-extensive with the state itself" (1979, 215). He even offered a detailed description of the close association between state formation and new forms of power relations. In a revealing passage, he asserted that the modern state used politics "as a technique of internal peace and order... to implement the mechanism of the perfect army, of the disciplined mass, of the docile useful troops, of the regiment in camp and in the field, on manoeuvres and on exercises. In the great eighteenth-century states, the army guaranteed civil peace no doubt because it was a real force, an ever-threatening sword, but also because *it was a technique and a body of knowledge* that could *project* their schema over the social body" (ibid., 168; emphasis added). If we take this argument seriously, then it appears that the new techniques of power did in effect come from one central strategic terrain, the state, to spread all over the social field during the creation of the modern bourgeois nation-state and the first phases of capital accumulation.

What is more interesting, however, is that Foucault did not restrict this historical account to the modern state and the crucial role it played in the formation of new modalities of power. He supplemented his narration with a similar argument concerning the constitutive role of capitalism and the bourgeoisie. Concerning the first, Foucault clearly recognized that "this new type of power, which can no longer be formulated in terms of sovereignty, is, I believe, *one of the great inventions of bourgeois society.* It has been *a fundamental instrument in the constitution of industrial capitalism* and of the type of society that is its accompaniment" (Foucault 1980, 105; emphasis added). This is not an isolated statement. A more detailed account of the intrinsic relationship among the state, capitalist accumulation, the ascending bourgeoisie and the new forms of power relations can be found in other major texts as well. There, we discover a precise and scrupulous, almost Marxist, reconstruction of the process by which "new forms of capital accumulation," "new relations of production," "the development of capitalist society," "the need for a constant policing" exhibited by the bourgeoisie, and the shifting balance of class power were the primary causes, the basis, of the new techniques and microphysics of power (Foucault 1979, 86–87). Note here the striking affinities between this account and Poulantzas's claim that it is impossible for power to evade economic relations and class struggles (Poulantzas 1978, 36). Indeed, this Marxist approach seems entirely consistent with Foucault's interpretation of the advent of new techniques of power. Take, for example, his discussion of prostitution, as a representative case for the emerging disciplinary power. Here the processes of the normalization, control, categorization, medicalization, and disciplining of prostitutes benefited directly the bourgeoisie and were functional to "the illicit circuits of profit and power of the dominant class" (Foucault 1990, 124–27). Exactly the same economistic and class-centered explanation informs Foucault's depiction of prisons, factories, and schools. Thus Poulantzas was on the right track when he accused Foucault of espousing "a kind of neo-functionalism," which "brings us back to nothing other than the old structural homology of structuralism" (Poulantzas 1978, 68).

This critique becomes even more pertinent when applied to Foucault's famous historiography of sexuality. Here again, despite all appearances and professed claims, he comes closer to (neo-)Marxism than anywhere else earlier. In the case of sexuality and the private sphere of intimacy, Foucault provides us with an economistic and class analysis. The deployment of new forms of sexuality was, according to Foucault, the direct and immediate result of a class conflict that unfolded on the private sphere to be inscribed in the surface of the body (Foucault 1990, 124–25). Foucault even goes so far as to speak of a "bourgeois sexuality" in his examination of the new techniques of power, which was nothing else than "class effects" of the "bourgeois hegemony" (ibid., 126–27). The new technologies of power operating on sexuality and the body, which took the form of "biopower," "was without question an *indispensable element* in the development of capitalism: the latter would not have been possible without the controlled insertion of bodies into the machinery of production and the adjustment of the phenomena of populations to economic processes" (ibid., 140–141; emphasis added). At this point, Foucault brings back in the state, as an important factor in the process of capital accumulation and the consolidation of bourgeois hegemony. The instruments of the state, characterized as "institutions of power," were created for "the maintenance of production relations"; similarly, the exercise of biopower was introduced for "the expansion of productive forces," "the differential allocation of profit," and for "the adjustment of the accumulation of men to that of capital" (ibid., 141).

The capitalist state, for Foucault, as Jean Cohen and Andrew Arato have correctly demonstrated, further developing Poulantzas's critique, appears, implicitly, to play two important roles. First, "the newly differentiated, centralized administrative state apparatuses also had an interest in abolishing the old, incalculable, and expensive personal forms of power and substituting its new techniques for them. The state, then, as a key actor in generalizing disciplinary power, does play a major role in Foucault's account of the transition to modernity." Second, "the state's interests also play a central role in the globalization of biopower... [and therefore] the state is the coordinating mechanism of disciplinary power" (Cohen and Arato 1992, 283, 286). Similarly, Peter Dews, also reproducing Poulantzas's point, has argued that Foucault's detailed concern for the multiplicity of disciplines and institutional settings of power relations not only does not dispense with the state, but it also reserves for it a privileged place in the social field, and all this despite Foucault's claim to the contrary. In fact, from within Foucault's narrative, bourgeois state intervention played a fundamental role in the coordination, shaping, and channeling of the new disciplines and techniques of power (Dews 1984, 145–46).

As a result, after closely reading Foucault's genealogical approach, we are inclined to think that the new disciplinary model of power did emerge from within the modern state, was functional and necessary to capital accumulation, and was exercised mainly by a socially, politically, and economically rising bourgeoisie. In fact, Poulantzas was right in affirming that "we should not attach too much importance to Foucault's second-order epistemological discourse. Several of his analyses are not only compatible with Marxism: they can be understood only if it is taken as their starting-point" (Poulantzas 1978, 68; 1979, 14–15).

Unfortunately, these last observations were not taken seriously by future commentators on Foucault, with the result that Foucault's work continues to be treated as an original theory of power with anti-Marxist and antistatist implications, whereas in reality his theory illuminated—in an ambiguous and confusing way, it must be said—the elective affinity between capitalism, new forms of power relations, bourgeois domination, and state authority.[10] By analyzing the emergence of a disciplinary capitalist society, Foucault was in fact reproducing a neo-Marxist argument and reaffirming its analytical and critical significance.

These limitations and contradictions in Foucault's theory reverberate in Mitchell's work as well, but in an exaggerated form. Mitchell too remains trapped within the idealist and metaphysical mode of thought, which claims to criticize—and this thanks to his monistic and one-sided conception of power. By taking Foucault's arguments to their ultimate logical conclusions, he comes a step closer to an ontologized conception of power. If Foucault claimed that the modern individual is merely one of the principal effects of power, Mitchell goes on to argue that, "like the modern subject, the world seems to be constituted as something divided from the beginning into neatly opposed realms" (Mitchell 1990, 546). From the genealogy of the modern soul, we have moved to the genealogy of modern reality. From a monistic *analytical* method, Mitchell shifts to a monistic *ontological* framework, within which a Hegelian *Geist* (as power relations) penetrates every particle of the social body, from the individual to the state.[11] This framework lacks a historical and sociological grounding: it dispenses with actual social relations, economic imperatives, class conflict, forms of exploitation, and political interests, and hence one is unable to distinguish among different types of power relations.

Thus, several questions remain suspended in Mitchell's framework: Is political power similar, equivalent, or comparable to other forms of power? If not, what is the criterion for distinguishing between them?[12] Are all forms of political power the same? How can we differentiate between a "totalitarian" and an "authoritarian" regime, and these from Western liberal, capitalist democracies? Are "normal" and "exceptional" states different, and in what respect? How can we differentiate, from Mitchell's perspective, among different "states-as-an-effect"? Are all states similar in the sense of being mere effects of the homologous modern discourses? Do modern power relations operate in the same manner in all modern societies irrespective of their social-cultural, economic, and political uniqueness? As Nancy Fraser has powerfully shown, the generality of Foucault's concept of power, which informs Mitchell's research, tends to explain everything and nothing. As she puts it, this theory of power "calls too many different sorts of things power and simply leaves it at that. Granted, all cultural practices involve constraints—but these constraints are of a variety of different kinds and thus demand a variety of different normative responses. . . . phenomena that are capable of being distinguished through such concepts (authority, force, violence, domination, and legitimation) are simply lumped together under his catchall concept of power" (Fraser 1989, 32). The result is not only that empirical analysis is hampered by this conception of the state, but also that normative and critical theory is undermined. For Mitchell, "distinctions between just and unjust social arrangements, legitimate and illegitimate uses of political power, strategic and cooperative interpersonal relations, coercive and consensual measures—distinctions that have been at the heart of critical social analysis—become marginal" (McCarthy 1991, 54–55).

Moreover, Mitchell's theoretical framework does not help us to account for the phenomena of political crisis, collective action, and lucid and deliberative strategies of resistance and transformation. If everything is power relations, how can we account for cases of emancipatory revolutions? How do radical changes in the balance of power occur? Are we faced with a continuous state of war with contingent outcomes? How do we move from one stable state of domination to another? Or, to put the question in a different context, if the ontological conception of power is a model for strategic intersubjective conditions of struggle, what is the antecedent cause of conflicts? Mitchell does not address these crucial questions, and one wonders whether he is able to address them at all, for his analysis operates at a very abstract and ahistorical level. Ultimately, de-differentiation, homogenization, and leveling are the outcomes of Mitchell's ontologized model of power. By focusing undifferentiatedly on society as the locus of power relations, Mitchell becomes vulnerable to Poulantzas's charge of "mystification": the paradigm of the social is perceived qua society as independent of its social-structural properties, material basis of existence, patterns of exploitation, and class struggles. From an ontological perspective, abstract unity takes the place of real diversity, the universal replaces the particular, the ideal type is superimposed on the concrete, the objective category is substituted for the historical finite and relative. What Mitchell criticizes as a bipolar conception of reality is what in reality he advocates. The actual relations of individuals and their struggles at the level of capitalist, liberal societies are leveled and concealed as the expression of an abstract form of power relations. What is missing from this explanatory model is exactly what one can find in Poulantzas's theory of power, that is, "a correct conception of the 'economic' that grounds the institutional specificity of modern power" (Poulantzas 1978, 68).

In a different context, however, Mitchell, like Foucault, opts for an economistic argument regarding the formation of disciplinary power. His debate with James Scott on the notion of moral economy is extremely helpful for better grasping the ambiguities surrounding the concept of "enframing" (cf. Scott 1976, 1985). Mitchell examines the emergence of a dichotomized view of the world in a small rice-growing village in northern Malaysia. In his response to Scott's argument that popular revolts are based on preexisting ethical principles and communal experiences threatened by the commercialization of traditional societies, he proposes an alternative explanation consisting of a three-stage periodization (Mitchell 1990, 567). The first stage refers to the emergence of market society and of "powerful land-owning interests" related to "an external capitalist accounting" (ibid.). In the second stage, "these new forces create an effect of fixity and permanence. The earlier, less coordinated forms of domination seemed always unstable. To maintain them required the innumerable techniques of euphemization, and the periodic acts of violence. . . . The new forms of domination, by contrast, appear fixed and enduring" (ibid.). Finally, in the third stage, the new social practices spread all over the social body: in school, mosques, party organizations, feasts, and so on. Ultimately, "these methods of programming consist of nothing more than particular social practices; but they are set up and regulated in such a way as to appear to stand outside ordinary practices. They correspond to the method of enframing . . . all of which [have] contribute[d] to this impression that life's meanings constitute a program or text that exists apart from the practical world" (ibid., 573).

Like Foucault, Mitchell seems to argue that the sources of the modern form of power and the illusionary bifurcation of reality are the new economic relations of a newly emerging capitalist society. Indeed, market relations shattered the older ones, establishing gradually a new worldview and a novel ordering of the real, based on a dualistic structure, in which techniques of power appear as independent, extrasocial institutions. Thus, the ultimate cause of the modern bipolar world is not abstract power relations and new elusive discourses, as Mitchell seems to claim, but rather the most trivial "new economic practices [which] create an order that seems to stand from landscape" (ibid., 571). Moreover, like Foucault's depiction of the rise of new techniques in the prisons, factories, and armies of a market society, Mitchell's story focuses on the crucial role of new dominant social groups, acknowledging at the same time that they were in fact parts of the broader structural changes brought about by the commercialization and diffusion of capitalism in Malaysia. Indeed, despite his criticism of Marxism, the independent variables of class, state, and economy are crucially involved in the emergence and the globalization of disciplinary practices. In his dispute with Scott, Mitchell adopts an analysis that reluctantly relates modern power relations to the capitalist market system, the newborn bourgeoisie, and the capitalist state in a third-world country during the process of its modernization.

Liberal Authoritarian Legalism

As I have argued, one of the major effects of political postmodernism has been to extinguish the state—to "deconstruct" it—not only from the academic field, but also, and more importantly, from the political geography of the left. Apart from a few isolated exceptions, the state as a valid domain worthy of investigation has fallen into oblivion. This absence of theoretical work on the state conforms rather well with the absence of more conjunctural and contextual political writings, firmly rooted in the immediate political problems of actual politics, exploring potential strategies of resistance, tactics of mobilization, and struggles of radical transformation of the capitalist-instituted reality, including its central site of domination, the state. In light of this lack of theoretical work on the state, liberalism has had no problem in recent years imposing the image of a benign, neutral, disinterested, and lawful state, based exclusively on the free consent of equal and rational individuals. Indeed, one major impact of the decline of the studies of the capitalist state was the neglect of the mechanisms of organized and centralized force and coercion, of the way they are linked with class struggles, and of their role in securing class domination and social cohesion. The repressive apparatuses of the state seem to have regressed to a minimum level of exercise, as if the state's monopoly of violence was secondary and inconsequential for its survival and reproduction.

And yet, less than twenty years ago leftist intellectuals criticized the authoritarian potentialities of the capitalist state. Poulantzas exemplified this trend of critical Marxism at its best when he coined the term *authoritarian statism* to describe the new historical form that the capitalist state had taken (Poulantzas 1976, 30, 38, 48–50, 90–93, 106, 124). Although he initially situated the emergence of authoritarian statism as a succession to military dictatorship, he quickly developed it into a broader theoretical category, designating the contemporary state of monopoly capitalism (1976, ed., 19–58; 1978, 203–47; and 1980, 600–608). Authoritarian statism, which represented a response to the intensification of class struggles, to the hegemonic crisis of the power bloc, and to the dilemmas of the interventionist, welfare state, was characterized by the subordination of the legislative branch to the executive (usually plebiscitarian in character), the abolition of the separation of powers, the rise of the administrative-bureaucratic state, the crisis of the rule of law, where the general, abstract, and universal laws are replaced by discretionary and arbitrary decrees, the decline of publicity and the formation of hidden centers of power—what Norberto Bobbio has termed the "invisible powers" (Bobbio 1987, 79–97; 1989, 17–21)—the crisis of political representation, the failure of the dominant mass parties to fulfill their traditional roles, and the significant accentuation of state repression. These transformations, Poulantzas argued, were accompanied by deeper political changes, such as the decline of democracy, the increase of social control and of techniques of normalization, the intensification of state intervention in economic and social spheres of life, a profound crisis of political legitimacy, and the dangerous curtailment of liberal, "formal" liberties.

Of course, these observations were not new (cf. Schmitt 1985; Agnoli 1990; O'Connor 1973; Habermas 1975, 1993; and Offe 1983). However, Poulantzas's merit rests primarily in bringing all these analyses into a selective but coherent and systematic left interpretive and political framework, which he injected into the center of the heated debates about the immediate political and strategic problems of contemporary socialism. More particularly, he directly linked the types of transformation of the contemporary state with the search for an effective and efficient strategy of radical transformation and a successful transition to socialism. For Poulantzas, therefore, it was essential to reach the most accurate conclusions. His theory of the authoritarian state was motivated by strategic considerations, political objectives, and the need to provide a sound theoretical base from which to confront the central problem of left politics: what is the best road to democratic socialism?

If we ask now what is the present validity and actual pertinence of Poulantzas's notion of authoritarian statism, we will have to respond negatively. The capitalist state now seems to have transformed itself once again (Jessop 1990, 70–71).[13] However, if Poulantzas's descriptions of the state are obsolete and of little political and strategic use, his broader theoretical framework and his conceptual tools provide a rich and fertile resource for starting to rethink the contemporary state. They remain as relevant and appropriate for a political investigation of the current forms of the capitalist state as when they were first elaborated. The limits of the present discussion do not afford me to develop this claim in detail. Here, I will restrict myself to a series of broadly sketched, and thus necessarily tentative, propositions, which need careful elaboration elsewhere. A systematic study, I believe, of the new form of state, which can be identified as "liberal authoritarian legalism," would need to theorize several recent political, economic, and social changes. Its basic developmental tendencies might be briefly summarized in the following preliminary positions.

First, liberal authoritarian legalism is characterized by the gradual transfer of political power from the executive and the legislative to the judiciary and the concentration of power within the latter. Key aspects of important social issues are settled not by legislative vote but by the decisions of the unelected judges of the Supreme Court. This counter-majoritarian tendency, which has become standard practice in the United States, is now exported and duplicated in many Western European countries, most notably in Germany, France, Spain, and most of the Central and Eastern "new democracies." This trend points to a larger structural shift toward the depoliticization and neutralization of democratic legitimacy and the divestment of the popular sovereign of its political responsibilities. Not surprisingly, the deliberations of the Supreme Court, which decided the outcome of the 2000 U.S. presidential election, have been elevated to the status of an ideal model for the consensual politics of liberal societies (Rawls 1993, 231–40). Moreover, the gradual appropriation by the judiciary of the power to take fundamental political decisions and the proliferation of powerful constitutional courts, endowed with generous powers of judicial review over legislation, have created a great confusion as to where ultimate political authority lies. Contrary to the previous subordination of the three powers under the executive, today they have taken a rather ambiguous and elusive form that makes it nearly impossible to locate and fix them at one specific institutional instance. This volatility of power has benefited the power bloc in its effort to unify its different fractions and allies.

Second, in a historical departure, we are witnessing a surprising revival and reinvigoration of the rule of law and liberal-formal legality. Against Poulantzas's contention of an alleged "decline of law" (Poulantzas 1978, 219)—which, needless to say, belonged to a broader intellectual current that insisted on the irrevocable "retreat from legality" (Unger 1976, 166–242)—liberal authoritarian legalism signals the sudden return of the juridical. This unexpected restoration of formal legality, in the form of procedural models of democracy, which have been adopted by the main currents of contemporary political thought, clearly threatens to empty, weaken, and neutralize the principle of popular sovereignty by reducing it to a mere "fact of plurality" and to the institutionalized competition among dominant political elites. This return is not completely unrelated to the neoliberal economic offensive of the last years and to the fact that bourgeois hegemony seems more stable and secure than ever before. Indeed, one might argue that the return of formal jurisprudence is directly associated with the concrete relations of forces among the social classes at this particular conjuncture. Hence, today, in the context of the general tendency to regulate everything by means of rules, procedures, and instituted norms, politics becomes confined to the institutional limits imposed by the dominant legality. The attempted impeachment of President Bill Clinton is an exemplary case of how the discourse of the rule of law can be used to undermine a popularly elected executive against the overwhelming will of the public. By strictly following the prescribed legal procedures, the Republican Party was able to transform private vices into public crimes in order to subvert the principle of popular legitimacy. What is most interesting and revealing in this case is that the entire process, which could have very well reversed the results of a democratic election, reminiscent of a constitutional, legal coup, was carried out without any violation of the constitution or any break with the law (Arato 1999, 155). On the contrary, its success was predicated on the precise and correct application of the established legal system, which demonstrates that when used properly, vigorously, and consistently, the rule of law can turn legality against democratic legitimacy, liberal constitutionalism against popular sovereignty, the abstract norm against concrete will, the law against its real and symbolic founding source: the people. As the historian Eli Zaretsky has persuasively argued, the impeachment must be interpreted as part of a broader historical context, including "a discrete attack, from the thirties, on the presidency as the democratic moment of politics," a presidency "that turned out to be the center of democratic aspirations in the United States" (Zaretsky 1999, 133–34; Arato and Cohen 1998, 61–66).

Third, this trend toward the juridification of politics becomes more obvious when we shift our attention from the political realm to civil society (penal, criminal law, etc.). Here, the coercive potentialities of liberal legality become more evident. The "return of the law" corresponds to an intensification of state violence, to an expansion of the repressive capabilities of the state, and to an amelioration of its controlling apparatus—thanks also to new technologies. Poulantzas did pay attention to the increase of state violence and was perceptive enough to relate it to authoritarian statism (Poulantzas 1978, 29–30, 80–82; 1980, 606–7). Whereas in the past, state violence corresponded to an arbitrary, discretionary, and in many cases extralegal and hidden use of the repressive instruments of the interventionist state (cf. Hirsch 1976, 1978; Preuss 1973), today political domination in liberal authoritarian statism is exercised in a modified form that entails two important differences with past practices.

On the one hand, the main function of the rule of law and legality is not to conceal state violence as it used to be; it is, rather, to provide the necessary semantic, normative, and institutional framework for its full expression and exercise. In contemporary liberal-capitalist societies, organized state oppression is not located below, next to, or against the law. It does not hide itself behind a veil of secrecy, nor does it represent an exceptional, extralegal moment of bourgeois hegemony. It exists mainly through and in the law. It is in full accord with the law so that it can be mobilized and deployed in a completely visible and public way. Precisely because it is a legal form of violence, it manifests itself proudly in the light of day. The violence of the rule of law represents the normal situation of the contemporary liberal-capitalist state. This does not mean that it has a real global and universal applicability or that illegal state violence has completely disappeared. It still remains the case that formal law is not applied equally to the entire population. Nor does it affect all social classes similarly. It operates selectively. Its targets continue to reflect policy and class discriminations. However, there are some relatively minor and detached developments that point to this more general phenomenon of the authoritarian dimension of liberal legality: the much-advertised war on drugs and (more recently) crime, the new repressive measures against illegal foreign workers, the tremendous increase of the carceral population, especially among the black population in the United States, the trial of juvenile delinquents as adults, the increase of the public visibility of police forces, preemptive policing, and the proliferation of forms of social control through the extensive public use of closed-circuit television for the surveillance of civic spaces (and not only) in the inner cities. All these phenomena establish a close link between liberal formal law and new forms of violence and repression, which are predominantly exercised against different sections of the working class.

On the other hand, there is another crucial difference with the past. No doubt, the idea of the juridification or colonization of the life-world is not a new one (Habermas 1987, 301–403). In the past, however, the critique of the juridification of social relations was intrinsically related to the welfare state, the growth of administration, its expansive economic and social role, and its detrimental impact on the formal and abstract structure of liberal law. For example, in the administrative state, the production of law was not confined to formal and general norms that could guarantee predictability and security and whose enactment was considered to represent the general interest of society. Instead, legal norms were subject to ever more elaborate specification by the administration that ruled through particular decrees and orders. Today, however, the crisis of the welfare state has diminished considerably the role, amount, and impact of arbitrary, administrative decrees. What we are witnessing today is a rather opposite phenomenon: the proliferation of general norms, associated with a neoliberal quasi-minimal state, and which, despite their universality and abstractness, still aspire to regulate and shape ever-greater domains of social life. Liberal legal authoritarianism is linked to the liberal, limited state rather than to the traditional bureaucratic regulatory state (Poulantzas 1979, 8).

Although state action that rests on general, public, relatively clear, and stable legal norms is indeed less prone to adopt unwanted and arbitrary forms of discretion than an administrative state is, this does not mean that it is less repressive. This can be explained by the fact that discretion is not the sole face of organized violence. It is one of its conditions, but neither the only one nor the most important. In liberal authoritarian legalism, formal and abstract legal codes contain tremendous capacities for oppression and social control, as mechanisms of securing the domination of the power bloc. For example, legal domination and its judicial appendage can create new forms of criminality. They might also institute new categories of legal subjects and establish new and more thorough procedures of investigation and persecution. They can, furthermore, invent new types of punishment as well as determine which legal transactions the law should regulate by means of formal power-granting norms and which not. Additionally, formal-abstract law can create new privileges in the forms of rights and have absolute control over the procedures of their acquisition, distribution, and transfer. One essential feature of the modern juridical machine is that it can expand the scope of its operation indefinitely by increasing the number of *social relations* that are to be transformed into *legal transactions*, which means adding new spheres of life under the direct control of legal coercion, state supervision, and judicial adjudication. Last but not least, law in liberal authoritarian legalism can function in such a way that the coercive apparatus can be endowed with the appropriate normative structure to induce the emergence of certain socially desirable relations and modes of behavior (usually in matters related to the economy, but not only). Poulantzas understood these aspects of the law rather well. If we leave aside his arguments concerning the relationship among law, discretion, and the interventionist state, which became outmoded after the crisis of the material legal paradigm (cf. Teubner 1988; Habermas 1996), his observations remain astonishingly pertinent. He realized that "law involves an eminently positive aspect: *for repression is never identical with pure negativity.* More than a conglomeration of prohibitions and censorship, law since Greek and Roman times also issued positive injunctions. . . . [Law] lays down things to be done, dictates positive obligations, and prescribes certain forms of discourse. . . . Law does not merely impose silence or allow people to speak, it often *compels* them to speak. . . . law is a constitutive element of the political-social field" (Poulantzas 1978, 83). I think that today Poulantzas would have said that law is *the* constitutive element of the organizational terrain of the capitalist state.

Not surprisingly, this productive and normalizing aspect of formal law is downplayed and relativized by liberal legal theorists, who insist on approaching law purely from the point of view of negative and prohibitory injunctions. Thus, they conceal the fact that these new forms of juridification do not presuppose an indeterminate and open-ended legal system or a discretionary potentiality or even a substantive content. They fit perfectly well with the liberal model of formal law and its emphasis on general, predictable, determinate, and abstract legal norms. Hence, it seems to me that they are inscribed in the very flesh of liberal legality and formal jurisprudence, as essential parts of its functioning. In fact, from a historical point of view, the periods that manifested greater state coercion in Western liberal societies—late-eighteenth-century and early-nineteenth-century England, France, and the United States—were precisely those in which the rule of law reigned unconstrained.

Under this new constellation of power, then, what might be the most effective strategies of political transformation? I would like to conclude by suggesting three possibilities with regard to modern law. What all these strategies share is a similar approach to the law as the main organizational terrain for the reproduction of the domination of the power bloc as well as for the unfolding of class struggle. More than ever, law has acquired today a central, constitutive, and instituting character with direct political implications. The juridical is the aspect of the state where class domination is reproduced. Therefore, it is important to grasp the mode in which class struggles are inscribed in the semantic and formal structure of modern law and how the latter condenses and shapes the existing relations of forces into a system of abstract, general, legal norms. Certainly, there is always the danger of falling into the trap of legal fetishism, by essentializing law or by thinking that it constitutes the only, or the superior, field of politics. Obviously, the law does not exhaust all of the strategic options of the left. However, under contemporary conditions, it seems to me that the specificity of the modern state refers to the relative separation of the juridical from the economic and to the dominant role the former plays in the organization and unification of the power bloc.

The first strategy refers to the politics of semi-illegality. An organized political movement of the left that aims at conquering the state in order to change it should be aware that once in power the limits of legality should be questioned from within and that a popular state should elaborate forms of breaking with liberal normative and legal constraints and make use of exceptional and emergency measures—even if these are not clearly included in the constitutional provisions (the case of Allende in Chile is a good example). Against the liberal politics of legality, the left should elaborate a counterpolitics of semi-illegality. I do not mean that it should drop institutionalized politics altogether and adopt exclusively illegal means. Nor am I suggesting that the popular state should become an "exceptional" state. This would be an absurd claim. What I am pointing to, to use Jean Cohen and Andrew Arato's terminology, is the need to find the proper point of encounter "between the boundaries of insurrection and institutionalized political activity" (Cohen and Arato 1992, 566), or between instituted and instituting politics. Such a two-track strategy will be able to confront the legal barriers imposed by the liberal law, which permeate the entire field of the state, without, however, disrupting altogether the existing legal and institutional framework and without representing a new, sudden revolutionary change. While remaining in the relational field of the liberal law, the left must also seek ways of acting outside the established juridical system to circumscribe and supersede the existing procedural mechanisms and legal limitations, particularly in those cases that these may favor, and entrench the reproduction of the existing relations of forces among classes and impede the implementation of a socialistic program. This ability to exploit the gray zone between legality and illegality, which might be interpreted in terms of a "normal, albeit extrainstitutional, dimension of political action" (ibid.), could permit popular power to counteract the "imperialistic" tendencies of the liberal juridical political system. Daniel Lazare has argued in an intriguing article that "The Fifth Amendment's entrenchment of bourgeois property rights renders socialism 'unrealistic' for anyone who accepts the permanence of America's constitutional structure. The enormous barriers that the constitutional system places in the way of new political parties all but guarantee that socialism will be effectively marginalized" (Lazare 1998, 32). If the left does not break with the current widespread cult of legal norms and the mystification of the juridical, the outcome will be a worsening of inequalities, an increasing of brutality toward the working class and the poor, a weakening of democracy, and a widening of class divisions. Under these conditions, this form of illegal action points to the possibility of preserving the "utopian horizon" of a democratic society, which, while presupposing the constitutional framework of an institutionalized democracy, extends the range of legitimate, even if initially extralegal, state activity.

Second, next to rediscovering law as a potential terrain of class struggle and as a strategic field, the left also needs to formulate and impose its own constitutional model to fill in the gaps that the politics of semi-illegality will create. This imposition entails not only a politics of legal or constitutional reform, which under particular circumstances might prove extremely useful; it also involves a piecemeal politics of original law creation and law transformation. The politics of the popular bloc should include a debate over the creation of a new legal order and the implementation of new legal relations governing both the private and the public spheres of society. The left, in other words, needs to develop a positive constitutional politics, aiming at the radical and profound transformation of the existing constitutional order (cf. Levinson 1996). A first step toward this aim could be the attempt to generate mass political support for the convocation of a new constituent assembly that will endow the hegemonic popular bloc with an instituting and founding content. It is important to start reexamining and reevaluating the role of a constituent assembly as a potential form of hegemonic politics and democratic founding. Such a strategy of transformation might be composed of five basic procedural steps (Schmitt 1928; Arato 1995, 203):

1. The dissolution of all previously constituted powers.
2. A popularly elected assembly with a plenitude of powers.
3. A provisional government rooted entirely in this assembly.
4. A constitution offered for a national, popular referendum.
5. The dissolution of the constituent assembly upon the ratification of the constitution that establishes a duly constituted government.

If one attributes the historical failure of socialism to, among other things, the absence of a systematic and constructive reflection on institutions, rules, and norms—an absence that permitted liberalism to monopolize the field of modern legal and constitutional theory—then the left needs to start rethinking issues bearing on the relationship among law, democracy, and socialism.

The absence of such reflection has created the impression that while democratic socialism is exclusively related to the question of how to change the material basis of society and how to equalize unequal economic relations, it has totally ignored the equally critical question of how to transform the political and juridical realm, a question confronted predominantly by liberal thinkers. Indeed, traditionally, socialism was conceived as a historically privileged form of concrete and substantive ethical life that has superseded the artificiality and subsidiary role of legal reality. The early socialists were confident that the sociable forms of life of freely associated workers would emerge spontaneously from properly organized production processes. Socialism was related to the vision of a homogeneous, totally pacified, monolithic society (with the exception of a small group of surviving class enemies). This conceptualization of the socialist society alluded to the overcoming of the two "circumstances of justice," as well as to the final removal of the fact of domination and economic exploitation. It was an absolute leap from the realm of necessity to the realm of collective freedom. In a self-ruled and self-reconciled society, law would be gradually absorbed by an increasingly expanding and democratically organized society and would ultimately wither away. Legal domination would dissolve into a transparent and rational self-administration. This fusion of an ethical system with the dominant social norms and the collective appropriation of the means of production would ultimately dispense with the need for a legal order. The state as a juridical structure supported by a coercive mechanism of law enforcement would progressively become restricted to the coercion of a hostile minority. This vision of the socialist society was of a society beyond law. Against the excesses of pure liberal legality, socialism appeared to evoke an equally extreme economist model, according to which the will of the people would be in a continuous, uninterrupted actuality, in a state of everlasting presence. This notion of socialism came at times perilously close to the self-deluding Marxian utopia of a society without institutions and without a modern structure of rights and liberties carving out autonomous spaces. Against this naive utopianism of classical socialism, the left needs today to take law more seriously and to investigate the different possibilities for the construction of a new socialist legal and constitutional order. Such an order must be capable of taking into consideration the complexity of highly developed and functionally differentiated societies and of presenting a viable and effective alternative to liberal legality. With this second strategy, the left will enter again, from a position of semilegality, into the domain of law, but in this case, it will be the law of a democratic, socialist society.

Although there are few theoretical works pointing in this direction, it should be mentioned that toward the end of his life, while still in prison, Antonio Gramsci contemplated the idea of a constituent assembly as a solution to the problem of fascism and the transition to a socialist regime (Athos 1973, 81–103; Quercioli 1977, 193–240). Taking into account his previous critique of liberal constitutionalism and constituent assemblies "as a vague and confused myth of the revolutionary period, an intellectual myth" (Gramsci 1977, 34–35), his description of the liberal constitution as "a codification of disorder and anti-human chaos," a "juridical fiction of the impartial and superior sovereignty of law... [that] was, in reality, the beginning of the dictatorship of the propertied classes, their 'legal' conquest of the supreme power of the State" (Gramsci 1994, 88), and his earlier insistence on the role of the Soviets and the dictatorship of the proletariat, this shift, I believe, is a key to understanding the instituting dimension of this strategy of constitutional politics (Cammet 1967, 182–86; Spriano 1979, 119–28). In fact, I would like to suggest that this change, rather than expressing an occasional tactical response to the specific conjunctural situation of Italian politics, reflects a deeper political and philosophical transformation related to the requirements of a hegemonic, thus democratic and popular, radical founding strategy (Buci-Glucksmann 1978, 238–39). Gramsci was inclined to define the constituent power as the "moment of an intensively collective and unitary national development of the Italian people" (Gramsci 1975, 2004). He even criticized Gioletti's party for "wanting a constituent assembly without a constituent assembly, that is, without the popular-political mobilization that leads to the convocation of a constituent assembly. They want a normal parliament to function as a constituent assembly reduced to its minimal term and domesticated" (ibid., 989, 1167). Here, Gramsci is alluding to the fact that only the constituent subject or a constituent assembly shaped by a popular alliance could create a new constitution. As he suggestively put it, "the '*Constituente*' represents an organizational form with which are expressed the most important demands of the working class" and prepares the ground for the founding of a new democratic order (Athos 1973, 88). It is unfortunate that we do not have more information about what Gramsci might have thought about the relationship between the hegemonic party and the constituent subject. It is legitimate to speculate, however, that, because in this same period he was deliberating about the need to re-create a new communist party no longer tied to the proletariat but open to different and broader social and intellectual forces, he might well have thought about the popular alliance as the main vehicle for the incarnation of the constituent power and as the central political force for the institution of a new Italian democratic republic based on the sovereign will of the masses.[14]

Finally, another strategy would be to strengthen and protect the existing institutional apparatuses and norms that are directly or indirectly related to democratic legitimacy and the popular basis of the liberal-capitalist states. This implies a fortification of the present constitutional and political venues for the expression of popular sovereignty. This is a classical strategy that entailed in the past the radicalization and extension of the positive aspects of liberalism, such as individual rights and political liberties. Poulantzas adopted this strategy by defending the liberal representative system of parliamentarism. In a similar way, the left should today consider the democratic potential of other established constitutional and political procedures and devices that are either malfunctioning or cast aside by the power bloc because they are detrimental to its hegemonic reproduction (referendums, plebiscites, popular initiatives, local decentralization, etc.).

In one of his last writings, Poulantzas understood the importance of law as a central target that the left needs to take seriously into consideration. The rule of law not only represents a main political terrain for the condensation of class struggle, it also constitutes one of the main fields of investigation. As he explicitly put it, "The same can be said of the study of the legal systems and of the law in general; although we have cast off traditional dogmas as to the merely 'formal' nature of democratic freedoms, we still do not have a real theory of justice. As a result we are unable to formulate a positive concept of human rights and freedoms clearly distinct from neoliberalism" (Poulantzas 1979, 15).

Notes

I wish to thank Mehmet Tabak for his insightful comments, which I have accepted only sometimes, but always appreciated.

1. This reconstruction of a critique of postmodernism from Poulantzas's writings acquires a unique meaning today, especially when the left is desperately striving to transform its growing dissatisfaction with poststructuralism into a coherent and cogent theoretical and political response (cf. Anderson 1983, 40–55; Callinicos 1990; Harvey 1990; Jameson 1991; Eagleton 1996; and Amin 1998, 93–122).
2. Barry Smart provides a completely distorted, inaccurate, and misleading discussion of the relationship between Poulantzas and Foucault (Smart 1983, 96–107).
3. For Marx, the modern factory created a new and pervasive form of domination and stratification, based on the division of labor and the despotic structure of the workplace. However, contrary to Foucault's critiques, Marx recognized that this new form of power relations was not exclusively confined to the factory. It spread to the whole social body and permeated other institutions and structures of civil society, as for example, the family (cf. Marx 1990).
4. The best and most concise definition of power is given by Foucault in his afterword to Hubert L. Dreyfus and Paul Rabinow, *Michel Foucault: Beyond Structuralism and Hermeneutics* (Chicago: University of Chicago Press, 1982). Foucault argues that "the exercise of power is not simply a relationship between partners, individual or collective; it is a way in which certain actions modify others." "The exercise of power consists in guiding the possibility of conduct and putting in order the possible outcome. Basically power is less a confrontation between two adversaries and the linking of one to the other than a question of government. . . . 'Government' did not refer only to political structure or to the management of states; rather it designated the way in which the conduct of individuals or of groups might be directed. . . . To govern, in this sense, is to structure the possible field of action of others. The relationship proper to power would not therefore be sought on the side of violence or of struggle, nor on that of voluntary linking (all of which can, at best, only be the instruments of power), but rather in the area of the singular mode of action, neither warlike nor juridical, which is government" (Foucault 1982, 219, 221).

5. Much like Foucault, Mitchell widens the field of investigation from the state to society as the final locus of modern power relations, independent and distinct from the sovereign state. Indeed, the state, rather than being the center of modern forms of domination, physical violence, and subordination, is reduced to a fraction of a broader process of new and pervasive forms of technologies/disciplines of power.

6. Mitchell's critique that Poulantzas's theory of the state remains helplessly trapped in the tradition of structuralism should be seen at best as a rhetorical move against an approach that threatens its own validity, and at worst as a complete misinterpretation of Poulantzas's writings that reveals a misconception about the evolution of Poulantzas's thought. There is total agreement among his interpreters that from the early 1970s on, Poulantzas moved away from structuralism and disassociated himself from Althusser's legacy. As Bob Jessop has keenly observed, "in eliminating the Althusserian influences in his work Poulantzas gradually abandoned the commitment to a structuralist interpretation of structural effects. He no longer treated the structural determination of hegemony or the class unity of the state as reflecting the functional imperatives of the self-production of the social whole.... From the notion of structural causality as formulated by Althusser he moved to the idea of structural selectivity formulated by Offe's early works.... Ever restless, Poulantzas then moved on from the idea of structural selectivity... to take up Foucault's ideas on power and strategy" (Mitchell 1991, 94; Jessop 1985, 134).

7. To realize the importance of Poulantzas's critique of Foucault, one has to be aware that it was the first serious and systematic critique articulated from a left-wing position. With the exception of a few isolated and scattered articles, left-oriented intellectuals started to engage critically with Foucault only in the early 1980s.

8. More broadly, Poulantzas characterized postmodernism as the return of the irrational. Although, he had particularly in mind Deleuze and Guattari, this characterization can also be applied to some ideas of Foucault (Poulantzas 1979).

9. The critique that Foucault absolutized and essentialized power has been repeated infinite times since Poulantzas (McCarthy 1991, 43–75; Flynn 1987, 80, 72).

10. The work of the urban geographer David Harvey combines Foucault's innovative propositions and Poulantzas's theoretical framework. Harvey's main claim is that the modern capitalist city not only is the product of capitalist accumulation, it is also made in such a way as to facilitate the dissemination throughout the social body of power relations that were articulated within the realm of production. The circulation of capital through the use of land explains the historical geography of the capitalist cities. "Factories and fields, schools, churches, shopping centres and parks, roads and railways litter a landscape that has been indelibly and irreversibly carved out according to the dictates of capitalism." For Harvey, capitalist production is not only the formative element in the making and remaking of cities, necessary to the overcoming of the problems of overproduction, but it also plays a key role in the shaping of class identity and the fragmentation of class solidarity. The process of urbanization has freed the microtechniques of power and has provided capitalism with a powerful tool in disseminating the practices of control and discipline, in a hidden, pervasive, and all-encompassing way. Harvey defines his project as the unmasking of the power relations that became dispersed through the creation of the modern "disciplinary" city by the process of capital reproduction. Where Foucault and Mitchell see "disembodied" power relations, Harvey detects

their material and historical roots. The emergence of asylums, workhouses, penitentiaries, hospitals and schools is directly related to "the manner in which industrialists in general, and the community of builders in particular, defined the quality of life for their workers and used to build the environment as part of a general strategy for inculcating bourgeois values and a 'responsible' work discipline.... A persistent theme in the history of the advanced capitalist countries has been to look for those improvements in the living place that will enhance the happiness, docility, and efficiency of labor" (Harvey 1982, 373; 1985, 50–51).

11. Of course, a major difference with Hegel is that power relations, contrary to *Geist*, have no hidden meaning, no final end, and no telos in the forms of self-realization.

12. In his later writings Foucault distinguished between domination and power. This distinction refers to the difference between "relationships of power as strategic games between liberties," where "some people try to determine the conduct of others," and "the states of domination... we ordinary call power." For Foucault, "power is always present: I mean the relationships in which one wants to direct the behavior of another.... These relations of power are changeable, reversible, and understandable.... Now there are effectively states of domination. In many cases, the relations of power are fixed in such a way that they are perpetually asymmetrical and the margin of liberty is extremely limited" (Foucault 1991, 19, 11–12). This definition, however, does not seem to advance and clarify the distinction between political power and other forms of power relations. First, it is based on a quantitative and empirical criterion, that of stability. What are the criteria for drawing the lines between a stable and an unstable power relation? Are we not in this case shifting the level of analysis to that of institutional structures? Second, what does "effectively states of domination" mean? We might have stable but ineffective states of domination. How are we to classify them? Third, this definition does not overcome the confusion between different types of domination. In other words, what are the differences between two stable and effective forms of domination, as, for example, the domination of the state and the domination within the family? Finally, although Foucault wanted to provide a descriptive, neutral, and value-free concept of power, he nonetheless introduced a crypto-normative element, as, for example, in the argument that "power is not an evil. Power is strategic games.... To exercise power over another in a sort of open strategic game, where things could be reversed, that is not an evil.... The problem is rather to know how to avoid... the effects of domination" (ibid., 18). But why are power games better than states of domination? Just because, as he said, they are "more attractive and fascinating" (ibid., 20)? In order to avoid the normative issues of legitimation and consent, Foucault equates questions of justice with aesthetic preferences. He fails to explain why something that is attractive is also the best choice. A way out of this impasse is to introduce a normative criterion that will justify why something that is fascinating for us is also worth struggling for, and similarly, why something that is repulsive or boring must be reversed and overthrown. Such a strategy of justification would not be far away from a classical utilitarian argument, which still operates within a normative, value-oriented framework.

13. Jessop has criticized Poulantzas's notion of authoritarian statism (Jessop 1990, 70–71).

14. This essay was written during the dramatic events in Venezuela, where a new constituent assembly was convoked following the elections of July 25, 1999. The stated purpose of this assembly, led by the president, was to draft a new constitution. The first act of the constituent assembly was to declare itself the "original source of the popular will and expression of the people's sovereignty." This means that the rest of the powers (especially, the judicial and legislative branches) are subordinated to the decisions adopted by the assembly. According to this decision, the assembly can intervene and reform any of the existing political powers. Following its inauguration in early August, the assembly focused on ways in which it could subordinate both the Supreme Court and Congress. The assembly spent the first month arguing over the creation of emergency commissions in charge of evaluating the performance of the judicial and legislative branches and determining the best form to intervene in them. This resulted in the resignation of the president of the Supreme Court, Cecilia Sosa, and the confrontation (physical and verbal) of the Congress with the constituent assembly. Despite many vacillations, most of the constitutional proposals that have been presented to the assembly, particularly those introduced by President Hugo Chávez, are aimed at deepening the process of democratization and at establishing social justice. The result is to be seen. Ignacio Ramonet has described these events as an "antiliberal revolution" (Ramonet 1999, 1). I wish to thank Michael Penfold-Becerra for discussing with me these events in Venezuela.

References

Agnoli, Johannes. 1990. *Die Transformation der Demokratie und andere Schriften zur Kritik der Politik.* Freiburg: Ça ira.

Amin, Samir. 1998. *Spectres of Capitalism: A Critique of Current Intellectual Fashions,* New York: Monthly Review Press.

Anderson, Perry. 1983. *In the Tracks of Historical Materialism.* London: Verso Books.

Arato, Andrew. 1995. "Forms of Constitution Making and Theories of Democracy." *Cardozo Law Review* 17(2): 191–231.

———. 1999. "Impeachment or Revision of the Constitution." *Constellations* 6(2): 145–56.

Arato, Andrew, and Jean Cohen. 1998. "Politics by Other Means? Democracy and the Clinton Crisis." *Dissent* (summer): 61–66.

Athos, Lisa. 1973. *Memorie. In carcere con Gramsci.* Milan: Feltrinelli Editore.

Babb, Hugh, ed. 1951. *Soviet Legal Philosophy.* Cambridge: Harvard University Press.

Bobbio, Norberto. 1987. *The Future of Democracy: A Defense of the Rules of the Game.* Minneapolis: University of Minnesota Press.

———. 1989. *Democracy and Dictatorship: The Nature and Limits of State Power.* Minneapolis: University of Minnesota Press.

Buci-Glucksmann, Christine. 1978. *Gramsci and the State.* London: Lawrence and Wishart.

Callinicos, Alex. 1990. *Against Postmodernism.* New York: St. Martin's Press.

Cammet, John. 1967. *Antonio Gramsci and the Origins of Italian Communism,* Stanford, Calif.: Stanford University Press.

Carvel, Terrell. 1998. *The Postmodern Marx.* Manchester, U.K.: Manchester University Press.
Cohen, Jean, and Andrew Arato. 1992. *Civil Society and Political Theory.* Cambridge: MIT Press.
Collins, Hugh. 1982. *Marxism and Law.* Oxford: Oxford University Press.
Connolly, William. 1991. *Identity/Difference: Democratic Negotiations of Political Paradox.* Ithaca, N.Y.: Cornell University Press.
———. 1993. *Political Theory and Modernity.* Ithaca, N.Y.: Cornell University Press.
Dews, Peter. 1984. *The Logic of Disintegration.* London: Verso Books.
Eagleton, Terry. 1996. *The Illusions of Postmodernism.* Oxford, U.K., and Cambridge, Mass.: Blackwell Publishers.
Flynn, Bernard. 1987. "Foucault and the Body Politic." *Man and the World* 20: 70–84.
Foucault, Michel. 1979. *Discipline and Punish: The Birth of the Prison.* Trans. Alan Sheridan. New York: Vintage Books.
———. 1980. *Power/Knowledge: Selected Interviews and Other Writings: 1972–1977.* Ed. Colin Gordon. New York: Pantheon Books.
———. 1982. "The Subject and Power." In Hubert Dreyfus and Paul Rabinow, *Michel Foucault: Beyond Structuralism and Hermeneutics.* Chicago: University of Chicago Press.
———. 1990. *The History of Sexuality.* Vol. 1, *An Introduction.* Trans. Robert Hurley. New York: Vintage Books.
———. Michel 1991a. "The Ethics of Care for the Self as a Practice of Freedom." In James Bernauer and David Rasmussen, eds., *The Final Foucault.* Cambridge: MIT Press.
———. 1991b. *Remarks on Marx: Conversations with Duccio Trombadori.* New York: Semiotext(e).
Fraser, Nancy. 1989. *Unruly Practices: Power, Discourse, and Gender in Contemporary Social Theory.* Minneapolis: University of Minnesota Press.
Gramsci, Antonio. 1975. *Quaderni del Carcere.* Turin: Giulio Einaudi.
———. 1977. *Selections from Political Writings: 1910–1920.* London: Lawrence and Wishart.
———. 1994. *Pre-Prison Writings.* Cambridge: Cambridge University Press.
Habermas, Jürgen. 1975. *Legitimation Crisis.* Boston: Beacon Press.
———. 1987. *The Theory of Communicative Action.* Vol. 2, *Lifeworld and System: A Critique of Functionalist Reason.* Boston: Beacon Press.
———. 1993. *The Structural Transformation of the Public Sphere: An Inquiry into a Category of Bourgeois Society.* Cambridge: MIT Press.
———. 1996. *Between Facts and Norms: Contributions to a Discourse Theory of Law and Democracy.* Cambridge: MIT Press.
Harvey, David. 1982. *The Limits to Capital.* Oxford: Basil Blackwell.
———. 1985. *Studies in the History of and Theory of Capitalist Organization.* Vol. 2. Baltimore: Johns Hopkins University Press.
———. 1990. *The Condition of Postmodernity.* Oxford: Basil Blackwell.
Heller, Agnes, and Fehér, Ferenc. 1988. *The Postmodern Political Condition.* Cambridge, U.K.: Polity Press.
Hirsch, Joachim. 1976. "Remarques théoriques sur l'État bourgeois et sa crise." In Nicos Poulantzas, ed., *La crise de l'État.* Paris: Presses Universitaires de France.

———. 1978. "The State Apparatus and Social Reproduction." In John Holloway and Sol Picciotto, eds., *State and Capital.* London: Arnold.
Honneth, Axel. 1991. *The Critique of Power: Reflective Stages in a Critical Social Theory.* Cambridge: MIT Press.
Jameson, Fredric. 1991. *Postmodernism, or, The Cultural Logic of Late Capitalism.* Durham, N.C.: Duke University Press.
Jessop, Bob. 1985. *Nicos Poulantzas: Marxist Theory and Political Strategy.* New York: St. Martin's Press.
———. 1990. *State Theories: Putting Capitalist States in Their Place.* London: Macmillan.
Kelsen, Hans. 1955. *The Communist Theory of Law.* London: Stevens and Sons.
Laclau, Ernesto, and Chantal Mouffe. 1990. "Post-Marxism without Apologies." In Ernesto Laclau, ed., *New Reflections on the Revolution of Our Time.* London: Verso Books.
Lazare, Daniel. 1998. "America the Undemocratic." *New Left Review* 232: 3–40.
Levinson, Sanford. 1996. "A Constitutional Convention: Does the Left Fear Popular Sovereignty." *Dissent* (winter): 27–33.
Marx, Karl. 1990. *Capital.* Vol. 1. London: Penguin Books.
Marx, Karl, and Frederick Engels. 1978. "The Communist Manifesto." In Robert Tucker, ed., *The Marx-Engels Reader.* New York: W. W. Norton.
McCarthy, Thomas. 1991. *Ideas and Illusions: On the Reconstruction and Deconstruction in Contemporary Critical Theory.* Cambridge: MIT Press.
Mitchell, Timothy. 1988. *Colonizing Egypt.* Cambridge: Cambridge University Press.
———. 1990. "The Everyday Metaphors of Power." *Theory and Society* 19(5): 545–77.
———. 1991. "The Limits of the State: Beyond State Theories and Their Critics." *American Political Science Review* 85(1): 76–96.
O'Connor, James. 1973. *The Fiscal Crisis of the State.* New York: St. Martin's Press.
Offe, Claus. 1983. *Contradictions of the Welfare State.* Cambridge: MIT Press.
Poulantzas, Nicos. 1976. *The Crisis of the Dictatorships: Portugal, Greece, Spain.* London: Verso Books.
———. 1978. *Political Power and Social Classes.* London: Verso Books.
———. 1979. "Is There a Crisis in Marxism?" *Journal of the Hellenic Diaspora* 6(3): 7–16.
———. 1980. "Research Note on the State and Society." *International Social Science Journal* 32(4): 600–608.
———, ed. 1976. *La crise de l'État.* Paris: Presses Universitaires de France.
Preuss, Ulrich. 1973. *Legalität und Pluralismus: Beitrage zum Verfassungslehre der Bundesrepublik Deutschland.* Frankfurt: Suhrkamp.
Quercioli, Mimma Paulesu, ed. 1977. *Gramsci Vivo. Nelle testimoniaze dei suoi contemporanei.* Milan: Feltrinelli Editore.
Ramonet, Ignacio. 1999. "Chávez." *Le Monde diplomatique* 547, 1.
Rawls, John. 1993. *Political Liberalism.* New York: Columbia University Press.
Schmitt, Carl. 1928. *Verfassungslehre.* Berlin: Duncker and Humblot.
———. 1985. *The Crisis of Parliamentary Democracy.* Cambridge: MIT Press.
Scott, James. 1976. *The Moral Economy of the Peasant: Rebellion and Subsistence in Southeast Asia.* New Haven: Yale University Press.
———. 1985. *Weapons of the Weak: Everyday Forms of Peasant Resistance.* New Haven: Yale University Press.

Smith, Adam. 1981. *An Inquiry into the Nature and Causes of the Wealth of Nations.* Indianapolis: Liberty Press.
Smart, Barry. 1983. *Foucault, Marxism, and Critique.* London: Routledge.
Spriano, Paolo. 1979. *Antonio Gramsci and the Party: The Prison Years.* London: Lawrence and Wishart.
Teubner, Gunther, ed. 1988. *Dilemmas of Law in the Welfare State.* New York: Walter de Gruyter, European University Institute.
Unger, Roberto Mangabeira. 1976. *Law in Modern Society: Toward a Criticism of Social Theory.* New York: Free Press.
Vadée, Michel. 1998. *Marx, penseur du possible.* Paris: L'Harmattan.
White, Stephen. 1991. *Political Theory and Postmodernism.* Cambridge: Cambridge University Press.
Wood, Ellen Meiksins. 1998. *The Retreat from Class: A New 'True' Socialism.* London: Verso Books.
Zaretsky, Eli. 1999. "Cultural Wars and the Assault on the Presidency: The Twin Stakes of the Impeachment Crisis." *Constellations* 6(2): 133–41.

CHAPTER SIX

Eras of Protest, Compact, and Exit

On How Elites Make the World and Common People Sometimes Humanize It

Richard A. Cloward and Frances Fox Piven

Until the last decade or so, virtually all European and American theorizing about the origins and development of the Keynesian welfare state (KWS) was evolutionary. True, there were disputes about theoretical orientations and methodological preferences. Nevertheless, the main body of work shared an underlying assumption that state provision would continue to expand, at least in the rich industrial nations, and that the forces impelling that expansion were rooted in the basic institutions of capitalist and democratic societies.

One group of evolutionary interpretations was functionalist. The most influential of these posited that the growth of social programs was a necessary response to economic growth and its demographic and social correlates. Industrialization and urbanization not only led to increased longevity, and thus a larger population of the dependent aged, but also disrupted traditional familial and communal methods of care of the aged or the indigent or the disabled or the unemployed. At the same time, economic growth created the wealth that could be tapped by the state to meet these new needs. And in the aftermath of World War II, these programs enlarged sufficiently to make them useful in managing and stabilizing consumer demand in mass-production economies.[1]

Or, in another variant of the functionalist approach, it is not industrialization as such, but capitalism, and the imperatives of accumulation and legitimation generated by industrial capitalism, that fueled the growth of the welfare state (see O'Connor 1973; Gough 1979). In a still further variation, feminist analysts argued that welfare state programs were developed to shore up the traditional family and to reinforce patriarchal gender roles (cf. Fraser 1989; Gordon 1994; Eisenstein 1981; Abramovitz 1988). Finally, some analysts, perhaps more sensibly, developed synthetic explanations, resting their case for the expansion of the welfare state on the interplay of conditions associated with industrialism, capitalism, and patriarchy, for example.

The second line of evolutionary argument was about power. Analysts argued that functionalist models were inadequate, and focused instead on political relations. Certainly, there were important intellectual precedents for this perspective: Marx rooted the growth of proletarian power in the inevitable development of industrial capitalism; Bernstein rooted the possibilities of working-class power in the development of electoral representative arrangements. Or pluralist analysts simply point to the power dynamics generated by liberal democracy itself, arguing that the growth of the welfare state is a result of electoral competition and/or the influence of organized welfare-state beneficiaries.

Among these political interpretations, the social-democratic perspective is the most widely accepted, melding as it does the economic evolutionism generated by industrial capitalism with the political evolutionism generated by electoral representative arrangements. Thus social-democratic power resources are said to grow in tandem with both industrial capitalism and electoral democracy (cf. Korpi 1983). Industrialism fostered trade-union growth, while electoral representative arrangements led to the development of labor or socialist political parties. Together the unions and parties promoted the expansion of social programs that ameliorated the condition of the working class and also shielded it from market insecurities and untrammeled employer power. In the happiest variants of this perspective, welfare-state programs promoted the "decommodification" of labor that increased labor power in market relations" (Esping-Andersen 1985, 31).[2]

A broadly compatible view of power as evolutionary is embedded in the work of the historians dedicated to recovering the history of "protest from below" in preindustrial Europe, such as Eric J. Hobsbawm, George Rude, Charles Tilly, and Sidney Tarrow. Hobsbawm captured the drift:

> Until the past two centuries, as traditional historiography shows, "the poor" could be neglected most of the time . . . because their active impact on events was occasional, scattered, and impermanent. If this has not

> been so since the end of the eighteenth century, it is because they have become an institutionally organized force. (Hobsbawm 1985, 293)

Tilly (1986) makes a similar argument with the sweeping claim that the advance of industrialization and the growth of the nation-state made possible the transformation of popular struggles from localistic and "reactive" protests to the national "proactive" strikes and popular electoral mobilizations that characterized the industrial and democratic era.

Whatever the institutions privileged, all these theories take for granted the continuing development of the welfare state because they lodge the forces that lead to welfare-state growth in fundamental social structures. Broadly speaking, the welfare state expands in response to imperatives generated by industrialism, or by capitalism, or by patriarchy, or in response to the political formations created by capitalist and democratic arrangements.

Events have now put these models in question. Welfare-state programs are under assault. By the mid-1980s, the programs were being whittled back in almost all the rich democratic countries, and in some countries big changes were under way, particularly in the United States, the United Kingdom, Australia, and New Zealand. To be sure, pension programs are tending to withstand the assaults, at least thus far, but all of the programs that reached the active labor force, such as sickness, disability, unemployment, and social assistance, have undergone tightening of eligibility requirements and cuts in benefit levels.

This reversal of evolutionary development might well have been expected to generate something of an intellectual crisis. Functionalist analysts have averted it, however, by positing the emergence of a new institutional order. They shifted from the general presumption that the Fordist or social-democratic welfare state was somehow functional for industrial and democratic societies to the presumption that it is dysfunctional for the postindustrial, post-Fordist, and presumably post–social-democratic future. Who better to capture the drift of recent commentary than Daniel Bell?

> In Europe, the major structural problems are social welfare costs and aging, inefficient industries propped up by subsidies. . . . A corollary factor is rigid labor market costs (the costs of reducing a work force by benefit payments), and the unwillingness or inability of workers to move. . . . The most surprising issue is social welfare. Forty or so years

> ago, Marxist theory said the capitalist state would spend for warfare, but not for welfare. But it is welfare that now may be strangling the capitalist state. (Bell 1994, 446)

Bell is speaking directly to the theorists of the KWS, and in their language. His sweeping neoliberal conclusion rests on what he believes to be a conviction shared by diverse analysts that the welfare state arises from institutional imperatives of the capitalist state, and is therefore ultimately functionalist. What Anthony Giddens called the "theory of industrial society" has thus been preserved, but adapted to the neoliberal program of cutbacks in welfare-state regulatory and redistributional programs.[3] Where the KWS was once treated as necessary, its development virtually inevitable, the neoliberal rollbacks are now treated by some analysts as necessary and inevitable because they are propelled by new institutional imperatives. What was functional in an earlier social order is not in the succeeding one.

But advocates of power models have no such easy way of sidestepping the intellectual crisis. Reversals in welfare-state programs, together with the enormous concentration of income and wealth that has taken place in advanced economies over the past several decades, expose the inadequacy of evolutionary models of power. What is missing in much of the work on the welfare state is an appreciation of the shifting and contingent dynamics of class power. We turn, therefore, to an effort to rethink the bearing on class power relations of the convulsive economic and political changes that have characterized capitalist history.

Interdependencies as Sources of Power

Capitalist societies organize production and exchange through networks of specialized and interdependent activities. These networks of cooperation are also networks of contention. They help to shape the interests and values that give rise to conflict. More important for our argument, networks of interdependency also generate widespread power capacities. Agricultural workers depend on landowners, but landowners also depend on agricultural workers, as industrial capitalists depend on workers, the prince depends in some measure on the urban crowd (Hobsbawm 1965, chap. 7), and governing elites in the modern state depend on the acquiescence if not the approval of enfranchised publics.

In other words, though agricultural laborers, industrial workers, the people in the urban crowd, are all at the bottom end of hierarchical relationships, and are kept so by dominant ideologies, by rules, and by raw coercion, they all also have potential power. Their power consists in their ability to interrupt a pattern of cooperation that depends on their continuing participation and contribution. We think of welfare-state arrangements as a social compact, forged over time in response to the threatened or actual exercise of this disruptive capacity. Of course, there are multiple other influences on the shape of the compacts that evolve in particular social formations. But everywhere the compact includes measures that are at least to some degree responsive to the grievances that provoke disruption (such as the right to vote, or to unionize, or income support programs) coupled with new rules backed by sanctions to enforce cooperation and limit future defiance. The capacity to disrupt that spurs efforts at conciliation and regulation is rooted in the underlying economic and political interdependencies that bind social actors together, and that the social compact of an era is intended to stabilize and maintain.

Actual power relations are, of course, enormously tangled and intricate. Urban, democratic, and capitalist societies generate multiple and crosscutting forms of interdependency—between husbands and wives, doctors and patients, students and teachers, beauticians and their clients, and so on. All of these interdependencies generate the potential for conflict and the exercise of power. And the exercise of power in one set of relations can work to dampen efforts to exercise power in another set of relations, as parents might succeed in dampening any inclinations to rebelliousness among schoolchildren, for example. All of this is complicated and interesting, and indeed preoccupies some power analysts, particularly those identified with "exchange theory" who study the dynamics of power in networks of individuals.

We take for granted, however, that some relationships are much more important than others. The dominant interdependencies—and the power constellations they make possible—develop within economic relationships, and within the political relationships that anchor state elites to the societies they rule. Thus dominant interdependencies, and dominant forms of power, reflect the cooperative activities that generate the material bases for social life, and that sustain the force and authority of the state. When we speak of classes and class power, we mean the economic interdependencies that develop between large aggregates of people bound together in systems of production and exchange, and divided by the typically exploitative character of those systems. These economic relations are, of course, intertwined with the interdependencies on which state authority is anchored—markets always depend on political authority—helping to explain why the state elites who ordinarily buttress patterns of economic domination sometimes intervene to modify them.[4]

Our emphasis on the power capacities shaped by the interdependent relations that constitute society is broadly consistent with important theoretical traditions. It is consistent, for example, with Norbert Elias's depiction of the development of European central states as propelled by the dynamics generated by the networks of interdependency of warrior societies (Elias 1982). It is also consistent with the Marxist view of working-class power as nourished by the role of workers in capitalist production. And it fits Schumpeter's model characterizing the capitalist state as the "tax state," which, because it depends on economic resources it does not control, ties state authorities in close interdependence with the owners of private property who do control those resources.

But doesn't this model of power also lend itself to an evolutionary perspective? After all, it would seem to follow from the argument we are laying out that popular power should have increased over the course of capitalist history, temporary setbacks notwithstanding. If power is rooted in interdependent social relations, then the increasingly elaborate division of labor that characterizes capitalist societies, as well as expanding penetration of the core into the periphery with the consequent absorption of previously marginal communities and societies into the capitalist division of labor, would diffuse power capacities more and more widely. This is the political implication of the growth of Durkheim's organic solidarity: a wider and tighter grid of interdependencies means that everyone in that grid has some power, at least under some conditions. This line of reasoning would lead us to reverse the conventional wisdom: it is not decentralization, but centralization and the integration it implies, that enlarges at least the possibility of popular power. The remote village may be shielded by its remoteness from a predatory state, but neither can it have influence on that state until it is brought, willy-nilly, into some kind of relationship with it.

Moreover, if people do in fact have some agency, which we take to mean some capacity for innovation, some ability to see through a dominant ideology, and some capacity to act outside the rules that ensure powerlessness, then the very fact of participation in this ever tighter grid of interdependencies should nourish agency as it nourishes power. So, perhaps popular power capacities have enlarged over the sweep of Western history.

But if popular power is evolutionary, that is true only over the broadest sweep of capitalist and democratic development. There have also been sharp reversals in the ability of lower-strata groups to exercise power. We appear to be witnessing such a reversal now. Reigning ideologies, systems of rules, capacities for organization, the deployment of the threat of exit, and the ability of class power groups to manipulate these conditions constitute important qualifications on a developmental and evolutionary view of power.

The Actualization of Power Capacities

In principle, all parties who make necessary contributions to economic or political processes have power. In principle, workers in a capitalist economy always have potential power over capitalists, whether they labor as agricultural tenants, or as industrial workers, or as technicians in a postindustrial economy. In principle, they have power because their contributions are necessary to ongoing processes of production and exchange. But the actualization of those power capacities is always conditional on the ability of parties to the relationship to withhold or threaten to withhold their cooperation, and this capacity depends on other features of these relationships beyond the fact of interdependency. To understand the terms of any social compact, and the power dynamics that underly changes in the social compact, and especially to understand the impact of postindustrial changes on worker economic and political power, we have to pay attention to the conditions that make it possible for people to realize the power leverage in actual systems of interdependent relations.

The first condition is that contributions must be recognized. This raises the complex problem of culture or ideology. Economic and political interdependencies are real in the sense that they have real ramifications in the material bases of social life and in the exercise of coercive force. But they are also cultural constructions. Although we cannot explore the full ramifications of this observation and its bearing on the very development of economic and political interdependencies here, we do need to make the point that culture, or ideology, or the Marxist problem of false consciousness, is critical to the realization of the kind of power we are examining. To be sure, at first glance it might seem that the very fact of participation in interdependent activities would incline people toward recognition of their own contributions, and therefore of their power capacities. Perhaps so, or at least to some extent, or at least under some conditions.[5] But such recognition must overcome deeply imprinted inherited interpretations that privilege the contributions of dominant groups,[6] as well as the continuing ability of dominant groups to project new and obscuring interpretations.

Second, and obviously, behavior in social relations is institutionalized, which is to say it is rule-governed, and rules are not neutral. Rather, the rules constraining behavior in interdependent relations tend to ensure the cooperation of people on the bottom end of social hierarchies, not only through the force of custom or habit, but through the force of law and the threat of coercive force that the law implies. Virtually by definition, rules that enforce cooperation in interdependent relations strip people of the capacity for exercising power in those relations, as laws against worker "combinations" and strikes strip workers of power in their relations with employers, for example, and laws governing plant closures may similarly limit the power of employers over workers.

Third, the relevant contributions to ongoing economic and political activities are often made by many individuals, and these multiple contributions must be coordinated for the exertion of effective leverage. This is the classical problem of organizing workers, or voters, or community residents, in order to deploy their leverage over those who depend on them, for their labor, or their votes, or their acquiescence in civil life.

Fourth, and this is both important and widely recognized, the power of an actor that derives from her contribution to a cooperative endeavor is only effective if other contenders for power in that endeavor cannot exit or threaten to exit at little or no cost. The threat of exit includes the threat of finding alternative partners, as when employers find replacement workers, or workers find alternative employment, or voters switch party allegiance. Moreover, employing the threat of exit implies the ability to endure at least the temporary suspension of the relationship, and that ability is almost always unequally distributed. Landholders can typically endure the material losses resulting from agricultural strikes far better than can the laborers whose very subsistence is at stake.

Institutional Change and Power Relations

Thus, although the premise that power is rooted in patterns of specialization and interdependence suggests a tendency toward equality, that premise must be sharply qualified. True, considered in the abstract, the capacity to disrupt ongoing economic or social or political processes on which power rests is widely distributed, and increasingly so as societies become more complexly specialized and interrelated. But the ability to mobilize and deploy contributions to social cooperation in actual power contests varies widely, and depends on very specific and concrete historical circumstances. To appreciate this, we have to forgo our tendency to speak in general terms of classes and systems. For some purposes, these abstractions are, of course, useful. But the interdependencies that sometimes make assertions of popular power possible do not exist in general or in the abstract. They exist for particular groups, who are in particular relationships with particular capitalists or particular state authorities, at particular places and particular times.

Economic or political change, especially rapid and uneven change, can alter power relations not because class interdependencies evaporate, but because the concrete particularities that govern the actualization of power are transformed. People recognize their leverage over particular employers or particular state leaders, not over capital in general or the state in general, although they are surely influenced by more general ideas about the relationship of employers to employees, of citizens to governments. They recognize commonalities and capacities for collective action among members of particular concrete groups far more readily than among the working class in general, although here too broader group identities and antagonisms may predispose them one way or the other. And people fear the loss of particular forms of employment to which they have access, and in the particular places where their lives are rooted, although once again they are surely more likely to be alert to these dangers if they think capital exit is a more widespread phenomenon. The decline of handloom weaving in nineteenth-century England is an example, for it did not mean that manufacturers no longer depended on labor. But it did mean that the handloom weavers and framework knitters could be abandoned as manufacturers turned to women and children to work in the new textile mills. And as this happened, the understandings, forms of solidarity, and strategies for limiting exit threats by employers that had developed in an earlier era of putting-out manufacturing eroded.

In our time, while capital still depends on labor in general, ongoing economic changes are undermining the ideas, the solidarities, and the strategies for curbing exit threats that were developed by concrete groups under the concrete circumstances of industrial capitalism. The old occupational categories—the miners, the steelworkers, the dockers, and so on—that were at the forefront of labor struggles have been depleted. And those who remain no longer have the confidence that they can act to "shut it down," paralyze an industry, much less make an entire economy falter. Meanwhile, the working-class towns and neighborhoods are emptying out, the particular working-class culture they nourished is fading. The unions that drew on all of this are necessarily enfeebled. They are enfeebled even more by employer strategies that take advantage of the decline of older forms of working-class power to launch new and terrifying exit threats—by hiring contingent workers and strike replacements, by restructuring production, or by threatening to close plants and shift production elsewhere.

Still, the power advantage yielded to elites by institutional change does not last forever. Spurred by new hardships or new opportunities, people gradually discover the power capacities embedded in particular patterns of economic and/or political interdependency, in a process influenced over time both by the experience of previous struggles and by the system of social provision yielded by those earlier struggles. Gradually, they develop interpretations that somehow counter reigning ideologies that deny the importance of their contributions to new economic and political relations. And they develop the solidarities and networks that make possible the concerted action necessary for effective leverage within these relationships, or they politicize existing solidarities and networks. The politics from below that forces the construction of a regulatory social compact develops over time, and it develops unevenly. But it does develop.

Protest, Compact, Exit, and the Poor-Relief Compact

For the purpose of this preliminary statement of our argument, we mark out three distinct eras in capitalist development: the rise of commercial agriculture and the poor-relief compact in the waning days of feudalism, with Britain in the lead; the era of industrial capitalism and the Keynesian welfare state that began in the late nineteenth century; and the new postindustrial era based on high-tech production systems and the accelerated globalization of trade and finance and accompanied by neoliberal welfare policies, with the United States in the lead.

With our provisos about the deployment of power in mind, we can begin to discuss the power dynamics that underlay the making and breaking of social compacts in the history of Western capitalism. Most of the academic work on the welfare state has been devoted to explaining its historical evolution, as well as variations between nations. If our emphasis on power is useful, it should help explain differences in welfare-state patterns between nations that functionalist perspectives elide. In particular, it should help account for the convulsive rather than evolutionary pattern of development, and for reversals where expansion might otherwise be expected.

The first precedents of the contemporary welfare state date from the secularization of relief for the poor, an innovation that seems to have spread across Western Europe between the thirteenth and the sixteenth centuries. In the background of the new concern with poverty and its regulation were the massive changes taking place in the feudal order of Western Europe as the peasantry began to gain personal freedom and, in the context of a rural labor surplus, to lose access to the land. "Poverty as such begins with the tiller's freedom," said Marx of this development (*Grundrisse*, 735, cited in Novak 1985, 3). And while the centuries-long severing of the peasantry from the land eventually created a wage-labor force, the demand for wage labor developed slowly and almost surely did not motivate the displacement of the peasantry, at least during earlier stages. More likely, the process reflected pressures on the feudal surplus—and on the feudal contract—resulting from population growth. After all, undergirding feudal notions of the responsibility of lord to vassal was the economic imperative of keeping the people who worked the land alive during periods of dearth (Hill 1952, 36). Population growth reduced the urgency—and raised the cost—of that imperative, and rural elites began shirking on their feudal responsibilities.

The loss of access to the land and subsistence inevitably led to deeper poverty, and increased vagrancy, begging, and theft. Starving rural people flocked to the towns, where their very presence was perceived as threatening, and particularly so because disease epidemics often followed in the wake of hunger.[7] But vagrancy, begging, and theft can be understood as something more than the blind responses of the poor to their desperation.[8] Transiency could also be a form of defiance of customary forms of labor regulation that bound the poor to their employers.

When the population equation shifted dramatically in favor of workers in the wake of the mid-fourteenth-century plague that killed off an estimated half of Europe's population, transiency actually seems to have escalated. The poor took advantage of the shifting population equation by taking to the road in vast numbers to better the terms of their employment.[9] Across Europe, the response of elites was to try to override the advantage yielded the peasantry by demographic collapse by freezing wages by law, limiting mobility, and requiring the unemployed to accept whatever employment was offered.[10] The English Parliament passed the first of many Ordinances of Laborers in 1349, directing all able-bodied men and women under sixty and without income to accept employment at wage rates that prevailed before the plague (Lis and Soly 1979, 48).

Judging from perennial complaints about vagrancy, these efforts to reshackle the poor could not have been very successful, and the unsettled poor continued to be a threat, a physical menace to persons and to property, if only because they wielded the age-old political weapons of theft and arson. And then also, even when the poor took to the road in an effort to better their condition, the strategy often entailed eking out a subsistence by begging or stealing—or, failing that, starving. And vagrancy was often simply an effort to cope with the dire need caused by bad harvests. Either way, the numerous, clamorous, and hungry poor, and the specter of epidemic they raised, threatened the better-off. "The permanent confrontation with the migrating possessionless became an obsession for the 'right-minded' European" (ibid., 115; see also Jutte 1994, 29, 35; Hill 1952). Moreover, the dispossessed seemed to think they had some rights, a residue perhaps of the feudal idea of the social contract between the king and his lords, the lord and his vassals (cf. Markoff 1996, 40; Jutte 1994, 27), and also of eclesiastical traditions of almsgiving as an exchange between the affluent seeking salvation and the poor seeking to survive (De Swaan 1988, 29).

The threats posed by a defiant poor shaped the gradual development of poor-relief systems as, from the thirteenth century on, municipal authorities made episodic efforts to establish secular control over charitable giving. Presumably, neither the church nor those who sought salvation through almsgiving could be relied on to condition their giving with the firm discipline that the rise in vagrancy and begging seemed to make necessary.[11] The main solutions—usually developed by municipal authorities, but occasionally enjoined by absolutist rulers as well—more or less described the principles that would govern several centuries of poor relief: some food in the form of "outdoor" relief, but not enough to sustain the poor, and sometimes shelter for transients, the sick, or the homeless in new charitable institutions such as hospitals or almshouses. Meanwhile, there were strenuous efforts to rationalize the collection of revenues and the giving of alms. Lists were maintained of paupers by categories signifying their worthiness, systems were established for monitoring their behavior, and so on (Lis and Soly 1979, chap. 1). And the aid that was given was coupled with strict prohibitions on begging, backed up by draconian punishments, and forced labor for the able-bodied (cf. ibid.; Jutte 1994; Geremek 1994).

In the two centuries after the passing of the Black Death in the mid-fourteenth century, episodes of rebellion forced the periodic revival of these sorts of poor-relief arrangements, which then were allowed to lapse when the threat from below subsided. True, after the Black Death, population grew rapidly, agriculture recovered, as did trade and the demand for manufactured goods, and so therefore did the towns where manufacturing was centered. Economic growth did not, however, put a halt to continuing rural impoverishment. The numbers of the rural landless increased, and even those with land, the smallholders, and sharecroppers on the continent, lived on the edge of subsistence, barely surviving in good years, and sinking into debt in bad years, precipitating the cycle of debt, borrowing, and property loss that typifies the rise of commercial agriculture.[12] Meanwhile, economic growth spurred the continuing expropriation of land by big landholders who were shifting arable land to pasturage, which meant demand for acreage increased while the demand for labor fell.

The sixteenth century, which had begun as a period of relative plenty, witnessed a series of bad harvests, in 1521–22, and from 1527 to 1534. Vagrancy assumed mass proportions, especially in the epidemic year of 1530, and peasant rebellions flared across Germany, Spain, the Netherlands, and France. In Italy, in the years 1527–29, whole provinces were said to be in ruins as marauders swept the countryside, transport routes were obstructed or destroyed, and crowds of starving peasants clamored at the gates of Venice. In Lyons, as prices soared, the poor swept through the streets, plundered the granaries, and pulled down the houses of the rich. In 1531, Lyons was again beseiged, this time by invading rural paupers (Geremek 1994, 120–57).

Rebellion spurred elites to attend to poor relief. The arrangements invented earlier were revived, and expanded. Absolutist rulers, including Charles V in the Low Countries (1531), Ferdinand I of the Austrian Empire (1552), and John George of Prussia (1535), issued edicts requiring communities to feed their indigenous poor, as did the parliament of Paris, which created the Great Bureau of the Poor, probably about 1545. All over Western Europe, municipalities undertook poor-relief reform, more or less following the principles developed earlier: centralized systems of revenue collection and almsgiving, fierce punishments for persistent beggars, and an even more strident emphasis on forced work, along with the invention of the first workhouses.[13] "The main problem," writes Hill of this period, "was to transform the mental outlook of the lower orders so that they no longer waited at the rich man's gate for charity, but went out to offer their services on the labour market" (Hill 1952, 36).

The Evolution of the Poor-Relief Compact

Once institutionalized, the social compacts brought into being by class conflict in a given era do tend to expand, and in a pattern that is evolutionary. The class forces that give rise to the compact continue to develop, and continue to press for advantage within the terms of the fledgling social compact. This pattern of expansion eventually became evident in the era of poor relief.

Although not for a long time. De Swaan (1988, 32) says of early poor-relief arrangements that they disintegrated into an "archipelago of small fortresses."[14] It is not hard to see why. Royal edicts notwithstanding, poor relief remained local, and despite the harsh terms, the towns that provided poor relief risked being overrun by armies of the desperate during periods of dearth. Not only that, the severe discipline that these systems tried to impose in exchange for alms was resisted, often by riot, and not only among the paupers, but among a larger population that still identified with the "sturdy beggars" (Hill 1952, 43). Not surprisingly, poor-relief arrangements inaugurated to cope with the unruly poor were allowed to languish when the crisis subsided, only to be reinvented when the poor again became threatening. Poor relief reflected a rolling social compact, a contractual arrangement between the well-off and the poor that had to be enforced by riot. Steinmetz's careful study demonstrating the impact of violent collective disruptions on poor-relief spending in German municipalities in the nineteenth century suggests that this rolling social compact remained in force in Germany for a very long time, indeed, well into the twentieth century (Steinmetz 1993, chap. 6). This kind of compact continues to describe the dynamics of American poor-relief programs to this day, as we first argued more than two decades ago, and events since then have strengthened our argument (Piven and Cloward 1993).

England was the pioneering capitalist nation, and the pioneer in the institutionalization of poor relief. England led Europe by several centuries in abandoning feudal property relations, ejecting the peasantry from the land in favor of a distinctive three-tier system of commercial agriculture: large holdings owned by the aristocracy were managed by market-oriented tenants, and worked by a rural proletariat. Ellen Meiksins Wood thinks this property system, and specifically the pivotal role of the middle-tier tenant farmers who were pressed by market competition to increase productivity, spurred the rise of capitalist agriculture, with all of its disruptive consequences (Wood 1991, 45).

Moreover, England had the advantage of a unitary state. At a time when absolutist rulers on the Continent were still maneuvering for advantage amid parcelized feudal sovereignties, the self-confident and united English ruling class governed through a legal system in which a universalistic common law and a system of royal courts that reached into every locality gave the national government scope and authority (Wood 1991, 45; Hill 1952, 37; Mann 1993, 490). England had the institutional capacity, in other words, to pioneer the stabilization of the poor-relief social compact. And, as the processes of engrossment of landholdings and ejection of the peasantry advanced, the English ruling class soon had the motive (Saville 1969). The displacement of the peasantry increased during the Tudor period, with the now-familiar consequences of vagrancy and beggary. Moreover, local revolts by this rural proletariat became more common, and some of the revolts were serious, "close to all-out war involving large military forces," says Wood (1991, 151).[15]

By the early sixteenth century, English rulers began to create a national poor-relief system. In 1531, Henry VIII made use of England's distinctive system of nationalized local authorities to order justices of the peace, bailiffs, and mayors to take a census of the poor in their areas, issuing licenses to beg to the sick or old or disabled. Those who sought alms without licenses were to be arrested and flogged. In 1535, a further edict ordered local authorities to provide support for the infirm, and work for the able-bodied, while children were to be apprenticed, all this to be financed by a voluntary fund that centralized almsgiving. Then, in 1536 and 1539, church property was secularized. In 1563, another law was passed making work obligatory.

Meanwhile, enclosure proceeded apace, and in the years 1594–97, poor harvests spurred another series of revolts (Geremek 1994, 163–77). In the years 1597, 1598, and 1601, a series of laws were passed requiring localities to establish local poor-relief systems. In 1640, these local poor-relief systems were made legally permanent. Over the course of the next century, as the enclosure of the commons and the displacement of the agricultural population proceeded, with the by now ritual riot and tumult, the poor-relief system was stabilized and expanded (cf. Geremek 1994; Cata Backer 1995). In short, although the terms remained harsh, the poor were fed.

In the late eighteenth and early nineteenth centuries, a new wave of enclosure was spurred by the opportunities for profit created by expanding urban markets for cereals and new agricultural methods, such as cross-harrowing. Between 1750 and 1850, six million acres, or one-quarter of the total arable acreage, had been engrossed by large landowners or holders. This, together with the collapse of the cottage-based handloom weaving industry early in the nineteenth century, spurred new waves of protest in the countryside, at the same time that the towns were racked by Luddism, radicalism, trade unionism, and Chartism. "At no other period in modern British history," writes Eric Hobsbawm of these years, "have the common people been so persistently, profoundly, and often desperately dissatisfied. At no other period since the seventeenth century can we speak of large masses of them as revolutionary" (1987, 55).

And so, "fear and pity united to sharpen the wits of the rich, and to turn their minds to the distresses of the poor," as Hammond and Hammond put it (1948). Relief expanded rapidly, along with a new innovation—variously called the allowance or relief in aid of wages or

Speenhamland system—in which relief payments were used to supplement declining agricultural wages (Polanyi 1957; Hobsbawm and Rude 1968, 48–49). The poor rate rose steadily, and by 1818 was more than six times as high as it had been in 1760.[16] Sidney and Beatrice Webb estimate that by the 1830s more than a million people were on the dole (1929, 105). Thus, there was evolution and expansion, within the framework of the poor-relief compact created in response to the protests provoked by a commercializing agriculture. Polanyi concludes that "by and large the nearly 16,000 Poor Law authorities in the country managed to keep the social fabric of village life unbroken and undamaged" (Polanyi 1957, 92).

Exit and the Smashing of the Poor-Relief Compact

Social compacts are made, and they are broken. Economic and political relations are dynamic, they change, and, as they do, so do the power capacities of contending groups and classes and the forms in which class conflict is acted out. This can result from changes in basic patterns of interdependency and the leverage that interdependency yields to all parties to economic and political cooperation. The power loom and the factory rendered the handloom weavers virtually helpless in their dealings with manufacturers, because they were no longer needed in the new system of factory production. They simply lost any direct leverage over the employing class, although they retained some leverage over the local political authorities who were exposed to the tumult they could create. More usually, however, economic and political reorganization does not so much totally marginalize people as undermine, at least for a time, their ability to recognize, organize, and deploy the power potential inherent in interdependent relations.

With the passage of the New Poor Law in 1834, the poor-relief system that had developed over three centuries was dismantled. Now there was to be only the workhouse for the able-bodied indigent, at least in legal principle.[17] People still protested. They demanded what they had by now come to see as their ancient rights. Richard Cobbett expressed their indignation, even equating the right to relief with property rights:

> Among these rights was . . . the right in case we fell into distress, to have our wants sufficiently reliefed. . . . When the Tithes were taken away . . . compensation was given in the rates as settled by the poor-law. The

> taking away those rates was to violate the agreement, which as much right to receive in case of need, relief out of the land, as it left the landowner a right to his rent. (Cited in Thompson 1963, 761)

Indeed, Dorothy Thompson thinks that the sustained and furious reaction against the New Poor Law was a major spur to the rise of the Chartist movement.[18]

But to little avail. It was, as we say, the end of an era. Underlying changes in economy and polity had made the disruptive protests of the rural poor less important. The reasons are familiar. As manufacturing grew apace, the locus of economic and political activity gradually shifted from the countryside to the towns, from the rural gentry to the new manufacturing class. The campaign of manufacturers and shopkeepers for the franchise, culminating in the Reform Act of 1832, resulted in their rising political influence, effected through the domination of the Whigs in Parliament. The New Poor Law reflected these newly dominant interests, specifically their material and ideological commitments to the creation of a "free" market in labor. The workhouse system was designed, Polanyi later said, to oil "the wheels of the labor mill." In other words, a form of exit had been taking place, not as a direct result of the class partner to an interdependency withdrawing or threatening to withdraw, but as a result of the class partner to an interdependency losing influence in a larger and changing economic and political constellation. The rural gentry and farmers who were exposed to the protest power of the poor and to their protest repertoire of riot and arson and mayhem had themselves lost power to a rising class of manufacturers who were far less exposed to the defiance of the rural poor, and who considered poor relief an impediment to the creation of a free market in labor.[19] An era had ended, with a compact smashed.

The Industrial-Era Compact

Some three centuries after the emergence of the poor-relief compact, a new system of interdependencies overtook the locally based economic and political relations of the largely agricultural early capitalist economies of Europe. Manufacturing expanded and urbanized, and the apparatus of the nation-state grew, and electoral representative arrangements also expanded. By the late nineteenth century, patterns of contention began to reflect these new interdependencies, as workers and then voting publics discovered new forms of leverage, and mobilized to use them.

As welfare-state analysts have been at great pains to argue, the industrial social compact was not by any means uniform. Although it developed over the course of an era in a pattern that may indeed be roughly evolutionary, it developed unevenly, in reflection of the exigencies that affect the actualization of class power. The historical case that the rise of industrial capitalism and the growth of the nation-state undergirded the mass strike and the political demonstration, the forms of popular protest that characterized the late nineteenth century, has been made by others (such as Tilly 1986; Tarrow 1994; Markoff 1996). And accounts of the role of mass strikes, unions, and labor-based political parties in the development of the KWS are also familiar. In our language, the emergence and growth of income support and regulatory programs reflected the new forms of power available to workers and mass publics as a result of the interdependencies generated by industrial capitalism and the rising nation-state. The growth of manufacturing meant the growing interdependence of employers and workers, and the concentration of workers in factories facilitated the growth of unions and of efforts to mobilize the leverage inherent in the employment relation. A parallel growth of the nation-state tied state rulers to the mass publics from whom they extracted the resources for state making, an interdependence ultimately institutionalized in the development of electoral representative arrangements. In both economic and political spheres, population concentration and the growth of communications encouraged popular efforts to actualize these new forms of power.

These developments created potential power that gradually came to be recognized, organized, and deployed at a time when capital exit, whether by replacing workers or disinvesting, was at least limited. As a result, and even apart from the sometimes sharp and precipitous influence of conflict spurred by market downturns, the industrial-era welfare state expanded, not in lockstep with the expansion of the industrial economy and the electoral representative institutions, but as a result of the variable and contingent deployment of the power capacities generated by those institutions.

Patterns of social provision varied for different strata of the population, and they varied between countries, as the literature on the welfare state reflects in its emphasis on the contrast between the more universalistic "social insurance" state and the "social assistance" or poor-relief state (exemplified by the United States), and in its preoccupation with explaining differences in aggregate "welfare-state effort" between nations, resulting in welfare-state leaders such as Sweden, and welfare-state laggards such as the United States. In our terms, the more generous and universalistic system of social provision secured by rights that we call social insurance reflects the larger power capacities of regularly employed workers in the core or metropolitan economy. Those working in more marginal sectors of the economy, or working irregularly, or not working at all, necessarily have less of the kind of power that inheres in interdependent economic relations—except, that is, for the power of the riot and other forms of civil disorder. Accordingly, because their power is only intermittently deployed, the social compact that regulates and stabilizes their use of that power is less secure, and provides fewer benefits.

However, the more marginal workforce continues to function as a reserve army, and in that sense, has an indirect and symbolically mediated relationship to production processes. For this reason, these strata may be at least partially shielded in the social compact earned by the power of core workers. Consistently, in countries where the exigencies of mobilizing worker contributions have made core workers politically and economically more influential, social insurance programs won by them are more likely to shield even marginal workers, and by doing so, reduce the corrosive influence of the reserve army on labor power.

As in the history of the poor-relief compact, early responses to the power challenges made possible by industrial society took the form of creating rules to suppress those challenges, as in the anticombination laws in England or yellow-dog contracts in the United States, or in the antisocialist laws in Bismarck's Germany. But, from the beginning, the emerging social compact included more than the bread and forced labor of the poor-relief compact. Rather, what developed was an intricate counterpoint of conciliation and regulation, of programs to ensure some economic security together with a net of civil and political rights that also channeled and constrained popular defiance. Thus Steinmetz, in his detailed examination of the interplay between unemployment, protests, and the strength of the parliamentary left in accounting for municipal public-works programs in nineteenth-century Germany, shows that strong social-democratic representation in municipal councils actually depressed city spending on public works: "Where the SPD [social-democratic party] was strongly 'municipalized,' as signaled by its successful engagement in conventional municipal politics, elites had less reason to fear the disruptive effects of unemployment" (Steinmetz 1993, 185–86).

Perhaps the lessons learned by German rulers from the experience with municipal programs help to explain why Germany, with its militant and organized industrial working class, was the leader in moving from poor relief to the insurance-style programs that defined the Keynesian welfare state. The first industrial accident insurance was introduced in 1871, a modest health program in 1883, and a pension program in 1889. Within two decades, most European countries had followed suit. Not surprisingly, nations that led in granting male suffrage also tended to be leading welfare-state innovators, suggesting that the responsiveness of these state authorities owed something to their new exposure to a mass electorate (Pierson 1991, 109–10).

By 1920, most of Europe had established the institutional framework of the welfare state, and the programs began to grow steadily, especially during the Depression years of the 1930s. Then, after the interruption of World War II and its aftermath, labor and youth movements—and, in the United States, minority protests—exploded in the 1960s, and so real program expenditures escalated, spiraling upward at a much faster rate than the growth of GDP (Organization for Economic Cooperation and Development, 1994). Even in the United States, where the initiation and expansion of welfare-state programs had lagged behind Europe, program spending rose rapidly. But, to most observers, it was Sweden that epitomized the industrial-era social contract. There, a "historic compromise" negotiated by the social democrats ensured unionization rights, full employment, and a panoply of government programs to reduce inequality, while guaranteeing Swedish capital both ownership and management prerogatives.

Postindustrialism and the Shattering of the Industrial Social Compact

We think the developments we call postindustrialism or post-Fordism are undermining the industrial-era welfare state partly because postindustrial conditions are changing power capacities, and partly because those changed capacities are being actively and strategically deployed by an activated capitalist class to reduce popular power. We stress this point because a different and functionalist explanation is rapidly gaining ascendance, namely, that under postindustrial conditions existing social programs are simply economically inefficient, impeding economic adaptation and growth. Thus, an OECD jobs study recommends curbing social spending in order to lower nonwage labor costs, increasing wage differentials (or lowering wages) to foster employment growth, lowering unemployment benefit levels and tightening eligibility checks, and so on. These and similar proposals to roll back the industrial-era welfare state are understood as the necessary and inevitable steps that will have to be taken to adapt to the conditions created by new technologies and globalization, an interpretation that appears to be shared by a good number of leftist analysts (e.g., Jessop 1993; Esping-Andersen 1994). These arguments are not wrong, as far as they go. But by resting the case on economic determinants, they obscure the changing power dynamics that these economic changes both reflect and create.

The impact of postindustrialism on the industrial-era welfare state is the consequence of shifts in power relations between classes that postindustrialism may facilitate but does not fully explain. To be sure, new information technologies, globalization, and the reorganization of production combine to once again allow capital increased mobility. In turn, these new capacities are being invoked in arguments about the necessary and inevitable triumph of international markets. Thus, postindustrial economic changes have become the basis for an ideological campaign that underlines and exaggerates the new power of capital by naturalizing it. Just as the advance of industrial capitalism was spearheaded by the rise of laissez-faire ideology that argued the inevitability and superiority of unregulated national markets, now the advance of postindustrial capitalism is spearheaded by the rise of neo-laissez-faire doctrine that expands the natural law of markets to an international scope. No matter the variable reality of international competition—and it varies greatly, from industry to industry and country to country—the argument is that capital now can and must withdraw its contribution to the production relationship by seeking lower costs and higher profits, by disinvesting in one locale and reinvesting elsewhere, or by replacing workers with technology, or by replacing full-time workers with part-time or temporary workers, and so on. In this campaign, it is not easy to disentangle the real from the ideological.

Moreover, what is taken as economic, and therefore as inevitable, is as often the result of institutional changes that do not originate in economic relations at all, but are rather constructed by states, and by the economic elites who influence state policies. Think of supranational organizations such as the International Monetary Fund, or the tax policies that reward offshore investments, or the trade pacts that facilitate international exchange. Or think of the important role that the European Union, the creature of nation-states, has assumed in enforcing what are presumably the tough terms of international markets on helpless national governments, and therefore helpless national publics.

The implications of this power mobilization by capital for the power of workers and for the industrial-era social compact are readily apparent. Employers still need labor, but their increased capacity for exit, especially in the context of new, politically constructed institutions that facilitate exit, and the deliberately bred fear of exit, reduces their dependence on any particular source of labor. This means that workers are more inhibited in trying to exercise power, while employers are less inhibited. And because employer power is more readily actionable, it can be the basis for strategies that further increase or pyramid employer power, by eroding the capacity of workers to resist, whether by weakening unions or by changing hiring policies so as to increase worker divisions and heighten worker insecurity.

And employer power is not restricted to workplace relations. The much-remarked upon decline of the nation-state may not be the decline of the functions of the nation-state—arguably, national governments perform ever more critical functions for postindustrial capital—but rather the ability of capital to threaten exit in its dealings with both central and local governments, and with voting publics, in order to get favored treatment in such matters as taxation or infrastructure, or in order to force the partial deregulation of local labor markets. The threat of exit is also a weapon in the politics of welfare-state policies, where employer groups can push for rollbacks that enlarge the industrial reserve army and thus further weaken the power of labor in market relations.

Of course, people resist new doctrines that justify the dismantling of hard-won protections. They resisted in the nineteenth century in poignant and desperate protests against the New Poor Law. And they resisted in the twentieth century in the rash of strikes and protests that spread across France, Italy, and Germany. In the nineteenth century, resistance was to little avail. Will it be different in the twenty-first century?

Notes

1. The initiators of this interpretation include Wilensky and Lebeaux (1965), Cutwright (1965, 1967), and Wilensky (1975). Our brief characterization of this and other perspectives on the welfare state does not do them justice. Most analysts also think industrialization and urbanization, or capitalism, or patriarchy, have complex cultural and political consequences, which mediate the translation of the needs generated by industrialization into new state programs. See, for example, T. H. Marshall (1964).

2. For the social-democratic perspective more broadly, see also especially Korpi (1983). On decommodification specifically, see Esping-Andersen (1985, 1990) and Piven and Cloward (1985). Other class analysts saw the welfare state less as the expression of working-class interests and more as the instrument for the domination of workers, although this analysis has lost salience as welfare-state programs have come under attack. See Gough (1979) and O'Connor (1973) for statements of this perspective.

3. Giddens calls structural functionalism the "theory of industrial society" (1976, 718).

4. See Mann (1986, chap. 1) for an exposition of societies as overlapping, intersecting power networks that generate "promiscuous" sources of power.

5. Barrington Moore, and before him Tocqueville, seemed to think that the recognition of interdependencies was inevitable when they argued that peasants would come to see the extractions of a predatory landed aristocracy as unjust unless those extractions were balanced by contributions to the peasant community.

6. This includes, of course, the interpretations produced by intellectuals that privilege the contributions of dominant groups. A curious example is in the literature on exchange theory, which advances a definition of power as rooted in the exchange of services and benefits, and is thus at the outset similar to our definition. But the drift of this literature, and particularly of the work of Peter Blau, is to define power in relationships as the result of furnishing needed contributions, a tautology that, of course, works to justify unequal power.

7. Lis and Soly (1979, 17–20) provide data on purchasing power in calories for manual laborers in Florence in the thirteenth century that show the precariousness of their circumstances.

8. Political challenge by the lower strata has often not taken obvious and explicit forms, for the reason that open challenge risks fierce reprisals, and in any case, the poor often have multiple opportunities for concealed resistance and evasion. On this point, see Piven and Cloward (1977, chap. 1) and Markoff (1996, 23).

9. Curiously, "tramping" later became a strategy employed by networks of artisans who traveled the country to take advantage of difference in local trade conditions. See Mann (1993, 516).

10. On the statute of laborers, see Chambliss (1976).

11. Medieval charity reflected a kind of doctrinal interdependence between the better-off who sought salvation through giving and the poor who sought alms. On

this point, see especially Geremek (1994, 19). Of course, a charity thus motivated could readily interfere with other economic and civil relationships. On the continuities between eclesiastical, Elizabethan, and contemporary poor-relief systems, see Cata Backer (1995).

12. Lis and Soly (1979, 62–63) estimate the proportion of rural landless at one-quarter to one-half the population in Tudor England, and as high as one-half in parts of the Continent.

13. For a compelling account of the relief system developed in Lyons during this period, see Davis (1966).

14. De Swaan considers that poor-relief systems were forged as a way of solving dilemmas of collective action among elites, dilemmas that pertained mainly to the distribution of costs

15. See also Pound (1978), who says that every Tudor monarch had to contend with at least one serious rising.

16. We should note that estimates vary sharply. But no one disagrees that the poor rates rose precipitously, and so did the numbers of people on relief.

17. In fact, the implementation of the New Poor Law was complicated both by local class sympathies and by the cost and difficulties of constructing the huge new workhouses that were required. For a detailed examination of the implementation of the law in Norfolk, see Digby (1978).

18. The class anger that the law apparently provoked is astonishing. See Thompson (1984, esp. 28–36).

19. This shift should not be overstated, as it sometimes is. See Trattner (1994, 52–53). The rural gentry, and especially the farmers who paid the poor rates, were themselves agitated by the precipitous rise in poor rates. See Ashford (1986, esp. 68).

References

Abramovitz, Mimi. 1988. *Regulating the Lives of Women: Social Welfare Policy from Colonial Times to the Present.* Boston: South End Press.

Ashford, Douglas. 1986. *The Emergence of the Welfare States.* New York: Basil Blackwell.

Bell, Daniel. 1994. "The Future of Europe." *Dissent* 41 (fall): 445–50.

Cata Backer, Larry. 1995. "Medieval Poor Law in Twentieth-Century America: Looking Back toward a General Theory of Modern American Poor Relief." *Case Western Reserve Law Review* 44 (3–4) (spring/summer): 871–1041.

Chambliss, William J. 1976. "The State and Criminal Law." In William J. Chambliss and Milton Mankoff, eds., *Whose Law, What Order? Conflict Approach to Criminology.* New York: John Wiley and Sons. 66–106.

Cutright, Phillip. 1965. "Political Structure, Economic Development, and National Social Security Programs." *American Journal of Sociology* 70: 537–50.

———. 1967. "Income Distribution: A Cross-National Analysis." *Social Forces* 46 (December): 180–90.

Davis, Natalie Zemon. 1966. "Poor Relief, Humanism and Heresy." Paper given at the Newberry Library Renaissance Conference in Chicago, April 16 (mimeographed).

De Swaan, Abram. 1988. *In Care of the State.* New York: Oxford University Press.

Digby, Ann. 1978. *Pauper Palaces.* London: Routledge and Kegan Paul.

Eisenstein, Zillah. 1981. *The Radical Future of Liberal Feminism.* New York: Longmans, Green.

Elias, Norbert. 1982. *Power and Civility.* New York: Pantheon Books.

Esping-Andersen, Gosta. 1985. *Politics against Markets.* Princeton, N.J.: Princeton University Press.

———. 1990. *The Three Worlds of Welfare Capitalism.* Princeton, N.J.: Princeton University Press.

———. 1994. "Equality and Work in the Post-industrial Life Cycle." In David Miliband, ed., *Reinventing the Left.* London: Polity Press. 167–85.

Fraser, Nancy. 1989. *Unruly Practices: Power Discourse and Gender in Contemporary Social Theory.* Minneapolis: University of Minnesota Press.

Geremek, Bronislaw. 1994. *Poverty: A History.* Cambridge, Mass.: Basil Blackwell.

Giddens, Anthony. 1976. "Classical Social Theory and the Origins of Modern Social Theory." *American Journal of Sociology* 81 (January): 703–29.

Gordon, Linda. 1994. *Pitied but Not Entitled: Single Mothers and the History of Welfare.* New York: Free Press.

Gough, Ian. 1979. *The Political Economy of the Welfare State.* London: Macmillan.

Hammond, J. L., and Barbara Hammond. 1948. *The Village Labourer.* London: Longmans, Green.

Hill, Christopher. 1952. "Puritans and the Poor." *Past and Present* 2 (November): 32–50.

Hobsbawm, E. J. 1965. *Primitive Rebels.* New York: W. W. Norton.

———. 1985. *Workers: Further Studies in the History of Labour.* New York: Pantheon Books.

———. 1987. *The Age of Empire, 1875–1914.* New York: Pantheon Books.

Hobsbawm, E. J., and George Rude. 1968. *Captain Swing.* New York: Pantheon Books.

Jessop, Bob. 1993. "From the Keynesian Welfare to the Schumpeterian Workfare State." Lancaster Regionalism Group, Working Paper 45, Cartmel College, University of Lancaster, England.

Jutte, Robert. 1994. *Poverty and Deviance in Early Modern Europe,* New York: Cambridge University Press.

Korpi, Walter. 1983. *The Democratic Class Struggle.* London: Routledge and Kegan Paul.

Lis, Catharina, and Hugo Soly. 1979. *Poverty and Capitalism in Pre-Industrial Europe.* Atlantic Highlands, N.J.: Humanities Press.

Mann, Michael. 1986. *The Sources of Social Power.* Vol. 1, New York: Cambridge University Press.

———. 1993. *The Sources of Social Power.* Vol. 2, *The Rise of Classes and Nation-States, 1760–1914.* New York: Cambridge University Press.

Markoff, John. 1996. *Waves of Democracy: Social Movements and Political Change.* Thousand Oaks, Calif.: Pine Forge Press.

Marshall, T. H. 1964. *Class, Citizenship and Social Development.* Chicago: University of Chicago Press.

Marx, Karl. *Capital.* 1974. Vol. 1. London: Lawrence and Wishart.

Moore, Barrington. 1966. *Social Origins of Dictatorship and Democracy.* Boston: Beacon Press.

Novak, Tony. 1985. *Poverty and the State.* Philadelphia: Open University Press.
O'Connor, James. 1973. *The Fiscal Crisis of the State.* New York: St. Martin's Press.
Organization for Economic Cooperation and Development. 1994. *The OECD Jobs Study.* Paris: OECD.
Pierson, Christopher. 1991. *Beyond the Welfare State?* University Park: Pennsylvania State University Press.
Piven, Frances Fox, and Richard A. Cloward. 1977. *Poor People's Movements: Why They Succeed, How They Fail.* New York: Pantheon Books.
———. 1985. *The New Class War: Reagan's Attack on the Welfare State and Its Consequences.* Revised and expanded edition. New York: Pantheon Books.
———. 1993. *Regulating the Poor.* New York: Pantheon Books.
Polanyi, Karl. 1957. *The Great Transformation.* Boston: Beacon Press.
Pound, J. 1978. *Poverty and Vagrancy in Tudor England.* London: Longman.
Saville, J. 1969. "Primitive Accumulation and Early Industrialization in Britain." *Socialist Register.*
Steinmetz, George. 1993. *Regulating the Social: The Welfare State and Local Politics in Imperial Germany.* Princeton, N.J.: Princeton University Press.
Tarrow, Sidney. 1994. *Power in Movement: Social Movements, Collective Action and Politics.* New York: Cambridge University Press.
Thompson, Dorothy. 1984. *The Chartists: Popular Politics in the Industrial Revolution.* New York: Pantheon Books.
Thompson, E. P. 1963. *The Making of the English Working Class.* New York: Vintage Books.
Tilly, Charles. 1986. *The Contentious French: Four Centuries of Popular Struggle.* Cambridge: Harvard University Press.
Tocqueville, Alexis de. 1955. *The Old Regime and the French Revolution.* Doubleday and Company, Anchor Books Edition.
Trattner, Walter I. 1994. *From Poor Law to Welfare State: A History of Social Welfare in America.* New York: Free Press.
Webb, Sidney, and Beatrice Webb. 1929. *English Poor Law History, Part II, The Last Hundred Years.* Vols. 1 and 2. London: Longmans, Green.
Wilensky, Harold L. 1975. *The Welfare State and Equality.* Berkeley: University of California Press.
Wilensky, Harold L., and Charles N. Lebeaux. 1965. *Industrial Society and Social Welfare.* Glencoe, Ill.: Free Press.
Wood, Ellen Meiksins. 1991. *The Pristine Culture of Capitalism.* New York: Verso Books.

CHAPTER SEVEN

The Withering Away of the Welfare State?

Class, State, and Capitalism

Rhonda F. Levine

Without a doubt, the Miliband–Poulantzas debate was a major turning point in Marxist theorizing on the capitalist state and social class. The debate broke the theoretical impasse that had hindered state theory, transformed the discourse within Marxist political theory, and unleashed a flurry of overlapping and competing perspectives. For many of us, this was indeed a most exciting intellectual time. The debate produced several "schools of thought" in the 1970s and many of us firmly identified with one school or another. There is no need to review all the schools of thought and theories and critiques; that has been done elsewhere in great depth (see Jessop 1990; Barrow 1993). But before moving on to address the question of whether the Miliband–Poulantzas debate provides a useful starting point for analyzing contemporary changes in the U.S. welfare state, it seems prudent to review, however briefly, some aspects of the debate itself.

The Rise and Fall of State Theory

In *The State in Capitalist Society,* Ralph Miliband primarily attempted to expose the distortions and mystifications of liberal pluralism, which perceives the state as a neutral instrument capable of use with equal effectiveness by any class or social force. Miliband was principally concerned with presenting empirical evidence that would demonstrate how state policies in the hands of state managers (biased in favor of the free-enterprise system) acted to preserve the interests of capitalism. It is neither accidental nor incidental that Miliband's book is dedicated to the memory of C. Wright Mills, the most influential "radical" thinker of the 1950s.

In his critique of the pluralist diffusion of power thesis, Miliband attempted to demonstrate that real political power was in fact concentrated in the hands of an economic elite. For Miliband, this economic elite was the dominant class and synonymous with the ruling class of capitalist society. In particular, he argued that the interests of the government elite (state managers) were basically identical with the economic elite. Even the institutions of social democracy and political freedom in advanced capitalist countries do not alter the basic purpose and function of the state in these societies.

Miliband further argued that governments do not see their commitment to capitalist enterprises as involving any element of class partiality. This is so because they view the national interest as being in fact inextricably bound up with the fortunes of the capitalist enterprise. Miliband viewed this commitment of the state to the advancement of the capitalist enterprise as crucial to understanding the role of the state in advanced capitalist society. According to him, state intervention does not adversely affect the interest of capital because the "bias of the system" ensures that the latter benefits automatically in the long run. This "bias of the system," from the point of view of the state, has been ensured by the ideological disposition of governments in capitalist society, which has made more acceptable to them the structural constraints imposed on them by the system. As such, it is easier for governments to submit to the pressures of the dominant class.

Miliband attempted to show that the state is a relatively independent institution with respect to the dominant class, while at the same time being structurally constrained to work in the interest of capital. Yet, a great deal of Miliband's efforts in explaining the distribution of power in capitalist society rests on illustrating the link between economic elites and state managers. Miliband argued that members of the capitalist class have in fact directly participated in the state apparatuses and government, that state managers and capitalists have overlapping social origins, and that personal ties of influence, status, and social milieu can be established. The state, according to Miliband, is capitalist because its bureaucracy is almost exclusively composed of members of the capitalist class and who, as politicians, are themselves ideologically committed to the advancement of capitalism.

Unlike Miliband, who was concerned with disproving liberal democratic theorists, Poulantzas's theory of the state is basically a critique of the traditional communist orthodoxy that viewed the state as merely an instrument of the ruling class (see Poulantzas 1973, 1974, 1975, 1976, 1978). Poulantzas conceived the state as a relation between classes and class forces rather than as an institution of power. The state is not external but internal to class contradictions, the latter being the chief determinant of the nature of its operations. The bureaucracy acts within the class contradictions.

One of the distinguishing characteristics of the capitalist state for Poulantzas is its relative autonomy from the dominant classes. Because the state is located within the contradictions of the mode of production, the state itself is wrought with contradictions and the very contradictions that arise within the state are a product of the basic contradictions of the mode of production. For Poulantzas, the capitalist class itself is internally divided. The internal conflicts of the capitalist class arise from the fact that units of capital are in constant competition with one another. The separation of capital into competing units of accumulation, isolated from one another and working against one another, is a necessary component of the accumulation process. These class contradictions and class conflicts, which arise from the nature of capital accumulation, are embedded within the very structure of the state and, as such, provide structural limits or boundaries to state activity. Because the state is relatively autonomous from any given class or class fraction, Poulantzas argued that state policy is able to mediate between conflicting fractions of the capitalist class and to channel working-class discontent within limits that are compatible with the overall accumulation of capital. The precise manner in which this mediation takes place is dependent on the balance of class forces represented throughout the state.

The differences that were attributed to Miliband and Poulantzas, in retrospect, had more to do with the audiences their work was directed at, in contradistinction to their theories in and of themselves. At the time, the fact that Miliband was debating the pluralists and Poulantzas the orthodox communists was overlooked in an attempt to distinguish the two as distinct Marxist approaches to the study of the capitalist state. And those of us in the United States lost sight that both Miliband and Poulantzas were writing in the context of debates that had relevance to European politics in particular, and that Poulantzas's specific point of departure and main antagonists, in particular, probably had little relevance to the reality of the American political landscape. In the United States, unlike Europe, the "left" was simply not a player in national politics during the 1970s, and even less so in the 1980s and 1990s.

A tremendous amount of Marxist theorizing on the state developed in the 1970s, much of which we will not concern ourselves with here because it had little impact on the American side of the debate (here I am referring to the so-called capital logic school). American contributions to the study of the state, such as G. William Domhoff's *Who Rules America?* (1967) and James O'Connor's *The Fiscal Crisis of the State* (1973), were either overlooked or ignored. Like Miliband, Domhoff developed a theory of power in direct opposition to the pluralists that, although not an explicitly Marxist theory, was certainly compatible with later Marxist theorizing on power and the state as applied to the politics of the United States. And, although O'Connor did not develop a theory of the state per se, he did develop a theory about the logic of capital accumulation and its dependence on various types of state spending. Unfortunately, these works, and other studies that followed, were labeled "economistic," "functionalist," and "instrumentalist," and then dismissed from the ongoing discussions on the state.

Whereas American contributions to the Marxist theory of the state remained somewhat limited during the 1970s, interest in the state and a concern for analyzing potential state autonomy certainly flourished. Interest in what has been labeled structural Marxism was evident in American Marxist circles, most notably with the formation of the journal *Kapitalistate* and various working *Kapitalistate* collectives. The "state" was indeed the topic of the day in Marxist conferences on both sides of the Atlantic. One's personal identity became entangled with being labeled either an "instrumentalist" or a "structuralist," however misleading those labels may have been.

The Marxist debate on the state seemed to be exhausted by the early 1980s. As Jessop (1990, 2–3) argues, much of the Marxist debate was pitched at such a high level of abstraction and consisted of such obscure formulations that it lost its potential audience. Moreover, the general crisis of the Marxist tradition as a whole in the late 1970s led to a theoretical as well as a political abandonment of Marxism. New interests in theories of democracy, new social movements, feminism, discourse theory, and the like shifted interest away from state theory. Theoretical interest in "postmodernism" and deconstruction became vogue among radical social scientists, having the impact of essentially deconstructing any hope for the further development of state theory (see, for example, Laclau and Mouffe 1985). With convoluted language, discourse theory and deconstructionism reduced any analysis of the state to an exercise in ideological hegemony. And within state research itself, "state-centered" theory challenged the so-called society-centered approach of Marxist state theory.

State-centered theory, with its focus on state capacities and the internal dynamics of political regimes, shifted the state debate beyond the generalized framework of Marxism and attempted to advance an alternative formulation of the state that purported to be more historically relevant. No one would deny that the state in the post–World War II era has expanded its domain. The complexity of class relations in late capitalism is compounded by the ever-widening role of the state in social and economic matters. For proponents of state-centered theory, the increased role of the state in economic management, in particular, made plain that analyses of the state and state activity cannot be understood simply in terms of forces that guide "civil society." State-centered theory is distinguished from society-centered theories by locating the state as an autonomous structure, with its own logic, separate from social and economic forces.

By the late 1980s, the Marxist theoretical debate was largely exhausted. Work on the capitalist state within American sociology in particular moved the debate over the nature of the state from its rather abstract level to the concrete world. American sociologists looked to the European debates and evaluated the usefulness of various conceptualizations in terms of whether or not they fit the historical development of the United States. These empirically based studies led to the growing popularity of the "state-centered" approach, which distinguished itself from "society-centered" analyses of the state. The state debate, so to speak, had moved from understanding the state and its relation to ongoing processes of accumulation and class struggle to examining the state in its own terms. As Bob Jessop so aptly commented: "as a revival of interest in the state has occurred twice in the past 20 years, we should not be surprised that this repetition of history assumes the usual dramatic form. For the first debate ended in tragedy, the second is proving a farce" (1990, 2).

In an effort to further a critical analysis of state theory, Jessop (1990) edited a collection of essays he wrote between 1977 and 1990. These essays probably present the best overview of developments in the state debate, as well as changes in Jessop's own thinking on the matter. Further developing Poulantzas's concept of relative autonomy, Jessop argues for a "strategic-relational" approach to the study of the state. By this he means that the state must be related to the wider social, economic, and political environment. Although state structures and institutions may indeed develop an independent logic, this logic cannot be understood in separation from larger social, political, and economic forces. In Jessop's words: "This means that the powers of the state are always conditional and relational. Their realization depends on the structural ties between the state and its encompassing political system, the strategic links among state managers and other political forces, and the complex web of interdependencies and social networks linking the state system to its broader environment" (ibid., 367).

Jessop's "strategic-relational" approach complements a "class-centered" approach that I called for in my earlier work (Levine 1988). At that time, I set down a set of propositions that I believed best presented a starting point for embarking on historically grounded research on the state. I am convinced that these propositions, with perhaps some further refinement, still provide a suitable framework for state analysis. Specifically, they are the following:

1. The capitalist state is internally divided by its location within the social relations of production. Because the state is located within the contradictions of capitalism, the state itself is a product of class contradictions. The state cannot be derived from either the intentions, wills, motivations, or goals of aggregated individuals or from the logic of capital. The capitalist state can no more be treated as a conscious subject than as a passive object or thing, to be manipulated or utilized. Both of these perspectives assume that the state constitutes a unity, a homogeneous entity. The state is a relation, or, in Poulantzas's terms, the "material condensation of class forces." More specifically, the state in theoretical terms cannot be understood separate from (or independent of) *both* the process of accumulation (with its attendant crises and contradictions) and the relations of class forces (i.e., the balance of class forces—or, put another way, the class struggle).

2. As a consequence of the forces that continually separate capital into distinctive competitive and antagonistic units, the capitalist state is

the political terrain for the adjudication of fractions of capital. By being relatively autonomous from various class fractions, state policy serves to mediate between units of capital by attempting to politically unify an otherwise disorganized capitalist class. Moreover, as a consequence of the antagonistic relationship between labor and capital, the capitalist state becomes the arena for assuring a consensus for capitalist rule. State policy simultaneously attempts to unify an otherwise disorganized capitalist class and to channel working-class struggle within elements compatible with capitalist social relations of production, thereby short-circuiting independent working-class political organization.

3. State policies always reflect, in Poulantzas's words, "strategic compromises." Although state policies attempt to maintain class rule by providing the conditions for profitable accumulation, they are formulated and/or implemented not according to any preestablished functional harmony, but in and through the struggle of antagonistic classes. There are multiple strategies for capital accumulation and the maintenance of class rule. The particular formulation and implementation of a specific policy is shaped by the nature and the dynamic of the class struggle in the particular historical time and setting.

4. Three levels—a theory of the capitalist state, the analysis of forms and regimes, and the concrete level of personalities, boards, and agencies—must be kept analytically distinct. As such, a historical investigation of the institutional composition of the capitalist state, though extremely important in terms of concretely understanding the specific ways in which state agencies, boards, commissions, and the like carry out specific policies after having filtered their content through various "selective mechanisms," is not a substitute for a theory of the state per se. State agencies, branches, boards, and the like often represent competing, rival, class and/or social interests.

These propositions provide a useful starting point for state research. By "bringing classes back" to the state debate, one-sided analyses that reduce a complex process of variable determinations to a unilinear explanation for the formation and implementation of state policy can be avoided.

The central question, nevertheless, remains: how useful is this framework for understanding the contemporary changes in the welfare state?

The "Crisis" of the Welfare State: Lessons and Legacies of the 1930s

The state debate in Europe during the 1970s stimulated American sociologists to evaluate the usefulness of various conceptualizations of the state in terms of whether or not they fit the historical development of the United States. The New Deal period provided rich historical material that lent itself to close scrutiny of rather abstract theoretical concepts. Poulantzas's concept of "relative autonomy" came under particular scrutiny as American sociologists attempted to explain various policy outcomes of the New Deal period. Because the New Deal period is critical in understanding welfare-state development in the United States, application of aspects of state theory to the New Deal should also, therefore, be relevant to understanding contemporary aspects of the welfare state.

Primarily influenced by Poulantzas, the class-centered approach just outlined conceptualizes the New Deal as the state response to the economic crisis of the 1930s. The world economic crisis of the 1930s provided the occasion for a fundamental restructuring of capitalist development in the United States. The dynamic of the class struggle and the manner in which state policies attempted to resolve class conflicts and class antagonisms and overcome obstacles to capital accumulation mediated the historical restructuring of capitalist social relations of production that were necessary for the expanded reproduction of capital.

The crisis of the 1930s represented three obstacles to capital accumulation in the United States: (1) too high a rate of exploitation, resulting in problems of realization, (2) unregulated competition, leading to problems of investments, and (3) a political structure that was not structurally conducive to the imperatives of the accumulation process.

Although New Deal policies did not in and of themselves lead to a renewal of capital accumulation, they did provide the political conditions and structural mechanisms for a renewed phase of capital accumulation in the post–World War II period. New Deal policies, by attempting to resolve class conflicts and class antagonisms, created the structural forms that regulated objected conditions for capital accumulation and the conditions under which future class struggles and conflicts would be waged.

The welfare state in the post–World War II period was an outcome of the manner in which state policies attempted to resolve class conflicts and antagonism during the 1930s and provide conditions profitable for the expansion of capital. Its growth and current status can be seen in relationship to the manner in which conditions created to overcome obstacles to capital accumulation during the 1930s have presented obstacles in a later phase of capitalist development. The class struggle waged during the 1930s directed the restructuring of capitalist development that took place in the post–World War II period. Briefly put, the state apparatus was reorganized, through a strengthening of the executive branch, which proved to be beneficial to large-scale corporate capital. State protection of industrial unionization, itself a product of labor militancy during the 1930s, made possible the institutionalization of collective-bargaining arrangements. These collective-bargaining arrangements served to overcome the problem of realization because of the bargaining rights of labor over the rate of exploitation. The purging of communists from the union movement provided the context through which collective-bargaining arrangements tended to isolate political struggles from economic struggles. The incorporation of the union movement into the national political bargaining process via the Democratic Party and collective-bargaining arrangements altered relations in production and relations of production. The specific aspects of the party system in the United States, and the incorporation of labor into the Democratic Party resulted in a severe weakening of left politics among the working class. What developed was a general ideological consensus for capitalist rule, and further fragmentation within the working class among the unionized and nonunionized labor force, as well as deepened racial splits.

The trajectory of capitalist development in the United States took a different course as a result of the upsurge of workers' militant activities during the 1930s. Labor militancy in demanding and using collective bargaining made it possible to overcome the resistance of large-scale capital to fundamental reorganization of wages and consumption. Nevertheless, monopoly capital was able to adjust to these working-class gains. Large-scale corporate capital—in the long period of economic recovery and expansion first generated by World War II and then by the political hegemony that the United States enjoyed on a world scale from 1945 to the mid-1960s—not only passed wage gains and benefits acquired by workers on to consumers (located throughout the world), but also used collective bargaining (particularly with the Taft-Hartley Act of 1947, which restricted the rights of organized labor) as a way to ensure labor peace. In the process, large-scale corporate capital was able to dominate key state agencies and become the hegemonic fraction within the power bloc. Increased state intervention not only aided the regulation of competition, but also resulted in further investment outlets. In brief, the obstacles to capital accumulation of too high a rate of exploitation were temporarily resolved through the institutionalization of collective bargaining and the incorporation of significant trade unions into the national political bargaining process. Problems of unregulated competition were temporarily resolved through state policies that reflected the growing divisions between monopoly and nonmonopoly capital over the "monopoly issue" of the 1930s. Moreover, the political structure was altered in such a fashion as to correspond more closely with the imperatives of the accumulation process by monopoly capital's dominating key state agencies and by the industrial union movement's being incorporated into a clearly subordinate position vis-à-vis monopoly capital on the political level. The incorporation of the industrial union movement into the national political bargaining process and into a more "cooperative" relationship via collective bargaining with monopoly capital, the purging of leftists and the resulting ideological consensus for capitalist rule, and the unchallenged political hegemony of monopoly capital all combined to produce the conditions for a renewed phase of capitalist development within the United States. The renewed phase of capital accumulation in the post–World War II period seemed to have all the elements for a seemingly lasting profitable capitalist accumulation.

The course of capitalist development on a world scale consists of phases. Obstacles to capitalist accumulation in one phase may be temporarily resolved to enable the continued expansion of capital in another phase. This was the case in the United States during the world economic crisis of the 1930s. However, the process of capitalist development is contradictory and the conditions created to overcome obstacles in one phase of capitalist development often come to present obstacles in a later phase. State policies as mediated through the historical class struggle created conditions that proved to be necessary for the expanded reproduction of capital in the post–World War II years, but these same conditions also served to provide the preconditions for the economic downturn and crisis of world capitalist development in the 1970s.

The expansion of social-welfare programs in the 1960s, however limited, can be understood as state response to massive social protest originating in the struggle for civil rights in the South. Yet, these programs were formulated on capitalist terms (see, for example, Piven and Cloward 1993, 99, 222–480; Quadagno 1993). This massive protest occurred outside of the union movement to a large extent. The struggles for racial equality during the 1960s resulted in the expansion of social-welfare programs. However, the power bloc remained unified, working-class opposition remained limited, and capital was able to make concessions in a way that led to further fragmentation and disorganization of working-class politics. The left never regained the position within working-class political organizations that it had during the 1930s, and continued racism and sexism within the union movement served to short-circuit a fundamental reorganization of political structures and to alter the course of capitalist development.

The increased competition on a world scale in the 1970s had a particularly negative impact on U.S.-based firms. The world economic downturn of the 1970s left capitalists, once again, in disagreement over the best way to renew capital accumulation. The power bloc was once again in disarray. But, unlike the 1930s, an increasingly disorganized working class in the post–World War II period was unable to take advantage of an otherwise conflicted capitalist class. Moreover, the working class looked very different from that of the 1930s. The globalization of capital during the post–World War II years had a tremendous impact domestically on the class structure. The shift from a manufacturing-based economy meant that fewer workers were engaged in basic industry, leaving the vast majority in service-sector jobs and employed on the low end of the ever-increasing high-tech industries. The overwhelming majority of the working class were outside of organized labor, and were increasingly made up of women and people of color.

With no movement from below directing a course for further expansion of the welfare state, the power bloc during the Reagan administration was able, without much contention, to embark on a strategy of restructuring capitalist development that attempted to dismantle the welfare state as we knew it. Vast social expenditures and the expansion of the federal government were viewed as the main culprits for the economic downturn. A conservative coalition successfully challenged the more liberal policies of the power bloc and directed social-welfare policies (Piven 1998; Quadagno 1998).

The austere strategy for economic recovery had its costs. In its wake, poverty increased, and the standard of living for the majority of Americans declined, while those in the top 1 percent enjoyed an economic boom. The growing gap in inequality coupled with increasing racial tensions did have political consequences. By the 1990s, the conservative coalition could not rule at will. Massive social protest of the 1960s had a lingering impact. Veterans of the movements of the 1960s began to occupy key political positions, and some of us, however mistaken we were, thought Fleetwood Mac playing at the Inauguration Ball in 1993 was a sign that things "they were a' changing." But we were reminded once again of the specific relationship between the state and the process of capitalist development when President Bill Clinton signed the Welfare Reform Bill in the summer of 1996. How could a Democratic president support such a measure?

The answer is quite simple if we move our analysis of the state to the analytical level of the balance of class forces and how they represent themselves not only politically, but also ideologically within the changing balance of class forces. In the absence of any concerted political opposition that would severely challenge capitalist rule, the strategy of maintaining social cohesion means to unify the capitalist class; the working class is already disorganized. Although capital may indeed be able to adjust to various working-class concessions and even to an expansion in social-welfare policies, there is no need to do so without a challenge coming from below.

Moreover, the strength of capital in the post–World War II period was reflected in the forging of an ideological consensus for a form of social cohesion that created a "crisis" in some welfare-state programs and led to the dismantling of others. More specifically (as others have pointed out in this volume), the relations between capital and the state have never been more evident than they are today. Beginning in the mid-1970s, business groups that had been dormant in the immediate past were revived, financing not only political campaigns within the Republican Party, but also think tanks and policy groups. Whereas business policy groups were able to formulate the Social Security Act in 1935 on their terms, by the late 1970s and throughout the 1980s business groups were able to launch an ideological campaign that, in effect, created a "crisis" in social spending and paved the way for an ideological consensus for cutbacks in other social-welfare programs (see, for example, Domhoff 1996, 117–76; Quadagno 1998). Capital's response to a set of increased benefits enacted in the late 1960s and early 1970s was a litany of articles and reports from conservative think tanks that argued that Social Security was near bankruptcy. Because of public support for Social Security, in terms of both old-age pensions and Medicare and Medicaid, no politician who expects to be elected or reelected will advocate cuts in Social Security. Yet, cuts in welfare for the poor, in what used to be known as Aid for Dependent Families, although a minuscule part of the federal budget, was a much easier target. Symbolically, cuts in welfare for the poor, and the attendant ideology that distinguished the deserving poor from the undeserving poor, have the potential of going a long way toward securing social cohesion under the ideological dominance of capitalist rule. If one clearly understands the nature of the capitalist state, as a relation of class forces, then it becomes quite evident that a campaign against further social-welfare cuts and a challenge to the entire premise that these cuts are built on are essential to change the current trends.

Where is this challenge likely to come from? We may be beginning to see the seeds of it. The AFL-CIO's organizing strategy recognizes the changes in the nature of the class structure and it appears to have a better handle on the complexities of capitalist development than it has had since the inception of the CIO. The existence of a Progressive Caucus in Congress is another indication that cracks in the power bloc are possible. There just may be the possibility of a liberal–labor coalition that can challenge the political hegemony of a conservative power bloc. How we make that history is a story yet to be told.

Conclusion

In retrospect, the Miliband–Poulantzas debate made us aware of the underlying class components of understanding the capitalist state. In particular, Poulantzas's concepts of "relative autonomy" and even "power bloc" provide us with a conceptual apparatus from which to analyze contemporary political issues. But, as Poulantzas himself said, he wrote for Europe. Poulantzas provided much for an abstract understanding of the relationship between the state, social classes, and capitalist development, but his theory offers us less of a guide for a specific analysis of the relationship as it historically unfolds in the United States; for the United States is far different from Europe, politically speaking. An analysis of the class structure and the political system becomes an empirical exercise, not one of theoretical generalizations.

With respect to social welfare in the United States, Piven and Cloward (1993) have provided us with that detailed empirical analysis, which complements the main thrust of a class-centered approach to the study of the state. From the more general theoretical perspective, and the more specific empirical analysis, we just may be able not only to understand more fully the contemporary "crisis" of the welfare state in the United States, but also to find the political strategy to alter its course.

References

Barrow, Clyde. 1993. *Critical Theories of the State: Marxist, Neo-Marxist, Post-Marxist.* Madison: University of Wisconsin Press.

Domhoff, G. William. 1967. *Who Rules America?* Englewood Cliffs, N.J.: Prentice Hall.

———. 1996. *State Autonomy or Class Dominance? Case Studies on Policy Making in America.* New York: Aldine de Gruyter.

Jessop, Bob. 1982. *The Capitalist State.* New York: New York University Press.

———. 1990. *State Theory: Putting Capitalist States in Their Place.* University Park: Pennsylvania State University Press.

Laclau, Ernesto, and Chantal Mouffe. 1985. *Hegemony and Capitalist Strategy.* London: New Left Books.

Levine, Rhonda F. 1988. *Class Struggle and the New Deal: Industrial Labor, Industrial Capital and the New Deal.* Lawrence: University Press of Kansas.

Miliband, Ralph. 1970. "The Capitalist State: A Reply to Nicos Poulantzas." *New Left Review* 59: 53–60.

———. 1973a. "Poulantzas and the Capitalist State." *New Left Review* 82: 83–92.

———. 1973b. *The State in Capitalist Society.* London: Quartet Books.

O'Connor, James. 1973. *The Fiscal Crisis of the State.* New York: St. Martin's Press.

Piven, Frances Fox. 1998. "Welfare and the Transformation of Electoral Politics." In Clarence Y. Lo and Michael Schwartz, eds., *Social Policy and the Conservative Agenda.* New York: Blackwell Publishers. 21–36.

Piven, Frances Fox, and Richard A. Cloward. 1993. *Regulating the Poor: The Functions of Public Welfare.* New York: Vintage Books.

Poulantzas, Nicos. 1969. "The Problem of the Capitalist State." *New Left Review* 58: 67–78.

———. 1973. *Political Power and Social Classes.* London: New Left Books.

———. 1974. *Fascism and Dictatorship.* London: New Left Books.

———. 1975. *Classes in Contemporary Capitalism.* London: New Left Books.

———. 1976. "The Capitalist State: A Reply to Miliband and Laclau." *New Left Review* 95: 63–83.
———. 1978. *State, Power, Socialism.* London: New Left Books.
Quadagno, Jill. 1993. *The Color of Welfare: How Racism Undermined the War on Poverty.* New York: Oxford University Press.
———. 1998. "Social Security Policy and the Entitlement Debate: The New American Exceptionalism." In Clarence Y. Lo and Michael Schwartz, eds., *Social Policy and the Conservative Agenda.* New York: Blackwell Publishers. 95–117.

CHAPTER EIGHT

Globalization and the National State

Bob Jessop

Poulantzas wrote well before the current hype about globalization took off and before claims about the death of the nation-state had became common. But his work during the 1970s did address some key issues involved in a serious Marxist analysis of the relation between *(a)* changes in the capitalist economy on a world scale and *(b)* the basic form and functions of the contemporary capitalist national state. These issues were first broached in a lengthy and important essay titled "The Internationalization of Capitalist Relations and the Nation State" (1973a in French, 1974b in English, but cited below from 1975, 37–88). They were further discussed in three books, *Classes in Contemporary Capitalism* (1975), *Crisis of the Dictatorships* (1976), and *State, Power, Socialism* (1978). My contribution to this volume will review Poulantzas's overall argument in the 1970s, noting how it changed in some key respects during this period, and distinguishing between his general theoretical approach and its particular application to Europe (especially France, Greece, Portugal, and Spain) in a specific phase of imperialism. I argue that Poulantzas's general approach is theoretically more sophisticated and strategically more relevant to the left than much of the current "globaloney" over the future of the national state in an era of globalization. However, I also suggest that his general approach was marred by class reductionism and that he also failed to anticipate future changes in the internationalization of capital. This in turn meant that his specific prognoses were, in key respects, mistaken. Nonetheless, his analyses can be improved by introducing additional theoretical considerations that are consistent with the overall Poulantzasian approach, as well as by noting certain novel features of the current phase of imperialism. Accordingly, my essay is divided into two main parts: first, a critical appreciation of Poulantzas's arguments, and second, an account of current changes in the national state from a modified Poulantzasian stance. It concludes with some more general comments on the relevance of Poulantzas's work and my own remarks to possible changes in the European Union considered in state-theoretical terms.

Poulantzas: Marxist Theory and Political Strategy

I have noted elsewhere (Jessop 1985) that Poulantzas's work, for all its oft-criticized "hyperabstractionism" and theoretical obscurities, was primarily motivated by his deep-felt political commitments to working-class and popular-democratic struggles in contemporary Europe. Thus, in addition to his concern with the theoretical positions advanced in classic texts by Marx, Engels, and Lenin, Poulantzas consistently engaged in trenchant critiques of alternative contemporary Marxist analyses of imperialism: these include theories of state monopoly capitalism, an ultra-imperialism organized under the hegemony of a U.S. superstate or the domination of stateless monopoly capital, an alleged continuity of contradictions among national states mobilized in defense of their own national bourgeoisies, and the view that the European Economic Community was becoming a supranational political apparatus to serve European capital in its struggle against the hegemony of American capital (1975, 38–40). This concern with political strategy is especially clear in his analyses of then current changes in imperialism and their implications for national states and class struggles in Europe.

Rereading his work after more than two decades of further discussion on changes in the world economy reveals the importance for Poulantzas of situating his analyses in terms of a careful periodization of the "imperialist chain" and of the class struggles with which it is inevitably linked.[1] For he insisted on posing the question of internationalization in terms of imperialism. Although the latter is something that is all too often neglected in recent work on "globalization," concern with its changing forms is essential to an adequate understanding of changes in the national state and much else besides. Accordingly, Poulantzas examined changes in the international division of social labor, which connects different imperialist metropolises and dominated social formations in a complicated matrix marked by uneven and combined development. He related such changes in turn to the changing rhythms of class struggle (especially in regard to the principal contradiction between bourgeoisie and working class), which both prompt shifts in bourgeois strategies and result from changes in the "imperialist chain." And he explored how these changes are reflected in the reorganization of the institutional materiality of the national state, the relationship between its economic and other functions, and the nature of its crisis tendencies.

It was in grappling with these issues that Poulantzas integrated his long-standing interests in state theory and political strategy more closely and more coherently with traditional Marxist economic themes. These latter had largely been ignored in his early state-theoretical work on the grounds that the capitalist economy was not only separate from the capitalist state but also largely capable of self-valorization once the "external" political and ideological framework for accumulation is secured through the state (1973b, 32–33, 55–56; for his own subsequent critique of this classic error in liberal political economy, see Poulantzas 1975, 100–101; 1978, 15–20). Substantive concern with economic themes first became prominent in Poulantzas's work on the internationalization of capital (1973a) and on *Classes in Contemporary Capitalism* (1975). They were later integrated relatively effectively with his own state theory in *State, Power, Socialism* (1978). But Poulantzas had also brought new insights to the traditional Marxist critique of political economy. In particular, he analyzed the labor process in terms of a complex economic, political, and intellectual division of labor in which the constitutive effects and actions of the state were always present; and, in a similar vein, he studied social classes from the viewpoint of their "*extended* reproduction" rather than from the "narrow" economic perspective of their place in production, distribution, and consumption. This extended reproduction encompassed economic, political, and ideological relations and involved the state and the mental-manual division, as well as the circuit of capital and noncapitalist relations of production. Indeed, Poulantzas always placed the social relations of production *in this expanded, or integral, sense*[2] at the heart of his analysis of class struggle. And he came to analyze social reproduction in terms of the reproduction of the interrelated economic, political, and ideological conditions bearing on accumulation (1973a, 1975, 1978). These were important advances.

This said, Poulantzas remained trapped within classical Marxist political economy; for his analyses were premised on the ultimately determining role of the mode of production for all aspects of societal organization, on the primacy of the fundamental contradiction between capital and labor, and on the driving power of proletarian class struggle in the transition to socialism. Only in his last year did he begin seriously to question these fundamental tenets of Marxism and try to move beyond them (Poulantzas 1979a, 1979b).

Imperialism

It is in this overall theoretical and strategic context that Poulantzas's 1973 extended essay on internationalization focused on the latest phase of imperialism and the upsurge of class struggle in the key imperialist metropoles, namely, Japan, the United States, and Europe (1975, 38). In particular, Poulantzas asked:

> Is it still possible today to speak of a *national state* in the imperialist metropolises? What connections are there between these states and the internationalization of capital or the multinational firms? Are new super-state institutional forms tending to replace the national states, or alternatively, what modifications are these states undergoing to enable them to fulfil the new functions required by the extended reproduction of capital on the international level? (1975, 38)

To answer these questions, Poulantzas proposed to analyze "the contemporary modifications in the imperialist chain and their effects on relations between the metropolises, and on the national states in particular" (ibid., 40–41).

Poulantzas divided capitalist development on a world scale along Marxist-Leninist lines into three main *stages:* a transitional phase, competitive capitalism, and monopoly capitalism (or imperialism). These stages overlap in the sense that precapitalist social relations as well as capitalist class relations corresponding to each stage of capitalism are subject to complex modes of conservation-dissolution as capitalism continues to develop in each social formation and in the imperialist chain as a whole (ibid., 44). According to Poulantzas, monopoly capitalism is marked by (1) a relative dissociation of economic ownership and legal ownership (seen in the rise of joint-stock companies); (2) the fundamental and determinant role of export of capital rather than export of commodities; (3) the displacement of dominance (both within social formations and within the imperialist chain as a whole) from the economic (i.e., market forces) to the political (the state); and (4) the displacement of dominance among the state's particular functions from the narrowly political (i.e., a juridico-political or "night-watchman" role) to the (now-transformed and much-expanded) economic function (1973b, 55–56; 1975, 42, 118–19). Each stage of capitalism can be divided in turn into *phases:* an unstable transitional phase, a consolidating phase, and a phase marked by the final consolidation of the typical features of that stage.[3] Different phases of imperialism correspond to specific forms of capital accumulation and to specific forms of the global relations of production and the international division of labor. They are also linked to different types of various "conservation-dissolution" effects on precapitalist, competitive capitalist, and other social relations of production and their respective social classes (1975, 43–44, 72, 142, 166–67).

A key feature of the "present" phase of imperialism (with Poulantzas writing, of course, in the early 1970s) was said to be the emergence of a "new dividing line within the metropolitan camp, between the United States on the one hand, and the other imperialist metropolises, in particular Europe, on the other" (ibid., 47). All metropoles were still struggling to exploit and dominate dependent formations, of course, but there was also a much sharper struggle for exploitation and domination within Europe (ibid., 47–48). This struggle was conducted not only through foreign direct investment (especially American capital), but also through American mergers with European capital and the more general establishment of the dominance of technical standards, know-how, and social relations of production typical of American monopoly capital inside European metropolises. A few years later, Poulantzas's analysis could easily have been rephrased in terms of the diffusion to Western Europe of the postwar American mode of growth, its social mode of economic regulation, and its more general mode of (mass) societalization to produce the phenomenon of Atlantic Fordism (cf. Jessop 1992; van der Pijl 1984). But there have since been events and emergent trends that he did not always fully anticipate that have changed the nature of imperialism. These include the crisis of Atlantic Fordism (albeit not of U.S. hegemony), the continued expansion of distinctive forms of East Asian capitalism (albeit under U.S. hegemony), the diffusion of "Japanization," and, something he did expect, the collapse of the Soviet bloc. My essay refers to some of these issues in the section titled "The Future of the National State."

Internationalization and Class Relations

Poulantzas linked the then current phase of imperialism to the international socialization of the labor process—a process, he suggested, that affects especially "global relations of production" (1975, 58–59). This process was allegedly prompted by the tendency of the rate of profit to fall (hereafter, the TRPF) and the search by capital for enhanced profit through continued indirect exploitation in dependent formations and increased foreign direct investment in other metropoles (ibid., 62–63, 62n). Later, Poulantzas would also argue that the southern European dictatorships (Greece, Portugal, and Spain) were also subject to American foreign direct investment (1976). They were thereby increasingly integrated into the circuit of Atlantic Fordism through their developing role as what Lipietz called "peripheral Fordist economies" (Lipietz 1987). In general, the principal countertendency to the TRPF was, according to Poulantzas, the intensified exploitation of labor power—extending beyond the labor process proper to include training, education, technical innovation, town planning, and forms of collective consumption (1975, 1976, 1978).

This "current" phase is associated with the reorganization of class relations within the bourgeoisie, as well as with changes in capital–labor relations. Above all, Poulantzas was concerned to show both theoretically and empirically that the traditional Marxist categories of national and comprador bourgeoisie are no longer adequate to grasp the specificities of relations among different fractions of capital in the current phase of imperialism. As is usual for Poulantzas, the structural determination of class position was referred not only to economic relations, but also to a class's place in the ideological and political structures (1975, 71). Thus, whereas comprador bourgeoisies have no autonomous domestic base for accumulation and are thereby triply subordinated (economically, politically, and ideologically) to foreign capital, national bourgeoisies are involved in economic contradictions with foreign imperialist capital and occupy a relatively autonomous place in the ideological and political structure (which facilitates alliances with popular masses) (ibid.). Poulantzas was particularly interested in how the current phase of imperialism undermined the position of the national bourgeoisie. It is being dissolved in favor of the interior (or domestic) bourgeoisie. The latter is neither a simple comprador class (it has its own bases of accumulation at home and abroad) nor a national bourgeoisie (it is multiply locked into the international division of social labor and into an international concentration and centralization of capital under American domination and thereby tends to lose rather than conserve its political and ideological autonomy vis-à-vis American capital) (ibid., 72). Nonetheless, there are still significant contradictions between the internal bourgeoisie and American capital and these are reflected in turn in European states in their relations with the American state (ibid.).

One effect of this is that power blocs, that is, long-term, structurally consolidated, class or class fraction alliances, are no longer, according to Poulantzas, located purely on the national level. In addition to an alleged general sharpening of internal contradictions within national power blocs, European bourgeoisies have been increasingly polarized in terms of their structural and conjunctural relations to U.S. imperialist capital. As a result, interimperialist contradictions are reproduced within each "national" European power bloc, national state, and wider social formation (ibid., 171). At the same time, each imperialist state is now involved in managing the process of internationalization among imperialist metropoles. Imperialist states "must take charge not only of the interests of their domestic bourgeoisies, but just as much of the interests of the dominant (sc. American) imperialist capital and those of the other imperialist capitals, as these are articulated within the process of internationalization" (ibid., 75). This does not mean, however, that "foreign" capitals directly participate as autonomous forces in power blocs: instead, they are represented by certain fractions of the interior bourgeoisie within the power bloc and also have access, through various channels, to the state apparatus (ibid.).

Internationalization and the National State

Although the terms of the debate in the 1970s differed from those that are prevalent today, Poulantzas made important points about the future of the national state in an era of increasing internationalization of capital. Above all, he insisted on the continued importance of the national state in spite (and, indeed, exactly because) of this increasing internationalization. Thus he argued that the national state will neither wither away in favor of some "superstate" standing over and above national states, nor in favor of a borderless and stateless world organized by multinational firms. His critique of the "superstate" was directed against forecasts of a "world state" organized under U.S. domination rather than at the prospects of an emergent European superstate. But the six criticisms he directed at the possibility of such a "world state" (detailed later) would also seem to apply to a European superstate. Indeed, Poulantzas firmly denied that every step that capital took toward internationalization would automatically induce a parallel "supranationalization" of states (ibid., 78). Such a *pari passu* claim would involve an unacceptable economism that denied the crucial political mediations of the internationalization process and the political overdetermination of the state's techno-economic functions (Poulantzas 1975, 1978). Similar arguments inform his rejection of what has subsequently been labeled a "borderless world" (e.g., Ohmae 1990); for he claimed that "every process of internationalization is effected under the dominance of the capital of a definite country" (1975, 73)[4] because national states remain central to the extended reproduction of their bourgeoisies (1978, 117).[5] In criticizing these two complementary (and still widespread) errors, Poulantzas was certainly not trying to suggest that nothing had changed as a result of internationalization. On the contrary, he argued that there were major modifications occurring in the form and functions of the national state (1975, 84; 1978). These called into question the legal concept of national sovereignty and were also linked to ruptures in the unity of national states, leading to nationalist revivals and institutional fragmentation (1975, 70, 80).

It was in this context that Poulantzas argued:

> The current internationalization of capital neither suppresses nor bypasses the nation states, either in the direction of a peaceful integration of capitals "above" the state level (since every process of internationalization is effected under the dominance of the capital of a definite country), or in the direction of their extinction by the American super-state, as if American capital purely and simply directed the other imperialist bourgeoisies. This internationalization, on the other hand, deeply affects the politics and institutional forms of these states by including them in a system of interconnections which is in no way confined to the play of external and mutual pressures between juxtaposed states and capitals. (Ibid., 73)

Overall, Poulantzas appears to reject the thesis of a supranational state on six grounds:

1. Internationalization is no longer limited primarily to purely external relations between autocentric national economies and states—relations that could perhaps have been coordinated from outside and above individual states in the manner of a night-watchman state.[6] Instead, it also involves the endogenization (internalization) of the contradictory relations among different metropolitan capitals, and especially the induced reproduction of the dominance of U.S. capital (ibid.). Arguments for a superstate imply that the now dominant economic function of the capitalist state could be largely dissociated from its articulation with the maintenance of political class domination and social cohesion in national states and transferred as such to some superordinate apparatus. At most, what one finds is a partial and conditional delegation of such functions in order to improve economic policy "coordination" across different states as part and parcel of each national state's new responsibilities for managing the process of internationalization (ibid., 81–82).

2. National states play a major role in the competitive positioning of their respective economic spaces vis-à-vis foreign capitals (including attracting foreign direct investment [FDI] and securing other advantages of foreign penetration), and they also promote the concentration and international expansion of their own indigenous capital in its competition with such capitals. This task could not be delegated to a supranational state because it pits different national power blocs and states against each other (ibid., 73).

3. As interimperialist contradictions also remain on many other points,[7] national states will still support their own nationally based (interior, national, comprador) bourgeoisies (ibid., 74) and, indeed, the "modern nation remains for the bourgeoisie the focal point of its own reproduction" (1978, 117). Together with the two preceding points, this seems to imply that supranational regimes or institutions will only be supported by national states to the extent that they are consistent with national interests (as modified by the process of internationalization).

4. The (national) state is never a simple instrument of the dominant classes (in which case, suggests Poulantzas, certain functions might, indeed, be passed up to a supranational apparatus step by step with each successive stage of internationalization) but is shot through with many class antagonisms and struggles. Thus the national state remains responsible for maintaining social cohesion in a class-divided national

formation that is now increasingly subject to uneven development owing to its insertion into the imperialist chain (1975, 78).

5. Indeed, each national state has its own distinctive, path-dependent, national balance of class forces, its own institutional and organizational specificities, its own strategically selective impact on the "national forms" of class struggle. This suggests in turn that, insofar as supranational politics is always already intergovernmental politics, it would reflect national specificities.

6. Finally, in each national state there are "social categories" (i.e., personnel divided perhaps by their place in class relations but unified by their common function) employed in the state apparatuses (e.g., civil servants, the police and military personnel, professionals, or intellectuals) that therefore have vested interests in the survival of the national state—which implies that they would resist the loss of the various capacities, prerogatives, and powers off which they live (ibid., 78–79).

Given that Poulantzas rejects the idea of a supranational state, as well as a borderless, stateless world dominated by multinational firms, how did he see the then "current" role of national states? His account is carefully located within his more general approach to the form and functions of the capitalist type of state. There are three key arguments relevant to this issue. First, a distinctive form of institutional separation from the capitalist economy marks the capitalist type of state and this separation limits the state's capacity to intervene effectively into the heart of the production process. Second, while this state's institutional materiality facilitates its role in politically organizing the dominant classes and disorganizing subordinate classes, it can never completely contain and domesticate the class struggle. And third, the state's three particular functions (i.e., techno-economic, more narrowly political,[8] and ideological) are always performed in the light of their broader implications and repercussions on its general (or "global") political function of maintaining social cohesion in a class-divided social formation (1973a, 1978, 160, 191–92).[9] According to Poulantzas, the changing forms of internationalization have had major effects in each of these three respects.

Thus, first, the forms of internationalization associated with the "current" phase of imperialism have transformed the forms of separation of state and economy—redefining their respective social spaces and structural coupling. Competitive capitalism allegedly involved a distinction between the state's intervention in the extended reproduction of the general conditions of production and its direct economic interventions (1975, 167–68). However, in monopoly capitalism (or imperialism), the various political and ideological "conditions" of production have come to belong directly to the valorization and extended reproduction of capital (ibid., 101, 168). This is reflected in a characteristic politicization of formerly (and still formally) extra-economic domains and increased state involvement therein to promote valorization and extended reproduction (ibid., 101). In competitive capitalism, the strictly economic functions of the state were subordinate to its more general repressive and ideological functions and were easily adapted to fit the changing exigencies of accumulation. But in monopoly capitalism, the state's political and ideological functions have themselves gained direct economic significance for the reproduction of the relations of production. Thus it has become increasingly difficult for the state to reconcile its responses to ever more insistent economic imperatives with the more general demands of securing political class domination and social cohesion (1975, 1978, 178).

Second, they have transformed the balance of class forces—notably through the emergence of an interior bourgeoisie that is itself internally divided according to its differential insertion into the imperialist chain. This means that national states now not only assume responsibility for their own nationally based capitals (comprador, national, or interior), but also serve the interests of other capitals with which they are affiliated in one way or another. This results in the disarticulation and heterogeneity of the power bloc and, according to Poulantzas, "explains the weak resistance, limited to fits and starts, that the European states have put up to American capital" (ibid., 74–75).

And third, they involve tighter subordination of the state's three particular functions to the mobilization of countertendencies to the tendency of the rate of profit to fall.[10] This makes the successful pursuit of the state's general function in maintaining social cohesion more difficult, politicizes its economic functions so that it can longer present itself successfully as a neutral arbiter above social classes, and intensifies generic crisis tendencies in the capitalist state to produce a permanent crisis of political instability and declining legitimacy (1978, 213, 244–45).[11]

"The Ideology of Globalization"

In this last section on Poulantzas's own arguments, I want to consider his response to the idea of globalization; for he critiqued the ideological term *globalization* (admittedly before its current popularity) on the grounds that it treats contemporary capitalism as if there were a single "world capitalist mode of production." This in turn prompts treatment of social formations as mere spatial concretizations of the "world capitalist mode of production" with differences among them being regarded as insignificant or reducible to a temporary uneven development. Against this approach, Poulantzas argued that "the ideology of globalization" (his own prescient phrase) tends to conceal the existence of the imperialist chain (1975, 50) and added that "uneven development . . . is the constitutive form of the reproduction of the CMP [capitalist mode of production]" (ibid., 49; cf. 78).

This general critique is reflected in turn in three particular lines of argument that could be redirected against current myths of globalization. The first concerns the alleged decline in power of nation-states in the face of globalization or the world market. This is one area where Poulantzas's unjustifiably notorious claim (first advanced in *Political Power and Social Classes*) that the state has no power of its own has a real cutting edge. Poulantzas proposed that state power is necessarily tied to class power through at least two crucial mechanisms. Class bias is always inscribed in the state's own institutional form and its insertion into the capitalist mode of production. And its powers (in the plural) are never exercised (or, owing to "non-decision making," not exercised) by state managers in isolation. They are always activated in a determinate but variable conjuncture of class struggles within, over, and at a distance from the state. And these struggles inevitably affect the manner in which the particular and global functions of the state are exercised. It follows that, if, within the limits established by its separation from the core of the production process, the state seems powerless in the face of this or that class (fraction), this occurs because of the class contradictions reproduced within the state apparatus itself. Thus, for Poulantzas, the inability of national states to control world markets would have far less to do with any alleged inherent "ungovernability" of footloose global capital than with real class contradictions within national power blocs as these are increasingly shaped by the process of internationalization itself. If we ask why agreement has not been reached to impose a modest transaction tax to reduce the speculative flow of "hot money" around the globe at the expense of stable conditions for production, for example, the answer will surely be found in the internal contradictions of capital itself rather than the simple incapacity of states to control financial capital.

The second argument concerns the relative autonomy (to purloin a phrase) of the nation. Thus Poulantzas argues that national social formations are still important because they remain "the basic sites of reproduction and uneven development . . . in so far as neither the nation nor the relation between the state and nation are reducible to simple economic ties. The nation, in the full complexity of its determination—a unity that is at the same time economic, territorial, linguistic, and one of ideology and symbolism tied to 'tradition'—retains its specific identity as far as the 'national forms' of class struggle are concerned, and in this way the relation of state and nation is maintained" (ibid., 79). Although there is a clear risk of class reductionism in certain features of Poulantzas's arguments on the nation, it is nonetheless salutary to consider the extent to which nationalism remains a focal point in economic, political, and ideological struggles. As Poulantzas himself noted, this not only affects the position of the national state in relation to internationalization and any potential "superstate," but also shapes forms of popular resistance to internationalization and the increasing tendency to authoritarian statism.

The third argument concerns those analyses of "strong" and "weak" economies that "pose the question of inter-imperialist contradictions in terms of the 'competitiveness' and actual 'competition' between 'national economies'" (ibid., 86–87). Although Poulantzas discussed this discourse in largely macroeconomic terms (e.g., rates of growth) rather than in relation to the more supply-side–oriented measures that are now in vogue, his criticism of their "futurological" tendency to extrapolate from short-term trends and their neglect of the effects of class struggle is still valid. He implied that the real problem was not so much a whole series of particular crises of national competitiveness as a general crisis of imperialism (admittedly under U.S. hegemony) (ibid., 87). This crisis of imperialism as a whole is by no means restricted to a crisis of U.S. hegemony over an otherwise stable system and so cannot be restricted to U.S. capital. If this were so, other national capitals might feel encouraged to lead popular struggles against U.S. imperialism to advance their own interests in the interimperialist conflict. According to Poulantzas, however, the principal contradiction in Europe is not one between specific national economies and American domination; instead, it involves the popular masses against their own bourgeoisies and their own states (ibid., 86–88, 155). This argument has interesting resonances with the current emphasis on "international competitiveness" and its deployment to justify the rolling back of past economic and social concessions to dominated classes.

Some Critical Comments

One can criticize Poulantzas's views on internationalization and the national state on at least three main grounds: (1) the adequacy of his general approach to the critique of political economy; (2) the adequacy of his general analysis of the relation between political power and social classes in contemporary capitalism; and (3) the adequacy of his particular account of the "present" phase of imperialism and its implications for the national state in Europe.

Regarding the critique of political economy, Poulantzas argued, in my view correctly, for the primacy of the capitalist production process in determining the overall dynamic of capitalism. He took the problematic valorization of capital seriously and linked it to the extended reproduction of social classes. In this context, he emphasized the need to link analysis of the "needs" of capital to the nature of class relations and class struggles—a lesson as valid today as ever. Thus changes in state intervention in the economy were always mediated through the balance of class forces and the problems of maintaining political class domination. He likewise offered some important theoretical observations on the changing separation of the economic and the political, and on the complexities of the "presence-action" of the state within the economic. And he emphasized the importance of the nation form and national states to the process of accumulation insofar as the extension of the capital relation on a world scale necessarily took the form of the uneven development of the inter- or transnationalization of capital. In practice, however, Poulantzas paid scant attention to the labor process itself, focusing instead on the changing relationship between the powers of economic ownership and possession within and across different units of production and economic decision-making centers. Likewise, despite his critique of a narrow conception of the economy or class relations, Poulantzas remained committed to residual forms of economism and class reductionism (for more details, see Jessop 1985).

Regarding political power and social classes, Poulantzas correctly saw the state as a social relation, as a form-determined condensation of a changing balance of class forces. This implies that the state does not have its own independent power that can either be fused with that of capital (in "state monopoly capitalism" or a Galbraithian "technostructure") or eliminated as a result of the growing counterpower of global capital (1978, 160).[12] This approach permitted a novel and interesting account both of the relative unity of the state apparatus(es) and of the basic limits of its capacity to function in a rational, coherent, and systematic manner on behalf of the power bloc. This is especially useful, as noted earlier, in dealing with the state's activities in relation to internationalization and its alleged loss of sovereignty in the face of globalization. However, in discussing the relative autonomy of the capitalist type of state, Poulantzas inclined toward a functionalist approach, limiting the state's relative autonomy to the twin tasks of organizing the dominant class(es) and disorganizing subordinate classes, and deriving its real power from the changing balance of political class forces. He also tended to ignore aspects of the state other than those attributable to capitalism and to downplay the significance of social forces other than class forces (e.g., 1975, 98).[13]

Regarding the "present" phase of imperialism, Poulantzas's empirical analysis was largely shaped by contemporary developments and conflicts within Atlantic Fordism. Thus he was preoccupied with establishing the primacy inside Europe of the interimperialist division between American and other capitals and with showing how the hegemony of American capital was being reproduced within each and every national economy, power bloc, and state in Europe. Although I do not deny the continued domination of U.S. capital and the American state in an allegedly "triadic" world, it is noteworthy that European and East Asian capitals have continued to catch up with American capital. Furthermore, the internal contradictions and conflicts within Europe's national power blocs now reflect structural and conjunctural links to East Asian as well as American and other European capitals; for the forms in and through which the relative closure of the gap between economic power and possession is being realized are now more complex, more flexible, more network-like, and more international than could have been anticipated by Poulantzas during the emerging crisis of Atlantic Fordism. In part this failure could be linked to his analysis of this crisis as an enduring crisis *of* imperialism as a whole (rather than as a possibly temporary crisis *in* imperialism owing to the crisis *of* Atlantic Fordism as its primary mode of growth).

Moreover, insofar as the emerging dynamic of capital accumulation on a world scale has begun to shift from the Atlantic Fordist mode of growth (and its extension through "peripheral Fordism") to the search for a sustainable "post-Fordist" regime in a triadic system, the manner in which the national state gets involved in managing the process of internationalization will also change. This is related in turn in a series of challenges to the continued dominance of the national state both as a *national* state and as a national *state* in managing this process. On the former point, indeed, interesting questions are being posed about the relative primacy, if any nowadays, of different scales of economic and political organization—thereby casting doubt on the continued dominance of the national level. In this regard, Poulantzas did not anticipate the growing integration within each triad region (North America, Europe, and East Asia), even though he correctly anticipated the continued importance of their interdependence under the hegemony (or at least dominance) of U.S. capitalism. And, on the latter point, there is increasing interest in the changing balance between government and governance in the overall organization of political class domination.

The Future of the National State: Twenty-five Years On

Having summarized and briefly critiqued Poulantzas's account, I now turn to the second task of this contribution: to consider the changing form and functions of the national state in relation to the most recent phase of imperialism. In undertaking this task, I propose, in line with Poulantzas, to treat internationalization (or globalization) as a process that involves the uneven development of the imperialist chain. But I will also depart from his approach by paying more attention than he did to the complex and tangled interplay of the different spatial scales on which accumulation can occur. In particular, as compared to Poulantzas's overwhelming interest in the national and the primacy he accorded to division between the United States and all other imperialist powers, I will give more consideration to local and regional spaces below the national level, to cross-border and interregional linkages at the subnational level, and to the emerging supranational blocs. Likewise, while subscribing wholeheartedly to Poulantzas's claim that the state is a social relation, I want to explore, in more detail than he himself managed, the division between "public" and "private" in the state's organization and operations and its implications for parallel power networks. In addition, albeit for different reasons, I will focus, as did Poulantzas, on current changes in the organization of European national states. Finally, also in his spirit, I will consider all these topics from the viewpoints of the rearticulation of the economic and political spaces of accumulation, the transformation of the state apparatus, and the continued significance of the national state.

The Rearticulation of the Economic and the Political

In this section, I deal with the rearticulation of the economic and political spaces of accumulation and extended reproduction by referring to changes in the so-called welfare state. Poulantzas had already argued in *Political Power and Social Classes* that this was "a term which in fact merely disguises the form of the 'social policy' of a capitalist state at the stage of state monopoly capitalism" (1973b, 193). He had likewise claimed that the welfare state illustrated a more general phenomenon in which "*the capitalist state undertakes massive interventions in order to adapt and adjust the system in the face of the socialization of productive forces*" (ibid., 272; emphasis in the original). He later emphasized that the welfare state is not intelligible purely as social policy nor simply in terms of concessions to working-class and/or popular struggles; for it plays a part in the state's general task of organizing the balance of forces in favor of the expanded reproduction of capital (1975, 184–85).

Two unstated assumptions behind these general claims about the nature of social policy in contemporary capitalism were the continued dominance of "Atlantic Fordism" and the existence of the Keynesian welfare national state. Poulantzas's account of the "current" phase of imperialism was marked by these closely related phenomena. Here I want to suggest that the crisis of Atlantic Fordism and the continuing search for a stable "post-Fordist" accumulation regime has been associated with a crisis of the "welfare state" as Poulantzas knew it and the tendential emergence of a new welfare regime. With the benefit of a hindsight not available to Poulantzas, it would appear that there has been a further rearticulation of the economic and political spaces of capitalism's extended reproduction. This transformation in the separation of the economic and political can be summarized in terms of a tendential transition from a Keynesian welfare national state (hereafter, KWNS) to an emergent Schumpeterian workfare postnational regime (hereafter, SWPR). The significance of these contrasting forms for extended reproduction can be expressed in terms of their respective functions in the valorization of capital and the reproduction of labor power (the following remarks draw on Jessop 1993, 1994, 1995).

As Poulantzas himself noted, during the postwar consolidation of imperialism, the metropolitan capitalist states sought to organize circulation and consumption as well as the production cycle. Their aim in so doing was to mobilize countertendencies to the tendency for the rate of profit to fall (TRPF) and to reproduce labor power. He noted how the state intervened not only through the provision of infrastructure, but also through monetary management, and how its intervention in the field of consumption was concerned more with collective than with individual consumption (1978, 178–79). These roles correspond to the Keynesian and welfare aspects of the KWNS, respectively. We can link these functions to the nature of Atlantic Fordism as follows. Economically, the KWNS aimed to secure full employment in relatively closed national economies mainly through demand-side management and regulation of collective bargaining. And, socially, it aimed to promote forms of collective consumption that supported a Fordist growth dynamic and to generalize norms of mass consumption. This in turn would enable all citizens to share the fruits of economic growth and thereby contribute to effective domestic demand within the national economy.

A third key feature of the KWNS was its organization primarily in and through the national state, for the international level was essentially a support for the virtuous circles of Fordist accumulation while local and regional states acted as relays for policies determined at national level. In particular, whereas macroeconomic policy was mainly determined and implemented at the national level, local states assumed an increasingly important role in infrastructural and social policy within parameters largely decided at the national level. In this sense, Poulantzas was quite justified in insisting on the central role of the national state during the then-"current" phase of imperialism, for this was precisely the period of expansion of the Atlantic Fordist system under U.S. hegemony and its subsequent crisis—a crisis that the national state was initially expected to resolve through the stepping up of its typical forms of intervention. Finally, although Poulantzas himself did not explicitly highlight this feature, it is important to emphasize the primacy of formal or public state apparatuses in securing the extra-economic conditions for the Atlantic Fordist mode of growth. This is reflected in the concept of the "mixed economy," in which the state corrects for market failures and introduces elements of imperative or indicative planning to guide the overall development of the national economy. It is this fourth feature that justifies the term *state* in the KWNS concept.

The emerging "Schumpeterian workfare postnational regime" involves quite different state activities and a shift in the sites, scales, and modalities of their delivery. Thus, economically, the SWPR tries to promote flexibility and permanent innovation in open economies by intervening on the supply side and tries to strengthen as far as possible the competitiveness of the relevant economic spaces. This involves a fundamental redefinition of the "economic sphere" insofar as "structural" or "systemic" competitiveness is held to depend not only on an extensive range of long-acknowledged economic factors, but also on a broad range of extra-economic factors. This is linked to the growth of new technologies based on more complex national and regional systems of innovation, to the paradigm shift from Fordism with its emphasis on productivity growth rooted in economies of scale, to post-Fordism with its emphasis on mobilizing social as well as economic sources of flexibility and entrepreneurialism, and to more general attempts to penetrate the microsocial level in the interests of valorization. Competitiveness is now widely believed to depend far more on formally extra-economic institutional forms, relations, resources, and values than in the past, and this belief is leading in turn to increased pressure to subsume these factors under the logic of capital. Indeed, this valorization of the extra-economic is a key dimension of current accumulation strategies oriented to so-called strong competition based on flexibility and innovation. Poulantzas had already hinted at this in his remarks on changing forms of state intervention in the economy in the 1970s (e.g., 1978, 167). Since then, the process and pace of the rearticulation of the economic and extra-economic have been reinforced and economic strategies have become more concerned with the social and cultural embeddedness of innovation and competitiveness, as well as more reflexive about how to promote accumulation. It is in this sense that we can describe the new mode of regulation as tendentially Schumpeterian.

Social policy is also affected by these changes. Although "conservation-dissolution" effects on past KWNS institutions and measures vary by national formation (as Poulantzas would have predicted), there is a clear trend among states at all levels to subordinate social policy to the discursively constructed "needs" of structural competitiveness and labor-market flexibility (see Jessop 1993, 1994, 1995). This is reflected in the increasing importance of "workfare" policies—which should not be understood in purely neoliberal terms, but actually embrace all forms of subordination of social policy to alleged economic imperatives. This policy reorientation is evident in new forms of labor-market policy, vocational training, the "learning society," housing policies, and so on. In addition, the social wage is now more and more seen as an international cost of production rather than as a source of domestic demand. This leads to attempts to reduce social expenditure where it is not directly related to enhanced flexibility and competitiveness within the circuits of capital. It also involves attempts to reduce or roll back the welfare rights that were established under the postwar class compromises associated with Atlantic Fordism.

Such changes also have major implications for the role of local and regional governments and governance mechanisms insofar as supply-side policies are supposedly more effectively handled at these levels and through public–private partnerships than at the national level through traditional legislative, bureaucratic, and administrative techniques. At the same time, the continuing internationalization of American capital (including in and through NAFTA) and the emergence of countervailing imperialist strategies in Europe and East Asia mean that the supranational has gained in significance both as a site for mobilizing countertendencies to the TRPF and for building strategic alliances and re-organizing power blocs. The increased importance of other scales of intervention and regulation justify the emphasis on the postnational character of the emerging system (see also the next paragraph). Finally, reflecting both the crisis in the mixed economy associated with the KWNS—which is linked to the perceived need to find ways to correct state as well as market failure—and the increased importance of extra-economic conditions for the valorization of capital, there is an increasing role for modalities of policy formation and implementation based on networking, public–private partnership, regulated self-regulation, and so on. The term *regime* in the SWPR concept serves to highlight this shift from the market–state couplet associated with the mixed economy of Atlantic Fordism to the more complex forms of governance associated with the search for a stable post-Fordist order.

The changes in economic and social policy associated with the shift from the KWNS to the SWPR serve to undermine the primacy of the national state as the site on which particular techno-economic, narrowly political, and ideological functions are undertaken in the interests of capital accumulation. They also reinforce the problems faced by national states in reconciling the increasing pressure to take measures directly and visibly beneficial to capital with the need to maintain political legitimacy and the overall cohesion of a class-divided social formation (cf. Poulantzas 1975, 1978). One response to this dilemma is the displacement of crisis through the reallocation of functions to different levels of economic and political organization[14] (the postnational moment of the SWPR) and/or to other modalities of intervention (the regime moment of the SWPR). Another is the strengthening of "authoritarian statism" and the concentration of power at the center (Poulantzas 1978). Nonetheless, in comparison with the Keynesian welfare national state, the Schumpeterian workfare postnational regime appears to give less direct support to Poulantzas's claims about the continued primacy of the national state in contemporary capitalism. Whether his thesis can be rescued in other ways remains to be discussed in the next two sections.

The Transformation of the State

This section advances three interrelated propositions about emerging trends in the organization of the state in the light of the rearticulation of the economic and political spaces of valorization and extended reproduction (for a more detailed and nuanced treatment, see Jessop 1997). In presenting these trends, I do not want to detract from Poulantzas's inspired analysis of the growth of authoritarian statism—which seems more relevant than ever for understanding the transformation of the national state in the economic and political spaces once dominated by Atlantic Fordism (see Poulantzas 1978). My aim is simply to highlight certain related changes that complicate his view of authoritarian statism and qualify his implied claim that the national state in its postwar guise has become a permanent feature of capitalism. At the same time, I want to subject my own earlier arguments to a Poulantzasian critique by noting in turn their limitations from his particular perspective on the dynamic of internationalization and the national state.

First, there is a general trend toward the *denationalization of the state* (or, better, statehood). This structural trend is reflected empirically in the "hollowing out" of the national state apparatus with old and new state capacities being reorganized territorially and functionally on subnational, national, supranational, and translocal levels.[15] There is a continuing movement of state power upward, downward, and sideways as attempts are made by state managers on different territorial scales to enhance their respective operational autonomies and strategic capacities. One aspect of this is the loss of the de jure sovereignty of national states in certain respects as rule- and/or decision-making powers are transferred upward to supranational bodies and the resulting rules and decisions bind national states. This trend is most apparent in the European Union but also affects NAFTA and other intergovernmental regional blocs. Another aspect is devolution of authority to subordinate levels of territorial organization and the development of transnational but interlocal policy making.

This trend should certainly not be mistaken for the rise of a "global state"—at least if the concept of the state is to retain its core meaning of the territorialization of a centralized political authority—such that a "global state" would become equivalent to a single "world state." Poulantzas himself gave sound reasons to reject such an interpretation. To these we could add that, even were a world state to be established, it would inevitably be subject to a tension between its juridico-political claim to unicity (sovereignty) and the harsh reality of plurality (particularistic competition among other states for influence in its counsels). It is for this reason that interstate politics on a global scale is often marked by the international hegemony of a national state that seeks to develop a hegemonic political strategy for the global system—with that hegemony armored, of course, by various forms of coercion and resting on a complex articulation of governmental powers and other forms of governance. This has been evidenced in the postwar period, of course, by the continuing hegemony of the United States within the interstate system. But there is also more to this trend to denationalization than changes at the supranational level; for we are witnessing a complex reconstitution and rearticulation of various scales of the territorial organization of power within the global political system. Thus denationalization involves more than the delegation of powers to supranational bodies and the resurgence of a reinvigorated and relatively unchallenged American "superstate" with revitalized capacities to project its power on a global scale. It also involves the delegation of authority to subordinate levels of territorial organization and/or the development of so-called intermestic (or interlocal but transnationalized) policy-making regimes.[16]

Second, there is a trend toward the *destatization of the political system*. This is reflected in a shift from govern*ment* to govern*ance* on various territorial scales and across various functional domains. There is a movement from the central role of the official state apparatus in securing state-sponsored economic and social projects and political hegemony toward an emphasis on partnerships between governmental, paragovernmental, and nongovernmental organizations in which the state apparatus is often only first among equals. This involves the complex art of steering multiple agencies, institutions, and systems that are both operationally autonomous from one another and structurally coupled through various forms of reciprocal interdependence. Governments have always relied on other agencies to aid them in realizing state objectives or projecting state power beyond the formal state apparatus. And, as Poulantzas notes, there is nothing new about parallel power networks that crosscut and unify the state apparatus and connect it to other social forces (1974a, 1975, 1976, 1978). But this reliance has been reordered and increased. The relative weight of governance has increased on all levels—including not only at the supranational and local or regional levels, but also in the transterritorial and interlocal fields. This increase in governance need not entail a loss in the power of government, however, as if power were a zero-sum resource rather than a social relation. Thus, resort to governance could enhance the state's capacity to project its influence and secure its objectives by mobilizing knowledge and power resources from influential nongovernmental partners or stakeholders. Moreover, in the light of shifts in the balance of class forces, the turn to governance could also be part of a more complex power struggle to protect key decisions from popular-democratic control (cf. Poulantzas 1973b, 1978). In both respects, it is important to resist the idealistic and erroneous impression that expansion of nongovernmental regimes implies that the state is no longer necessary. Indeed, the state retains an important role precisely because of the development of such regimes;

for it is not only an important actor in many individual governance mechanisms, but also retains responsibility for their oversight in the light of the overall balance of class forces and the maintenance of social cohesion.

Third, there is a complex trend toward the *internationalization of policy regimes.* The international context of domestic state action has extended to include a widening range of extraterritorial or transnational factors and processes; and it has also become more significant strategically for domestic policy. The key players in policy regimes have also expanded to include foreign agents and institutions as sources of policy ideas, policy design, and implementation (cf. Gourevitch 1978; Doern, Pal, and Tomlin 1996). This trend is reflected in economic and social policies as the state becomes more concerned with "international competitiveness" in the widest sense (cf. my earlier comments on Schumpeterian workfare postnational regimes). Neoliberalism pursued in the name of globalization is the most obvious and vocal manifestation of this trend; but its long-term social impact is also proving to be the most disastrous. This trend would not surprise Poulantzas, of course; it is an excellent illustration of his own arguments about the interior bourgeoisie and the increasing importance of the national state in managing the process of internationalization. But it should be noted that this trend also affects local and regional states below the national level and is also evident in the above-mentioned development of interregional and cross-border linkages that connect local and regional authorities and governance regimes in different national formations.

These trends have been presented thus far in a one-sided and undialectical manner. Each of them is linked to a countertrend that both qualifies and transforms its significance for political class domination and accumulation. This involves more than a simple reference to what Poulantzas described as the complex "conservation-dissolution" effects associated with successive stages in the development of capitalism. Such effects certainly exist insofar as past forms and functions of the state are conserved and/or dissolved as the state is transformed. Thus the tendential emergence of the SWPR is linked with different types of conservation-dissolution effects on the KWNS across different spheres of state intervention as well as across different national formations. The countertrends referred to here can be interpreted as reactions to the new trends rather than as survivals of earlier patterns. This is also why they should be seen as countertrends to the trends rather than vice versa. Let me now briefly present these countertrends.

Countering the denationalization of statehood are the attempts of national states to retain control over the articulation of different spatial scales. However, although it might be thought that there is a simple continuity of function in this regard (cf. Poulantzas 1975), I would argue that a major discontinuity has been introduced through the "relativization of scale" (cf. Collinge 1996) that is associated with the "current" phase of imperialism. In Atlantic Fordism, the national level of economic and political organization was primary: the postwar international order was designed to support its national economies and states and local and regional states acted as relays of the national state (cf. Jessop 1997). The current period of globalization involves a proliferation of spatial scales (whether terrestrial, territorial, or telematic; cf. Luke 1994), their relative dissociation in complex tangled hierarchies (rather than a simple nesting of scales), and an increasingly convoluted mix of scale strategies as economic and political forces seek the most favorable conditions for insertion into a changing international order (cf. Jessop 1995). In this sense, the national scale has lost the taken-for-granted primacy it held in the economic and political organization of Atlantic Fordism; but this does not mean that some other scale of economic and political organization (whether the "global" or the "local," the "urban" or the "triadic") has acquired a similar primacy. Indeed, this relativization of scale could well be seen as a further factor contributing to the growing heterogeneity and disarticulation of national power blocs that was noted by Poulantzas and, a fortiori, to the apparent loss of power by national states. Nonetheless, in the absence of a supranational state with equivalent powers to those of the national state, the denationalization of statehood is linked to attempts on the part of national states to reclaim power by managing the relationship among different scales of economic and political organization.

Countering the shift toward governance is government's increased role in *metagovernance*. Interestingly, Poulantzas identified one of the features of authoritarian statism as "the massive development of parallel state networks of a public, semi-public or para-public character—networks whose function is to cement, unify and control the nuclei of the state apparatus . . . and whose creation is directly orchestrated by the commanding heights of the State in symbiosis with the dominant party"

(1978, 239). This indicates both the expansion of governance and the extent to which governance operates in the shadow of government; for governments (on various scales) are becoming more involved in organizing the self-organization of partnerships, networks, and governance regimes. They provide the ground rules for governance; ensure the compatibility of different governance mechanisms and regimes; deploy a relative monopoly of organizational intelligence and information with which to shape cognitive expectations; act as a "court of appeal" for disputes arising within and over governance; seek to rebalance power differentials by strengthening weaker forces or systems in the interests of system integration and/or social cohesion; try to modify the self-understanding of identities, strategic capacities, and interests of individual and collective actors in different strategic contexts and hence alter their implications for preferred strategies and tactics; and also assume political responsibility in the event of governance failure. Although Poulantzas did not discuss such tasks in any detail (referring simply to the functions of parallel state networks), there are good reasons for taking seriously his more general argument that all such tasks will be conducted by the state not only in terms of their contribution to particular state functions, but also in terms of their implications for political class domination.

Somewhat ambiguously countering yet reinforcing the internationalization of policy regimes is the growing importance of national states in struggling to shape the development of international policy regimes in the interests of their respective national bourgeoisies. This phenomenon was emphasized, albeit in a different context, in Poulantzas's critique of the "world state." A second, and equally ambiguous, countertrend is the "interiorization" of international constraints as the latter become integrated into the policy paradigms and cognitive models of domestic policymakers. This phenomenon was also extensively discussed by Poulantzas (1975, 1976, 1978). However, in line with my own earlier remarks, I would note here that *interiorization* is not confined to the level of the national state: it is also evident at the local, regional, cross-border, and interregional levels, as well as in the activities of so-called entrepreneurial cities. The relativization of scale makes such "interiorization" significant at all levels of economic and political organization and, indeed, leads to concerns with the complex dialectics of spatial articulations that is reflected in such phenomena as "glocalization."

The Continued Significance of the National State

This section deals with the principal question that exercised Poulantzas in his comments on internationalization: is it still possible today to speak of a *national state* in the imperialist metropolises? Poulantzas's own answer was that the national state was irreplaceable. Indeed, one might argue that he saw the national state as, in a certain sense, "self-substituting."[17] My remarks have been concerned with revealing some of the complexities in the transformation of the contemporary state; but they have been placed in a framework that is broadly consistent with Poulantzas's approach. It remains for me to suggest that the various changes, trends, and countertrends that I have considered do not amount to a fundamental challenge to the national state as such. Instead, they seem to involve a transformation of the *Keynesian welfare national state* that was a key feature of the European social formations of most interest to Poulantzas in the postwar period. This does not exclude the transformation of state form and functions in ways that maintain the "nation" as a matrix of political organization and safeguard a continuing and central political role for the national state.

There can surely be no doubt that the latter remains an important level of political mobilization despite (and, indeed, precisely because of) the denationalization that has followed the crisis of the Keynesian welfare national state. In this context, I would like to suggest, in a quasi-Gramscian vein, that the state *in its integral sense* is reproduced in and through continuous changes in the articulation of government and governance. This reflects the "part–whole" paradox that lies at the heart of the modern national state and that has fueled so much debate about the nature and purposes of government; for, although the state is only one among several institutionally separated ensembles within a social formation, it is uniquely charged with overall responsibility for maintaining the cohesion of the class-divided social formation of which it is but a part (cf. Jessop 1990, 360). In exercising this responsibility, it must continually look beyond its own limited strategic capacities to secure the institutional integration and social cohesion of the wider society to which it belongs. This paradox in turn generates the strategic dilemma that, if sharing power tends to diminish the distinctive unity and identity of the state, not sharing power threatens to undermine its effectiveness (cf. Offe 1987). This dilemma is presented in class-theoretical terms by Poulantzas in his comments on the growing complexity of forming a national power bloc and securing its hegemony over the popular masses (notably 1973b, 1975, 1978). In this context, it may be that the shift from government to governance reflects a reordering of the national state's general (or "global") function: it has now become responsible for organizing the self-organization of social forces so that it reflects the "general will" and/or serves the "public interest." This would represent a rearticulation of the state in its integral sense as "political society + civil society." Indeed, unless or until supranational political organization acquires not only governmental powers, but also some measure of popular-democratic legitimacy, based on an international or cosmopolitan form of citizenship, the national state will remain a key political factor as the highest instance of bourgeois-democratic political accountability. How it plays this role will depend on the changing institutional matrix and shifts in the balance of forces as globalization, triadization, regionalization, and the resurgence of local governance proceed apace.

Concluding Remarks

Poulantzas's major theoretical contribution was to develop a view of state power as a social relation that is reproduced in and through the interplay between the state's institutional form and the changing nature of political forces. This was associated in turn with growing emphasis on the nature of the state as a system of *strategic selectivity* and on the nature of political struggle as a field of *competing strategies* to attain hegemony. He also tried to link these arguments to the changing forms of imperialism and the national state.

Building on Poulantzas's work, I have suggested that the relation between internationalization and the national state has changed in several key respects since he wrote. First, some of the particular technical-economic, more narrowly political, and ideological functions of the national state are being relocated to other levels of state organization. I have referred to this as the denationalization of statehood. Second, some of the particular technical-economic, political, and ideological functions previously or newly performed by the national state have been increasingly shared with, or wholly shifted to, other (i.e., parastatal or private) political actors, institutional arrangements, or regimes. I have referred to this as the shift from government to governance. And, third, in line with Poulantzas's own arguments, the international context of domestic state action has become of greater significance to national, regional, and local states and their fields of action for domestic purposes have been expanded to include an extensive range of extraterritorial or transnational factors and processes.[18] All three of these trends are associated with a partial redefinition of the particular functions of the state. Obviously, more detailed studies of the restructuring and reorientation of the national state would need to look at each trend in more concrete and complex terms. It should be evident too that, if each of these three trends can vary, the manner and extent of their interaction must be even more varied. This said, it is important to consider all three trends in their interaction rather than focus on just one or consider each in isolation.

Overemphasis on the first trend runs the risk of confusing the particular functions or tasks of a particular form of the national state in a particular period with the generic (or "global") functional activities of the capitalist type of state in any capitalist social formation. For the moment, this latter function, as Poulantzas emphasized, remains firmly anchored in the national state. In this sense, "denationalization" should be seen as a partial and uneven process that leaves a rearticulated "national state" still exercising the generic function of the capitalist type of state. It certainly does not imply that a full-fledged "supranational" state has already emerged to maintain institutional integration and social cohesion in an extended, class-divided, supranational social formation. This is especially clear regarding the still-limited development of the European Union's role in promoting "social cohesion" in the face of the uneven development and discontinuities generated by regional economic integration and international competition.

A unilateral focus on the second trend runs the risk of confusing changes in the specific institutional arrangements associated with particular regimes with the erosion of the state in its integral sense; for the tendential shift from government to governance need not weaken the state apparatus as a whole or undermine its capacity to pursue specific state projects. Much will depend on the ways in which new governance mechanisms are linked to the pursuit of changed state goals in new contexts and to the state's capacities to project its power into the wider society. This is reflected ideologically in the neoliberal claim that an overextended state is a weak state—which implies that, only by confining its activities to those that the state apparatus alone can (and must) do, can it be sure to perform even these effectively.

Too narrow a concern with the third trend runs the twofold risk of neglecting the ways in which the national state has previously managed the insertion of national economic space into the wider economy and, alternatively, of minimizing the real discontinuities in the state's current concerns for the structural competitiveness of nationally based capitals at home and abroad. American hegemony and intergovernmental cooperation in the postwar period rescued the "national state" and, although the KWNS was particularly concerned with the macroeconomic management of a relatively closed national economy, it did so in the context of a plurinational Atlantic Fordist economy. Even more telling, perhaps, is the fact that small open economies in this plurinational system were committed to maintaining the structured coherence of their national economies despite their dependence on exports. They appeared to have managed their national economies and secured the unity of the power bloc and people despite levels of internationalization that would now be said to imply a loss of sovereignty. This reinforces the point made earlier (and drawn from Poulantzas) that the power of the national state in the face of internationalization depends critically on the cohesion of the power bloc. If national states now seem powerless in the face of financial capital and/or footloose industrial capital, therefore, it could well owe something to the induced reproduction within these states of interimperialist and/or interfractional conflicts.

Finally, in relating these trends, whether individually or together, only to changes in the economy, one risks economistically underestimating the importance of politics (Evers 1994, 117). This error could occur in at least two ways. From an economic viewpoint, even paying due attention to the social embeddedness and social regularization of capital accumulation, it would be wrong to explain these general trends in terms of economic changes without noting how these latter are first translated through struggles into political problems for state action and their solution is mediated through the specific, structurally inscribed, strategically selective nature of the state. This is an error that Poulantzas cautioned against. Likewise, from a more state-centric viewpoint, it would be wrong to suggest that these trends are attributable solely to (politically mediated) economic changes; for there could also be sui generis political reasons prompting state actors and other political forces to engage in institutional redesign and strategic reorientation (cf. Jessop 1994). It is here that Poulantzas's Marxist emphasis on the primacy of political class struggle deserves further development.

My conclusion is that the "extended reproduction" of capitalism and social classes in the erstwhile economic space of Atlantic Fordism is no longer linked politically to the Keynesian welfare national state with its local relays, corporatist bias, and international supports. It has been relocated in a more internationalized and localized Schumpeterian workfare postnational regime. The particular functions of the latter have been dispersed among several institutional levels of territorial organization and are shared with an extended range of functionally relevant (and politically and ideologically defined) stakeholders. Yet the generic political function of maintaining social cohesion is still exercised at the level of the national state within this restructured and reoriented political ensemble. Hence, the typical features and generic functions of this national state are quite different from those of the Keynesian welfare national state and the strategic context in which it operates has also been significantly transformed.

For the foreseeable future, the most one could expect to see in Europe is some movement toward an *integral economic* regime oriented to achieving structural competitiveness and social cohesion in a European economic space that it co-defines with other major economic and political actors in the international order. At the highest level, this regime will involve a public power that combines features of a "condominium" of key players in governance mechanisms and a confederation of national states.[19] Thus, on the one hand, as governance mechanisms proliferate from below as well as being imposed from above and are to be found on various spatial scales and serving different functional purposes, the supranational public power will seek selectively to coordinate them to enhance its Schumpeterian workfare roles and to assist in projecting its power beyond its own organizational and institutional boundaries. This is especially important given the current restrictions on its resources and the limited nature of its own supranational state apparatus; for efforts to promote governance at the expense of government could succeed either in bypassing national states or in securing their compliance in other ways. On the other hand, it should be evident that national states themselves are not only key players in many governance mechanisms (and thus inevitably drawn into European politics), but are also trying to coordinate these mechanisms at the national level in ways that may contradict European-level preferences (so that the Euro-polity is inevitably drawn into national politics).

Moreover, given the continued importance of the generic or "global" political functions of national states and the continued "democratic deficit" of Europe's public power, the latter must draw and lean heavily on national states both for legitimacy and for assistance in securing compliance with Europe-wide policies (cf. Hirst and Thompson 1995). Even with the "interiorization" of the interests of European and/or global capital in the accumulation strategies and hegemonic projects of national states (cf. Poulantzas 1973a, 1975), there is still wide scope for conflicts over how to manage an inherently uneven national insertion into a changing international order. Likewise, even though European commitment to the principle of subsidiarity may enhance local and regional states and their cross-border linkages, it also enshrines a key role for national states—especially if they are unitary rather than federal. Thus, whether crisis- and erosion-prone or not in its integral economic *Keynesian welfare* features, the postwar national state remains significant as a general *political* force.

In short, the future of the European political system will reflect, in intensified form, the future of the national state. Both are subject to the three general trends outlined earlier. But the European political system, which many unrealistically hoped would prove to be an embryonic European national state, is now subject to growing pressures to move toward a future beyond the postwar national state. Indeed, lacking its own entrenched institutional legacies of a national state character, the European political system reveals more fully and transparently the current tendencies in the rearticulation of the economic and political moments of the capital relation. Yet, precisely because it lacks its own entrenched institutional legacies of a national state character, the European political system is also inclined to draw on real, if crisis-prone, national states to lend it legitimacy and to assist in policy implementation. Whether it can break out of such paradoxes, dilemmas, and contradictions by developing a new "social contract" on a European scale remains to be seen. If it does, it will be as a "denationalized, governance-based, Schumpeterian workfare regime" on a European scale.

Notes

1. Poulantzas noted that a periodization "does not derive from the supposed 'tendencies' of the mode of production itself, this being simply an abstract object. It is only social formations that can be periodized, since it is in them that the class struggle is enacted: a mode of production only exists in the specific conditions—economic, political, ideological—which determine its constitution and reproduction. . . . Social formations are in actual fact the sites of the reproduction process; they are nodes of uneven development of the relationship of modes and forms of production within the class struggle. This means that the site where the CMP [capitalist mode of production] is reproduced in the imperialist stage is the imperialist chain and its links" (1975, 48).

2. This phrase derives from Gramsci's analysis of the state: he defined the state in its integral sense as "political society + civil society" (Gramsci 1971). Likewise, Poulantzas analyzed classes from the viewpoint of their expanded reproduction (1973a, 1975, 1978). Indeed, with the exception of his overly politicized and ideologistic view of the petite bourgeoisie in *Fascism and Dictatorship* (1974a), he always defined classes in terms of the social relations of economic exploitation, ownership, and control. At the same time, however, he stressed that other institutional orders (notably the state) were deeply involved in reproducing the social relations of production.

3. Poulantzas dated these phases, respectively, from the late nineteenth century to the early years of the interwar period, the crisis of the 1930s, and the period from 1945 onward (1975, 45–46, 63).

4. But he would also note that "capital which overflows its national limits certainly has recourse to national states—not only to its own state of origin, but to other states as well. This gives rise to a complex distribution of the role of the state in the international reproduction of capital under the domination of American capital, which can lead to the exercise of the state functions becoming decentred and shifting among their supports, which essentially remain the national states. According to the conjuncture, any one or other of the metropolitan national states may assume responsibility for this or that international intervention in the reproduction process, and for the maintenance of the system as a whole" (ibid., 82–83).

5. In addition to the empirical arguments offered by Poulantzas himself on this point for the 1960s and early 1970s (Poulantzas 1975), one could also cite the more recent evidence marshaled by Hirst and Thompson (1995) against the globalization thesis in favor of an emphasis on the continuing importance of the "national" bases of internationalization.

6. This argument makes most sense on the assumption that an autocentric national economy is one in which the organization of the decisive sectors of production (as the ultimately determining moment in the circuit of capital) is controlled by a national bourgeoisie and also provides the basis for a coherent national accumulation strategy. In this context, external relations can be understood as commercial and financial relations that leave the productive core of the national economy largely untouched; and as diplomatic, security, and military relations.

7. Poulantzas nonetheless notes that "these antagonisms do not at present form the principal contradiction within the imperialist ruling classes" (1975, 74).

8. The narrowly political functions of the capitalist state concern its activities

in securing its own material and symbolic reproduction and its institutional integration as an ensemble of diverse branches and apparatuses on different territorial scales.

9. "The state's economic interventions in favor of monopoly capital are not simply 'technical' interventions deriving from the requirements of 'monopoly production', but like any state economic intervention, they are political interventions. In their specific forms and modalities, they generally take account of non-monopoly capital and the need for cohesion on the part of the power bloc, and in this way non-monopoly capital finds expression in certain *pertinent effects* within the very structure of the state's monopolist 'economic policy'" (1978, 160).

10. "Now, given that the State's present role in the economy alters the political space as a whole, economic functions henceforth occupy the *dominant place* within the State. . . . the totality of socio-economic fields is subordinated to the capital accumulation process" (ibid., 168, 169).

11. There are growing problems owing to the clash between the policy requirements of accumulation and the needs of organizing hegemony: "the strictly correlative expansion of state space and the space-process of the reproduction of capital" leads to "overpoliticization" of state actions (ibid., 169).

12. Galbraith's (1967) notion of "technostructure" was analogous to the state monopoly capitalist concept of the fusion of the state and monopolies into a single instrument of economic exploitation and political domination.

13. Thus "relative autonomy is inscribed in the very structure of the capitalist state by the relative 'separation' of the political and the economic that is specific to capitalism; it is in no way a function of the state or 'political instance' as such, but rather derives from the separation and dispossession of the direct producers from their means of production that characterizes capitalism. In this respect, this relative autonomy is simply the necessary condition for the role of the capitalist state in class representation and in the political organization of hegemony" (1978, 98).

14. On this aspect, see also the quotations from Poulantzas (1975 and 1978) in notes 4 and 15, respectively.

15. "At a time when the role of the state is more crucial than ever, the state seems affected by a crisis of representativeness in its various apparatuses (including the political parties) in their relations to the actual fractions of the power bloc: this is one of the reasons behind the controversies over 'state control', 'regionalization', and 'decentralization', at least in the form that they assume within the bourgeoisie itself" (Poulantzas 1978, 171).

16. *Intermestic* is a term coined by Duchacek to refer to the expanding area of international connections between local authorities. See Duchacek, Latouche, and Stevenson, 1988.

17. "Self-substitution" occurs when the crisis of an institution leads to its replacement by an equivalent institution. Thus the elimination of markets leads to black markets, and the suspension of parliamentarism leads to what Gramsci called "black parliamentarism" (Gramsci 1971). Similarly, one might argue that a crisis of a specific form of national state leads to its self-transformation or self-substitution with a new form of national state.

18. In addition to the international context of domestic state action, imperatives of international economic competition continue to highlight the domestic context of international state action.

19. I have purloined the concept of condominium from the work of Schmitter (1992) and his collaborators. However, although Schmitter and colleagues link "condominio" to functional rather than territorial organization, I link it here to governance as opposed to government. In this respect, my approach is also inspired by Tömmel (1992, 1993).

References

Collinge, Chris. 1996. "Spatial Articulation of the State: Reworking Social Relations and Social Regulation Theory." Birmingham: Centre for Urban and Regional Studies, University of Birmingham, unpublished paper.

Doern, G. B., L. A. Pal, and B. W. Tomlin, eds. 1996. *Border Crossings: the Internationalization of Canadian Public Policy.* Don Mills, Oxford University Press.

Duchacek, I. D., D. Latouche, and G. Stevenson, eds. 1988. *Perforated Sovereignties and International Relations: Trans-sovereign Contacts of Subnational Governments.* New York: Greenwood Press.

Evers, Detlev. 1994. "Supranationale Staatlichkeit am Beispiel der Europäischen Union: Civitas civitatum oder Monstrum." *Leviathan* 1: 115–34.

Galbraith, John Kenneth. 1967. *The New Industrial State.* London: Hamish Hamilton.

Gourevitch, Peter. 1978. "The Second Image Reversed: The International Sources of Domestic Politics." *International Organisation* 32(4): 881–912.

Gramsci, Antonio. 1971. *Selections from the Prison Notebooks.* London: Lawrence and Wishart.

Hirst, Paul Q., and G. Thompson. 1995. *Globalisation in Question: The Myths of the International Economy and the Possibilities of Governance.* Cambridge: Polity Press.

Jessop, Bob. 1985. *Nicos Poulantzas: Marxist Theory and Political Strategy.* London: Macmillan.

———. *State Theory: Putting Capitalist States in Their Place.* Cambridge: Polity Press.

———. 1992. "Fordism and Post-Fordism: A Critical Reformulation." In M. J. Storper and A. J. Scott, eds., *Pathways to Regionalism and Industrial Development.* London: Routledge. 43–65.

———. 1993. "Towards a Schumpeterian Workfare State? Preliminary Remarks on Post-Fordist Political Economy." *Studies in Political Economy* 40: 7–39.

———. 1994. "Post-Fordism and the State." In Ash Amin, ed., *Post-Fordism.* Oxford: Blackwell. 251–79.

———. 1995. "Regional Economic Blocs, Cross-Border Cooperation, and Local Economic Strategies in Post-Socialism: Policies and Prospects." *American Behavioral Scientist* 38(5): 674–715.

———. 1997. "Die Zukunft des Nationalstaats: Erosion oder Reorganisation? Grundsätzliche Überlegungen zu Westeuropa." In Steffen Becker, Thomas Sablowski, and Wilhelm Schumm, eds., *Jenseits der Nationalökonomie? Weltwirtschaft und Nationalstaat zwischen Globalisierung und Regionalisierung.* Berlin: Das Argument. 50–95.

Lipietz, A. 1987. *Mirages and Miracles.* London: New Left Books.

Luke, Timothy W. 1994. "Placing Power/Siting Space: The Politics of Global and Local in the New World Order." *Environment and Planning D: Society and Space* 12(4): 613–28.

Offe, Claus. 1987. "Die Staatstheorie auf der Suche nach ihrem Gegenstand. Beobachtungen zur aktuellen Diskussion." In T. Ellwein et al., eds., *Jahrbuch zur Staats- und Verwaltungswissenschaft*, vol. 1. Baden-Baden: Nomos Verlag. 309–20.
Ohmae, Kenichi. 1990. *The Borderless World: Power and Strategy in the Interlinked Economy. Management Lessons in the New Logic of the Global Marketplace.* New York: HarperCollins.
Poulantzas, Nicos. 1973a. "L'Internationalisation des rapports capitalistes et l'État-nation." *Les Temps modernes* 319: 1456–1500.
———. 1973b. *Political Power and Social Classes.* Trans. Timothy O'Hagan. London: Sheed and Ward.
———. 1974a. *Fascism and Dictatorship: The Third International and the Problem of Fascism.* Trans. Judith White. London: New Left Books.
———. 1974b. "The Internationalization of Capitalist Relations and the Nation State." *Economy and Society* 3(2): 145–79.
———. 1975. *Classes in Contemporary Capitalism.* Trans. David Fernbach. London: New Left Books.
———. 1976. *Crisis of the Dictatorships: Portugal, Greece, Spain.* Trans. David Fernbach. London: New Left Books.
———. 1978. *State, Power, Socialism.* Trans. Patrick Camiller. London: Verso Books.
———. 1979a. "L'État, les mouvements sociaux, le parti." *Dialectiques* 28.
———. 1979b. "Interview with Nicos Poulantzas." *Marxism Today* (July): 198–205.
Schmitter, Philippe C. 1994. "Representation and the Future Euro-Polity." *Staatswissenchaften und Staatspraxis* 3(3): 379–405.
Tömmel, Ingeborg. 1992. "System-Entwicklung and Politikgestaltung in der Europäischen Gemeinschaft am Beispiel der Regionalpolitik." In M. Kreile, ed., *Die Integration Europas.* Opladen: Westdeutscher Verlag. 185–208.
———. 1993. "Die Europäische Gemeinschaft: supranationaler Staat oder politische Agentur des Marktes?" *Links* 6: 28–29.
van der Pijl, Kees. 1984. *The Making of an Atlantic Ruling Class.* London: Verso Books.

CHAPTER NINE

Relative Autonomy and Its Changing Forms

Constantine Tsoukalas

Old Questions and New Realities

It is more than a quarter of a century since the "crisis of the dictatorships" announced the "definitive" consolidation of democracies in Western and Southern Europe, a fact that was generally interpreted by the left as signifying the emergence of a new and more optimistic period of class struggles. We may, however, entertain growing doubts as to the nature of these triumphant democratic achievements. Despite the extension and formal consolidation of democracies, the capitalist state is becoming more and more arrogant, self-righteous, and authoritarian.

The old Marxist question is still unanswered and unanswerable: how can it be that an increasing majority of nonowners continue to remain under the democratic dominance of a shrinking minority of property owners? Why should the many accept the continuing domination of the few? To put it more accurately, how does an increasingly inegalitarian democracy remain viable? The mechanisms that secure the continuity of the system thus appear as the most crucial of political issues. The fundamental role of the state in ensuring the reproduction and political cohesion of capitalist class societies remains the most important question of political theory.

Thus, the famous controversy between Poulantzas and Miliband may be seen as having a renewed significance. Indeed, at the time, this debate inaugurated an entirely new field of inquiry, at least in Marxist theory: the long-neglected question of the structure and functions of political power under capitalist conditions was seen as central to all the strategic considerations of the working class. But, since then, the preoccupation with the "political" has receded. State functions tend to be taken for granted, in ways that contribute to the restriction of most debates within leftist political movements to tactical or operational considerations—even if, in some ways, the esoteric and often cryptic jargon surrounding the debate itself may seem to be antiquated and pointless, and, despite the enormous theoretical difficulties of producing a coherent conception of the articulation between the economic and the political levels, we are obliged to face the problem anew.

Within this framework, the question of the *relative autonomy* of the state (the question of the particular way the state participates in the extended reproduction of capitalist society) remains paramount. The term *relative autonomy,* coined by Poulantzas and adopted by Miliband and many others, however critically, still remains vague, however, in that it is a general and flexible concept, not a measurable quantity. Miliband's question, "How relative is relative autonomy?" is far less significant than more general questions about the eventual "limits" of the structural articulation between economic relations and the state; for, as Miliband noted, "the notion of autonomy is embedded in the [state's] definition of itself, is an intrinsic part of it." If the state can by no means pursue its own independent aims, it should also not be seen as a "committee" executing the direct orders of the capitalists: "classes," after all, do not issue orders. It is much more important to elucidate the continuing functions and structural limits of the capitalist state's interventions than to come up with any kind of quantitative "measure" of the state's autonomy. The main questions to be answered are thus not centered on an elusive, impossible, and undefinable "essence" of relative autonomy. They are centered on the concrete historical transformations of a relative autonomy that must be considered a property of all capitalist states.

As Poulantzas argued, the *forms* of relative autonomy must be constantly *transformed* in response to more general modifications in the capital accumulation process. It is these changing forms and functions that have to be elucidated for the "post-Fordist," "post-Keynesian," or "postmodern" era. It may be undeniable that the "independent" organizational functions of traditional territorial states have been decreased in relation to the recent past. It is also true that there has been a marked delocalization of capitalist activities, a transmutation of class struggles, and a dominance of neoliberal ideologies. However, such transformations may be seen as a new structural circumscription of the individual state's interventionist capacities. In this sense, it may well be that the state's relative autonomy is being redefined by new structural limits.

In this context, the political and ideological differences between Poulantzas and Miliband seem much less pronounced today than they did at the time. Even if their respective epistemological foundations are still clearly distinguishable, if not totally opposed, their political analysis and predictions lay hand in hand. Both were critical of social-democratic strategies. Both had been right in assessing the importance of structural factors pushing toward "authoritarian statism" as the new dominant state form. Both were fundamentally right in their skepticism regarding the long-term effects of European social democracy and the welfare state. Miliband recognized that social-democratic forces "undermine the strength of the defense organizations of the working class," while Poulantzas insisted on the need to overcome the traditional forms of social-democratic "statolatry." Finally, both insisted on the necessity to preserve, enrich, and "deepen" representative parliamentary forms.

In this sense, probably more important than the explicit terms in which the debate itself was pursued, are the real political problems raised and discussed. Self-indulgent "democratic pluralism," attacked by Miliband and Poulantzas, has now emerged as the virtually uncontested world paradigm. More than obviously, the dissolution of the Soviet Union has been both a factor and a result of the global realignment of sociopolitical and ideological fronts. No longer content with the "end of ideology," mainstream thinkers now go as far as to proclaim the "end of history." Even if the age of class struggles is not over, the political world is increasingly apt to disregard them. The specter of revolution is by now invested with the elusive features of an impotent and benevolent Canterville ghost.

For all these reasons, the most critical issue is still the articulation between class domination and political power. One must consequently continue to ask the same old questions: In what sense is the problem of the relations between the state apparatus and capital different from what it was in the 1970s? And to what extent has the relative autonomy of the state been modified? Can one observe new specific forms of reproduction of social relations within both dependent social formations and those belonging to the capitalist "core?" And how is the new situation reflected on the level of social practices and class struggles?

It is my contention that some tentative answers to these questions can be offered by drawing on Nicos Poulantzas's analysis of what he identified as the new phase of imperialism. In this period, interimperialist antagonisms are present not only in "interstate" political confrontations, but also—and I would add mainly—*within* all countries concerned, dependent or not. The phenomenon of the "internal reproduction" of imperialist antagonisms is crucial in this connection. No longer can one speak, in Lenin's terms, of a geographical partition of the globe into more or less defined zones of imperialist influence and dominance. The growing mobility of capital and new productive and information technologies have led to a concomitant mobility and fluidity of the economic bases of accumulation and exploitation. Direct exploitation of labor can potentially be pursued by capital in almost all countries simultaneously, but under very different conditions.

This tendential "deterritorialization" and destabilization of exploitative forms, already anticipated in the 1970s but considerably accentuated since, has been accompanied by a universal rise of the rate of exploitation, which has been countering the tendency of the rate of profit to fall. At the same time, the period of *national* Keynesian welfare states with differentiated norms of redistribution has come to a close in the face of a new orthodoxy intent on reversing all welfarist trends on a *universal* scale. In all developed countries, including the metropoles, and even more so in dependent formations, economic inequality is rising rapidly. Simultaneously, socially accepted "tolerance levels" of unemployment, poverty, and misery have been rising everywhere. When, in countries like Spain, a quarter of the active population is *registered* as unemployed, one may well ask at what point the "acceptable" or "inevitable" begins and ends, and whether there are *normatively determined limits* to exploitation and misery. What seemed to be socially unthinkable some years ago is now accepted as a matter of course. On the level of political representation, internalized "social equilibriums" are being rapidly supplanted by what are now seen as "sociotechnological equilibriums." Ethical controversies and policy considerations are being recast in terms of, and in some cases supplanted by, purely functional, performative considerations. It is no exaggeration to say that, against all expectations, economic inequality and massive unemployment do not seem to be important political issues anymore.

In what follows, I touch very briefly on four specific points that, even if more elaborately analyzed by Poulantzas, are far from being absent from Miliband's problematic: first, the question of the precipitous decline, or even structural impossibility, of a "national bourgeoisie" capable of retaining a relatively autonomous basis of capital accumulation, and of the new resulting internal equilibriums in the dominant power blocs; second, the growing fragmentation of the laboring population into numerous, mobile, differentiated, and largely antagonistic fractions, with all that this implies for the process of dislocation and disorganization of traditional forms of class struggle; third, the new functions of the capitalist state, which, in its increasingly authoritarian form, assumes overall reproductive responsibility by means of a growing *regulation of the deregulation process* (this is generating an unprecedented fusion, or confusion, of the state's economic and ideological functions); fourth, the new developing forms of articulation between the various state apparatuses and the professional political personnel occupying their summits, on the one hand, and the representatives of big capital, on the other.

The National Bourgeoisie

All these issues are linked to the traditional territorial fragmentation of the world into relatively coherent "national" social formations in the specific context of which capitalist social relations are materialized and reproduced. Obviously, territoriality itself has not evaporated. Indeed, the internationalization of relations of production can by no means be understood to imply that economic activities take place in a transterritorial class vacuum. Exploitation must always take place somewhere—in other words, within the territories of specific societies organized as sovereign states. Whatever the organizational forms taken by accumulation, their concrete operationalization must remain by definition "domestic."

Thus, irrespective of the processes and mechanisms employed by capitalists in their search for profit, the main question to ask must concern the various forms of social activity of the bourgeoisie, or fractions thereof, within the given domestic socioeconomic environments. If the constitution of domestic power blocs and their internal antinomies and political antagonisms can only be properly understood in conjunction with their transterritorial entrepreneurial capacities, they must nonetheless also always operate within definite borders, however loose their dependence on internal markets may be. Even if capital may be controlled in the ethers, it must be accumulated on earth.

In this respect, Poulantzas proves to have been quite prophetic. The pertinent question is, In what sense can the nationally operating capitalist forces be "national" at all? Conversely, we are obliged to ask ourselves about the limits of *accumulative autonomy* of the dominant fractions of capital within national formations. Poulantzas underlined the gradual decline of traditionally autonomous national fractions of the capitalist class. Against the prevailing positions on the left in the early 1970s, not only did he pin down the decline and historic supersession of the accumulative autonomy of national bourgeoisies, but he also insisted on the necessity of a new concept, the "domestic bourgeoisie." In contrast to both the national bourgeoisie and the comprador bourgeoisie, the new concept served to denote the emerging and thereafter dominant fraction of a domestically operating capital that was already permeated by, and was thus reproducing, "external" interimperialist contradictions. In other words, it was becoming obvious already in Poulantzas's time that there could no longer be a dominant fraction of the domestic ruling classes that might continue the accumulation process within the narrow horizon of the domestic market.

Indeed, it is by now clear that with the partial exception of the United States, Japan, and, to a lesser extent, some European countries, there is less and less a question of autonomous national bourgeoisies. Globalization has brought about a *further* restriction on the accumulative autonomy of immobile domestic capital. This is evident in the proliferation of new developments that are undermining the traditional organization, technologies, and strategies employed by national firms. The spread of horizontal and vertical joint supranational ventures, the prevalence of transterritorial technological and information networks, and the total liberation of trade and capital movements have transformed the competitive horizon of domestic capitalists. In this changing environment, the contradictions and antagonisms of international capital are now directly present within national socioeconomic formations. Transnational concentration has reached previously unheard-of levels. At the end of the 1960s, the two hundred largest multinational firms controlled 17 percent of the gross world product. By now, their activities are estimated to be of the aggregate order of eight trillion dollars annually, almost one-third of the planet's revenue.

Nevertheless, a major problem remains unresolved. The dominant discourse on globalization tends to neglect the fact that the process is neither unambiguous nor conceptually clear. On the one hand, it refers to forms of transterritorial mobility, to the vertical or horizontal integration of productive activities and to mechanisms of international capital circulation. On the other hand, globalization refers to new joint forms of control and to new strategies of capital accumulation. The two facets are certainly interrelated, but not identical. Organizational transterritorialization does not necessarily bring about any kind of supranational transterritorial control. Metropolitan imperialist centers that remain ideologically, politically, and economically bound to their national contexts compete for world hegemony. Even if accumulation tactics are delocalized, power strategies are still organized on the basis of definable interimperialist antagonisms, all the more so as long-term advantages seem contingent on a relative military, economic, political, and symbolic strength that can be represented and made use of only on the level of organized national territories. In this sense, deterritorialization is by no means incompatible with intensified interimperialist struggle.

Indeed, to the extent that national states are not abolished, there can be no deterritorialized imperialism. If the fragmentation of organized political systems can be instrumental in permitting and encouraging mobile and delocalized forms of accumulation, at the same time, these organized state entities provide the framework for the universal pursuit of collective power. In this context, new contradictions have given birth to new and complex capitalist strategies. On the organizational level, growing mobility has brought about a worldwide free market, which is reproduced by means of a conjunction of purely economic flows and the interplay of hegemonic interventions of national territorial interests. It may well be that the dominant capitalist mode of production is gradually putting in place a new original political superstructure that more perfectly corresponds to the perceived long-term interests of the competing metropolitan nations. If the relative autonomy of small and dependent states has traditionally been challenged by direct diplomatic, political, or military interventions, by now utter dependence vis-à-vis the core countries is being enhanced and strengthened through the intermediation of what is conceived as a universally globalized capital that is free to impose its allegedly transnational will. Together with exploitation, imperialism is hiding behind the "neutral" logic of a supposedly uncontrolled transnational market logic. This may well be one of the most important overall ideological effects of the globalization discourse.

Following Poulantzas, it is now even more true that the contradictions between fractions of capital within national states are already "internationalized." As a consequence, the disarticulation and heterogeneity of the national bourgeoisies is further accentuated. Indeed, it may be doubtful whether any capital factions other than domestic and comprador actually exist. The recent dismantling of national plants by Renault, a public and therefore by definition national firm, is a striking sign of the new era. Poulantzas's domestic bourgeoisie may well prove to have been only a transitional form of organization in a period when the internationalization of capital was not yet completed. It is clear that the last remnants of these autonomous national bourgeoisies have been almost totally transformed into mobile and potentially delocalized "inter-national" capital. Even if ultimate control remains in the hands of firms and cartels maintaining strong national affiliations, and this is obviously the case in the strongest metropolitan capitals, both investments and profits are potentially increasingly delocalized.

A manifestation of this new situation is the total repudiation of policies advocating "import substitution." "National" capital cannot be protected anymore, for the simple reason that there is no material domestic structure that must be protected. Domestic deregulation is only an induced effect of international deregulation. Characteristically, the further liberalization of international trade institutionalized by the Uruguay Round—and, incidentally, the complete collapse of protectionist "anti-imperialist" third-world solidarities in the United Nations and elsewhere—was imposed against residual protectionist tendencies both in the United States and in Europe. Within the intercapitalist front, national bourgeoisies are being increasingly marginalized and defeated both economically and politically.

A word of caution is called for, however. It would, of course, be totally unwarranted to maintain that new supranational agencies directly reflecting the interests of world capital, such as the International Monetary Fund or the Group of Seven, have supplanted territorial state sovereignty, directly imposing the concrete terms of national economic interventions. Far from constituting themselves independently as new sources of autonomous political and economic power to which states are forced to submit, these agencies reflect state-sponsored processes of globalization. In this sense, the nation-state remains as always the central terrain of class struggle.

The case of Europe is instructive on this point. Despite the rhetoric of integration, European member states are far from having fused into a single ideological and organizational structure giving birth to a coherent and relatively homogeneous system of class relations. There still is no European working class or European national bourgeoisie. If the Maastricht Treaty imposed a certain number of common fiscal and economic policies, it carefully refrained from anticipating the eventuality of common social policies. The overall responsibility for reproducing internal class relations and equilibriums resides with national states. The Maastricht "criteria" only refer to quantitative macroeconomic standards of economic, monetary, and fiscal "performance." Despite the rhetoric on the dangers of social exclusion, the European Union does not demand that its members succeed in reducing unemployment, restricting poverty, or minimizing social exclusion. In no sense does the impending emergence of a monetary union imply the construction of a "social Europe." Social coherence, forms of exploitation, and class conflicts remain purely internal affairs. There still can be only one kind of political sovereignty: state sovereignty. And this is precisely the reason why the most pertinent political question today remains that of the relative autonomy of the *national* state.

Nevertheless, there can be no doubt that the internal forms of sovereign domestic political decision making have been substantially modified. More than anything else, the free-trade, austere public budgets and tight monetary policies called for by the Maastricht Treaty reflect the new limits of the autonomy of responsible bourgeois states and the power blocs they are called on to represent. They also reflect an incapacity, self-induced or otherwise, to imagine autonomous forms of domestic planning and economic intervention.

Indeed, the mobility of capital is so overwhelming that all locally bound investment decisions are increasingly dependent on the adequacy of domestically secured rates of profit. Domestic productivity and exploitation rates can in practice not be raised other than by further squeezing "social costs." If they are to survive the growing competition, the dominant fractions of domestic capital (in alliance or not with fractions of mobile world capital) must always be able to disinvest and delocalize their activities, if need be. A territorially restricted capital can no longer compete with its mobile counterpart. And this is the reason why all capital is now capable of blackmailing the national system within which it chooses to pursue the accumulation process. Any substantial increase in the "social costs" of redistribution will result in the threat of capital flight.

The political responsibility of states is consequently geared mainly toward maximizing domestic productivity and exploitation rates on the terms of mobile capital. Once more with the partial, but significant, exceptions of the great American metropolis and Japan, investment forms adopted by big capital evoke the particular independence of the historically delocalized shipping industry. By dint of the fact that "flags of convenience," which permit exploitation rates that are not burdened with any but minimal social costs, are eminently present and available, wages and labor security will tend to be restricted everywhere. Free interterritorial mobility brings about a "free market" of labor power that is indirectly reflected in the general fall of the relative remuneration of labor. All the more so with the collapse of "actually existing socialism," now that the political risks of subversion, risks that impeded free universal mobility, have been effectively minimized on a world scale.

The Fragmentation of the Laboring Population

Transformations in the labor process and working-class organizations have accompanied these processes of capitalist restructuring. Scientific developments in cybernetics, automation, and computer science since the 1970s have contributed to an enormous increase in the productivity of labor and have rendered a growing fraction of the working population functionally redundant. Concurrently, the continuous rise in life expectancies and longer periods of education have increased the percentage of people technically and structurally excluded from the production process. The absolute and relative costs of social welfare, including education, have been constantly rising as a result—a development that, if not reversed, results in the "fiscal crisis of the state." Thus, the combination of the overaccumulation of capital, growing intercapitalist competition, and soaring social costs has led to a universal trend toward a "renegotiation" of the overall terms of labor contracts and for a concomitant reorganization of the exploitation patterns in the world economy.

Within this context, and in view of growing intercapitalist competition, post-Fordist strategies have pushed toward either actively circumventing or simply abolishing most traditional forms of labor protection. In more and more employment sectors, hours are becoming longer, job security is eroding, and the protection of the unemployed is greatly reduced. Labor power is rapidly regressing into its nineteenth-century prototype: it is, once again, seen as one commodity among others. The corporatist arrangements of the late 1960s to the 1980s were thought capable of eliminating class conflicts through the typical tripartite negotiations of labor with the representatives of capital and public authorities. It is becoming increasingly clear that the containment of labor struggles within such procedural limits was feasible only within the context of social formations where consensual redistribution was an open and generally accepted political and ideological issue. The capitalist system was being reproduced by means of a constant appropriation of a part of the overall gains in productivity by the working population.

Consensual redistribution and the presence of the working class within the power blocs of advanced capitalist societies is increasingly rare. The combined effect of a global reduction in growth rates and the deterritorialization of productive activities acted to disarticulate and disorient working-class organizations everywhere. The de-proceduralization of labor conflicts undermined solidarities and further disorganized class affiliations, threatened as they were by the adverse sociopsychological effects of the new technologies that transformed the subjective representations of organized productive units. Even more to the point, the gradual but uncontainable increase of unemployed and unemployable masses led to a further fragmentation of the working class. Consequently, technical and economic progress has been internalized in increasingly nonpolitical terms: working-class organizations, which had been previously led to believe that they would actively and permanently participate in the decision-making process and thus negotiate the overall terms of income distribution, were once more pushed to the sidelines. While still nourishing hopes for uninterrupted progress toward petty consumer paradise, they suddenly found themselves to be more or less ousted from the power game. Internal political systems were subsequently pressured to accept and regulate redistribution norms according to the dictates of the free market. This was only one of the developments signaling the spectacular retreat of responsible public initiatives into new forms of regulative inertia. States have been progressively unburdening themselves of the task of shaping both the present and the future. The responsible "pastor-state" is being rapidly dismantled.

The working class faces a genuine dilemma in its struggle to defend what is left of its postwar gains in the real and social wage. In the best case, organized labor may succeed in clinging to some gains from the previous era, such as free education and Medicare. In the worst case, labor seems obliged to accept, however reluctantly, that, with further redistributional demands considered an impediment to "competitiveness," the gloomy present must be permanently traded off against the doubtful hope of a sunnier future, or at least the doubtful security of the status quo. The uncertain temporal dimension of labor struggles is absolutely novel both in its strategic implications for and in its tactical effects on the ideology of the left. Flexible representations of time, flexible labor forms, flexible individual strategies, and the flexible internalization of social roles necessitate a flexible class consciousness and equally flexible forms of mobilization. Disorganized and uncoordinated activities have tended toward a further political and social fragmentation of the working class. Indirectly, the long-term strategy of the bourgeoisie, which has always aimed at dividing the working class into fractions, has thus met with a good deal of success. As a side effect, post-Fordist organizational realities have led to a growing and cumulative political segmentation and fragmentation of workers and dispossessed alike.

Meanwhile, growing numbers of desperate and largely unemployable masses are pushed toward adopting unorganized individual survival strategies. Predictably, the new forms of informal survival are closely tied to "postmodern delinquency" practices. New "illegalisms" are being constantly promulgated within societies where increasing police controls and extending penitentiary systems are becoming more and more crucial mechanisms not only of social control, but also of class regulation. The combination of the legal inviolability of social goods (transport, communications, energy, etc.) and of intolerant cultural attitudes (drugs, tobacco, homelessness, loitering, etc.) results in a deliberate and generally accepted "illegalization" of all demands from below as "public nuisance." The threat of social and political marginalization permits the exacerbation of a growingly systematized authoritarian control. After more than a century of paternalist regulation, the main forms of class struggles of the dispossessed and unemployable classes are thus becoming, if not illegal, at least "antisocial," and, consequently, apt to be energetically repressed.

If we were to define, with Poulantzas, political power as the "capacity of a social class to realize its specific objective interests," we should conclude that never before has the capacity of the bourgeoisie been so uncontestably ubiquitous. And, if Poulantzas's remark that "the reproduction of social classes is materialized in and by the class struggle at all stages of the division of labor" is as correct as his assertion that "the structural determination of classes is not restricted to places in the production process alone but extends to all levels of the social division of labor," then, it seems obvious that the political and ideological "retreat" of working-class struggles since the 1980s is a "pertinent effect" of the new phase in the process of reproduction of class relations. It is an effect that is not isolated within the strictly economic sphere, but is also determined by the remarkable ideological and political forms of the overall victory of the bourgeoisie.

The New Functions of the Capitalist State

Within this context, the tendencies described by Poulantzas in the early 1970s have been largely consolidated. The economic functions of the state are being progressively amalgamated with its repressive and ideological functions. In this respect, the rise of technocratic "developmental" authoritarianism may precisely be understood in light of the fact that the "interior" field in which it is called upon to operate is already circumscribed by the contradictions of the dominance of mobile inter-national capital. More and more, the main economic functions of the state must therefore be geared toward ensuring the institutional and ideological conditions of the internationally imposed deregulation of economic and labor relations, as well as to contributing to the general acceptance of the alignment of public policies to the norms of international competitiveness. As already mentioned, above and beyond the project of developing the national economy, the demand for unregulated competitiveness must reign supreme. In this sense, the most pressing ideological task of the state is to convince everyone of the need to deinstitutionalize and "desubstantialize" all previous forms of consensual negotiation of redistribution—that is, to *dis*incorporate social classes.

It is thus no accident that, irrespective of the ideological and political "colors" of the government in power, it is only within the strongest core countries (e.g., Germany, France, Sweden, Canada) that the new authoritarian techno-orthodoxy may still be somewhat resisted in order to maintain existing equilibriums. Weaker links in the imperialist chain, even if formally run by social democrats (e.g., Italy, Spain, Greece), are obliged to accept induced forms of labor division and deregulation much more unconditionally. As things stand, it is only in the few countries that constitute the hard imperialist core that domestic class contradictions can still be politically negotiated. Wherever "national economies" are weak, states feel obliged to deflect or simply neutralize redistributive demands.

In this respect, the ideological functions of the state are of crucial importance. Never before has the ideological notion of the international competitiveness of the national economy been more compulsively central. Under the auspices of the state, all ideological apparatuses (schools, media, parties, mainstream intellectuals, trade unions, etc.) are systematically geared toward the dominant developmental tenets, characteristically modified to suit the new imperatives. If long-term development is synonymous with deregulated competitiveness, the very terms in which the socially desirable is defined are fundamentally modified. In lieu of an "autonomous," "sustained," and "autocentered" national development—the overriding myth of the 1960s and 1970s—international productivity and competition now appear as the new objectivized gods.

The first preoccupation of state intervention is thus to convince people of the developmental ineluctability of "modernization" via technocratic deregulation. The restitution of the inherent "sovereign rights" of the market lurks behind all public rationalizations. It is no accident that in contrast to the social-democratic period, which relied on social, political, and ideological arguments, the burning issue of nationalizing or denationalizing industries and utilities is now seen uniquely in terms of its repercussions on quantitative economic "performance." Deregulation is the new dominant theme, and unlimited performative deregulation is not only a specific form of active intervention, but also the main ideological tenet that must prevail. Intervention in the deregulating process is, however, an internally contradictory process. The constant public attention needed to bring about appropriate institutional and legal reforms calls for increasingly authoritarian state forms. The state is present to ensure that the "national economy" is organized so as to compete with the other "national economies" under the best possible terms. Furthermore, this general assertion is made acceptable precisely because of its alleged technical validity. The obvious Hobbesian metaphor may be expressed in military terms: states are at "war," each to protect its national economy—the true enemy being, however, not other states, but each state's domestic subjects (i.e., its working class).

In this context, the concrete effects of competitiveness on the forms of class struggle, and even the question of who gains and who loses, may appear as irrelevant and "ideological." Regardless of the nationality of the bourgeoisie that is to profit from market deregulation, it should be encouraged to make full use of its class prerogatives. The main agents of class struggle are a deterritorialized and integrated bourgeoisie versus a territorially tied and fragmented working class. This "geosocial" imbalance is only the latest expression of the structural power asymmetry between capital and labor. And the exacerbation of these asymmetrical terms seems to impose new structural limits on the accepted forms of class conflict, as they must be secured, imposed, and legitimated by the state.

In this sense, as Poulantzas was the first to note, the internationalization of capital "neither suppresses nor by-passes nation-states, either in the direction of a peaceful integration of capitals 'above' the state level (since every process of internationalization is effected under the dominance of the capital of a definite country), or in the direction of their extinction by the American super-state." On the contrary, national states provide the necessary mechanisms and "take charge of the interest of the dominant imperialist capital in its development within the 'national' social formation." Indeed, on the material level, deregulation, labor fragmentation, productivity, and profit maximization can only be ensured within a juridically given territorial context. In this sense, far from dispensing with national states' functions and services, the extended reproduction of the accumulation of international capital is totally dependent on their constant intervention.

Thus, the institutional and economic prerequisites of capital accumulation rest on the national states' capacity to guarantee the new forms of accumulation internally. It is precisely in this sense that the political and ideological cohesion of social formations, still materialized only by and through states, provides the basis for reproducing the (interchangeable) coherent socioeconomic and legal environments necessary for any productive organization. The jurisdictional fragmentation of sovereign political formations can consequently be seen to correspond ideally to the interests of delocalized capital. Whereas the organized state remains a necessary mechanism for securing the external conditions of production and reproduction, these conditions are far better served if all states are separately induced to reproduce their internal institutional and ideological order on the universal deregulatory model. On the contrary, the eventual appearance of a universal democratic "metastate" could lead to the resurgence of political autonomies liable to curtail unlimited capitalist power.

The fragmentation of relatively autonomous sovereign territorial political jurisdictions thus corresponds to the interests of deterritorialized capital. If nothing else, this justifies Poulantzas's assertion that one should not *stricto sensu* speak of "state power": the "postmodern," "postindustrial," or "post-Fordist" national state system provides a perfectly suitable institutional and ideological setting for ensuring the reproduction of transterritorial forms of accumulation.

Relations between the Personnel of the State and Capital

Finally, the state of affairs just described has some further important implications for the objective forms of articulation between political personnel and big capital. This is one point at which the question of relative autonomy may be concretized and empirically substantiated. One of the central objects of discussion between Miliband and Poulantzas in the 1970s referred to the theoretical relevance of relations between the personnel occupying the "summits" of the state and big capital, respectively. Whereas Miliband insisted on the importance of demonstrating the bourgeois class origin of political personnel and their special class links to the management of big firms, Poulantzas completely disregarded class origin and underlined the objective character of relations between the ruling class and the state apparatus. Poulantzas was mainly preoccupied with the structural determination of state interventions; he considered that whatever motivations, behavioral tendencies, and personal links there might be between political personnel and big capital, the operation of these objective relations was a simple effect of the objective cohesion of public apparatuses, necessitated by their overall function.

On the epistemological level, I would tend to side with Poulantzas. Recent developments, however, may suggest new objective reasons as to why the "personal links" between capital and political personnel are henceforth not only empirically ascertainable, but, in another way, structurally determined, if not inevitable. Regardless of their class origin, and independent of whatever class allegiances they might feel, those at the summits of state bureaucracies are increasingly tied to the private sector. The objective cohesion of the state apparatus, including that of political parties, calls for new "particularistic" forms of structural articulation between high public officeholders and private capital. Indeed, it is my contention that, in a convoluted and indirect way, the new internalized functions of the capitalist state have contributed to a growing political and economic dependence of political personnel on capital.

Very briefly, this emerging tendency may be suggested in a number of points:

1. The universal domination of competitive instrumental rationality has led to a restriction of the economic policy options of most states. The growing disillusionment and depoliticization of the population at large is an immediate consequence. Most developed countries seem to be advancing in the steps of the United States, where the crystallization of political antagonisms does not immediately correspond to clear class alternatives.

2. An important result of this new conjuncture is the dwindling "internal" basis for financing political parties. Less and less are labor and professional organizations capable of mobilizing their members in collective actions aimed at intervention and struggle on the political level. Hence the prevalence of fragmented and individualistic free-rider attitudes—described as "natural" by liberal organizational theorists—in growing sectors of social life. Inevitably, contributions of funds and energy by individual militants are being drastically curtailed.

3. In a related development, political conflict is concentrated on secondary debates and cannot directly reflect well-established and internalized class issues. To the extent that earlier collective images animating political struggle have been rapidly eroding, political discourse is

suffering an increasing loss of substance. The social alternatives opened up by democratic political antagonisms must be constantly reiterated on the level of collective representations. In this sense, one may legitimately speak of a growing "theatricality" of internal political conflict, still organized in parties. Political competition, in which parties constantly struggle to increase electoral and ideological influence, is developing into a subsystem ever more detached from any social and class foundations.

4. However desubstantialized, controversies are becoming more and more expensive, in both absolute and relative terms. On the one hand, organization costs have soared far beyond available organizational resources. On the other hand, the very fact that the issues separating the main contenders for political power are becoming far less visible increases the importance of what is now termed "political communication." The everyday political game of propaganda and public image making is now an integral part of political life. Elections increasingly are won or lost not according to the relevance of issues that are increasingly beyond the grasp of the population at large, but as a result of the success or failure of pervasive public-relations activities. Persons and parties are thus forced to rely on expensive media coverage and on the services of highly paid professionals. On all fronts, the costs of democratic competition are accumulating.

5. If direct contributions are dwindling and costs are soaring, the democratic political-electoral game must be suffering an increasing deficit. To the extent that the costs necessary for the reproduction of the political system cannot be covered by the voluntary microcontributions of individual party members, and external financing becomes a functional necessity, the question of new sources of "political money" must inevitably be raised.

6. At the same time, an increasing amount of public decision making consists of making contracts with big business. Privatization, military expenses, public works, and all kinds of political choices, translating into contracts with the private sector, represent a growing fraction of public budgets. Obviously, deregulation refers to the capital–labor relation and not to the importance of public contracts, which, if anything, have been growing in inverse proportion to the restriction of economic activities directly organized under the auspices of the state. It is

no accident that interterritorial "bribes" are now not only widely acceptable, but also accorded tacit official approval: in most European countries, "unsuccessful" bribes are considered to be a legitimate business cost to be taken account of in domestic tax exemptions. Even if it is frowned upon, transnational corruption is officially legitimated as part of the game. Inevitably, the articulation between "domestic" public decisions and "deterritorialized" private profits is thus more structured and continuous than ever before.

7. Like all forms of capital, state-linked big business reproduces on the domestic scale all the contradictions and antagonisms of delocalized international capital. Competition for particularistic state favors and contracts is becoming wider and deeper. The "domestic" bourgeoisies, together with their international linkages, are engaged in constant (oligopolistically organized) struggles in the expanding international market for public works, contracts, licenses, and interests.

8. Against this background, bids from national and international firms tend to be accompanied by more or less open offers of payoffs. The question of *functional corruptibility*, endemic in dependent countries, has rapidly become an objective structural feature of most, if not all, state structures. Indeed, the gravity of the problem is reflected in the fact that, like the United States, most European countries have recently implemented severe restrictions on electoral costs. Public financing of parties and elections is only one of the solutions that has been proposed. However, numerous studies have demonstrated that official public funds can account for only a fraction of soaring political costs. Political costs are virtually unlimited and uncontrollable. Whether this implies a growing structural corruption of political personnel—a fact that not only seems obvious but is amply corroborated by empirical studies—or whether this constant input of resources from the private sector to public and party decision making is used exclusively to promote the organizational interests of parties and collective public entities, is irrelevant to my argument. The main point to underline is that, objectively, political personnel and parties seem obliged to solicit and accept large private "contributions" in order to reproduce themselves as communicationally viable candidates for public office. Apart from the question of corruption and all the normative issues associated with it, it is a fact that new systemic factors are pushing the political structure toward an

increased dependence on unofficial and usually hidden forms of financing. "Personal links" are in this way structurally determined.

This development, in turn, exacerbates the general disillusionment with democratic forms. If general depoliticization results in a growing dependence of political organizations on an uninterrupted flow of resources originating in the private sector, and to the extent that this new objective link between politicians of all shades and their respective (or common) economic "sponsors" becomes public knowledge, the depoliticization process will become cumulatively more pronounced. "Lobbies" and "sponsorships" are both functionally and organizationally integrated. By dint of their very success, the new forms of articulation between capital and top state personnel thus seem to be undermining general political credibility and further exacerbating both the financial deficit of the political game and its resulting financial dependence on capital.

Conclusions

What may be inferred from the preceding discussion is that what has changed is the specific *form* of articulation of a particular branch of the state—indeed, the most important and powerful branch, the elected political summit—and not the *principle* of the relation of articulation itself. The new dominant forms of capital accumulation on a world scale are precisely reflected in the new forms of relative autonomy of the capitalist state. The international tendency toward restricting the external regulation of capitalist competition has called for a concomitant circumscription of public decision-making processes within new limits. The symbolic and functional presence of national states is more necessary than ever for the cohesion of social formations at the same time that their economic and ideological interventions are far more "deregulating" than before. This poses new dilemmas for the successful reproduction of the state.

It may well be that one of the growing contradictions within the contemporary capitalist state resides in the novel discrepancy between the professed aims of the political personnel responsible for the regulation of deregulation, on the one hand, and the established state bureaucracy entrusted with the symbolical, juridical, and ideological cohesion of national social formations, on the other. Antagonistic relations between government and traditional public organizations—such as schools, local administrations, and health and welfare institutions—seem to be emerging on a scale that transcends the predictable response to threats to public services. Privatization and rationalization touch the core of what was the main institutional and political manifestation of the overall relative autonomy of a state apparatus guaranteeing social cohesion. The new obsessive doctrine of a quantifiable productivity applied to all organized state functions—from the judicial to the administrative and from the military to the educational—introduces a universal technical-economic measure of assessment to functions that were traditionally legitimized through their autonomous value. In a convoluted way, this may be seen to effectively diminish the relative autonomy of the state. Obviously, to the extent that market logic is introduced directly into the evaluation of public functions, not only is the internal system of organization tendentially transformed, but, more to the point, public services and functions are becoming detached from their original functions. Whereas the desirability of free urban public transportation was still an open issue in the 1970s, by now the debate is centered uniquely around the question of the possibility of running public transportation in "efficient" ways. The very principle of redistribution serving the needs of social reproduction is blurred by the notion that all services and mechanisms, private or public, must "naturally" bow to the technical prescriptions of profitability and competitiveness.

This development suggests another potential contradiction between the elected summits of the state personnel, who must direct the regulation of deregulation, and the rest of the state apparatus, which remains responsible for the day-to-day social and symbolic cohesion of society. On the level of representations, this contradiction may be summed up in the ostensible incompatibility between "public neutrality" and "particularistic preferentiality." These incommensurable principles must be actively reinterpreted by the state to open up new possibilities for a resolution. The state must be capable of taking preferential deregulatory decisions while simultaneously preserving the mask of bourgeois respectability. This is precisely what happens when the state summits and the organized political subsystem form direct financial links with capitalists in ways that uphold their assumed autonomy, while the normative "separation" between private and public still reigns supreme. The ideological consistency of the system must confront the growing discrepancy between the "neutrality" of the state and the functional dependence of its summits. Techno-authoritarian discourse provides a way out. But the price to be paid is the growing delegitimation of democracy. More than ever before, the social contract is reduced to an increasingly unconvincing procedural legality.

For all intents and purposes, it is capital itself that assumes the soaring costs of reproduction of the entire political subsystem in the narrow sense of the word: a new kind of *faux frais,* or false political cost, is thus emerging as a structural prerequisite for the smooth functioning of the state system. This fact largely explains why, as a matter of course, big capital offers direct and simultaneous financial support to all serious contenders for elected political power, regardless of ideological shade. For the representatives of the domestic bourgeoisies, divided as they are among themselves, the issue is not so much one of maintaining political personnel on their direct payroll, but rather, one of sustaining a system of political representation that is dependent on direct inflows of uninterrupted capital "subventions."

One may conclude that although relative state autonomy still remains important, this autonomy is more and more structurally selective. In the contemporary international setting, the overall function of national states is being rapidly reconfigured by pseudo-autonomous forms of articulation between the political and the economic. But this pseudo-autonomy is not reflected in the same way throughout the various branches of the state apparatus in all their growing interrelation and complexity. Henceforth, if the mass of the state apparatus, including the judiciary, is still governed by the overall class contradictions, and thus continues to intervene in the interests of overall social reproduction, state "summits" must assume the ambivalent but now essential role of imposing the required forms of deregulation.

Under these circumstances, *one might well speak of a differentiated relative autonomy, reflected in the internal contradictions between the various "branches" of the state apparatus.* It is precisely these contradictions that mark the character of the present phase. Indeed, if state summits function in ways that bring to mind the most schematic of Marxist formulations, one is more and more tempted to return to instrumentalist conceptions; the state's overall role must still consist in securing a minimum of social cohesion under the hegemony of the dominant class, a cohesion whose costs are by now mainly "political." In addition, one might add, the political and ideological dangers emanating from the political personnel's incapacity to reproduce itself in a visibly autonomous way is counterbalanced by the further fetishization of the professed technical and ideological neutrality of other branches of the state apparatus. The more obvious it becomes that the specific objective forms of articulation between the state summits and the bourgeoisie are increasingly ambiguous and suspect, the more it is ideologically fundamental to cling to the illusions of public meritocracy and technocratic neutrality. If possible, these internal contradictions between branches of the state, in respect of the forms of their relative autonomy, must be masked behind a wider techno-authoritarian discourse covering the entire function of what is still considered to be the public sphere.

I hope to have shown here that the newly crystallized forms of articulation between the political and the economic must be reexamined in view of the global effects of a growing noncorrespondence between the "national" scale of political-ideological organizations and struggles, on the one hand, and the "inter-nationalized" and deterritorialized scale of capital accumulation, on the other. In this respect, the national state, still the fundamental instance ensuring the reproduction of social cohesion, has been led to modify spectacularly the form of its specific interventions, as well as its functional role in neutralizing the dominant forms of class struggles, both on the economic and on the political-ideological level. In this context, new contradictions between the various components and functions of the state apparatus have appeared, endangering its internal cohesion. As a consequence, the ideological and political prevalence of the new dominant techno-authoritarianism assumes a paramount importance.

One of the main political consequences of the present conjuncture is that it has become clear that working-class struggles have entered a new phase and face unprecedented challenges. The contradiction between the national and international loci of class struggles has led to a growing disorganization and demoralization of the victims of exploitation. Obviously, I cannot suggest the ways in which these new trends may be overcome. But it seems to me beyond doubt that it is impossible for the various fragments of the working class to advance toward new strategies and tactics if the political implications of complex new forms of state intervention, and the concomitant question of the modes of its relative autonomy, are not once again given the highest priority. This alone, I believe, justifies the importance we must, once more, attribute to the contributions of and debate between Miliband and Poulantzas. The answers may not be there, but the questions are as urgently valid as ever.

III

Beyond Miliband and Poulantzas

CHAPTER TEN

Unthinking the State

Reification, Ideology, and the State as a Social Fact

Peter Bratsis

> The philosophers have only *interpreted* the world in various ways; the point is to *change* it.
>
> —KARL MARX, *Theses on Feuerbach*

After Marx first penned these famous words, we find that he did not stop "interpreting" the world or cease in his theoretical pursuits. Rather, he followed a very specific theoretical project that does not simply "interpret" but attempts to transform reality through a critical and demystifying understanding of it.[1] A "philosophy of praxis" (Gramsci) or "class struggle in theory" (Althusser) is the intended character of such a theoretical project; Marxist political theory takes as its goal the transformation of society through the production of a critical and subversive understanding of it.[2]

Does state theory succeed in advancing this goal of Marxist theory? Has state theory produced sufficiently critical and demystifying knowledge? Without doubt, the production of critical knowledge has been an explicit goal for state theory. For example, Ralph Miliband framed *The State in Capitalist Society* as a critical response to the pluralist hegemony inside and outside the academy (Miliband 1969, 1–7). Nicos Poulantzas intended *Political Power and Social Classes* to be for the political moment of the capitalist mode of production what Marx's *Capital* was for its economic moment, a rigorous and demystifying understanding of its specificity and dynamics (Poulantzas 1973, 16–23; Jessop 1985, 59–60). Even behind the presumed obscurity and theoreticism of their debate, we see that Poulantzas stressed the critical function rather than simply the methodological or epistemological content of Miliband's arguments. Although Poulantzas praised Miliband's critique of pluralist theory, he found the way Miliband does this counterproductive because Miliband ended up sharing most of the epistemological and methodological assumptions of the theories he attempted to refute (cf. Poulantzas 1969). This sharing of assumptions is counterproductive because it limits the questions Miliband can pose (his problematic) and in this way presents a limit to the critical content of Miliband's arguments (because he is unable to question various essential assumptions of pluralist theory). The essence of Poulantzas's critique of Miliband is that he fails to sufficiently demystify the state.

Unfortunately, almost all of Marxist state theory fails in this regard. This follows from the tendency of all Marxist theories to take the state as a given. Although state theory has placed great emphasis on explaining why the state does what it does (and in this area can be said to have succeeded in its production of critical knowledge), it has not taken the state itself as something to be explained. State theory has yet to explain the state by examining the processes that may serve as its causes and conditions of existence. As Bob Jessop has noted:

> Much Marxist theorizing has focused on the state's functions for capital; the better sort has examined its form and shown how this problematizes these functions; none has put the very existence of the state in question. (Jessop 1990, xi)

The strategic defect contained in this lack of interrogation is the tendency to reify and legitimize the state. This tendency in political theory was noted by Marx himself in his "Contribution to the Critique of Hegel's *Philosophy of Right.*" For Marx, Hegel's misrecognition of the state as universal and as possessing a privileged ontological status in relation to "civil society" functioned to legitimize the state. As Jean Hyppolite has noted:

> When, in turn, Marx criticizes Hegel for having opposed bourgeois or civil society to the State, for having arrived by deduction at the constitutional monarchy and Prussian democracy, giving them an aspect of the eternal, he is simply revealing an essential tendency of Hegelian thought, which is to legitimate existing reality by conceiving it philosophically. (Hyppolite 1969, 108)

> The truly concrete subject, the bearer of predicates, is *man as social being*, who belongs to what Hegel called bourgeois society, and the State, which Hegel mistakenly took for the Subject, as Idea, is in fact a predicate of man's social nature. The Idea—in reality, the product of man's social activity—appears in Hegel as the authentic which results in "a mystery which degenerates into mystification," as Marx puts it. (Ibid., 112)

Of course, no Marxist state theorist says that the state is an a priori, that its existence is not a product of social relations or practices, that it does not have a cause. Nonetheless, state theory acts "as if" this were the case. Precisely because state theory does not explain the existence of the state, because state theory takes the state as its point of departure and fails to demystify its existence through explanation, all state theory proceeds "as if" the state were indeed a universal a priori predicate to our social existence rather than a product of our social existence. This "as if" act by state theory is a fetishizing act (and thus reifies the state) because it endows the state with ontological qualities not its own and abstracts its existence from the realm of social relations.[3]

The State as Subject and as Object

This reification is present in both dominant conceptualizations of the state within Marxist state theory: the state-as-subject and the state-as-object. State-as-subject conceptualizations understand the state to be a social actor distinguished by a common subjectivity among the people who occupy state positions. In its Leninist form, this conceptualization considers the state to be an appendage of the bourgeoisie by virtue of the bourgeois class consciousness of those who "control" the state (cf. Lenin 1932). For Lenin, the state functions as an "instrument" of class domination.[4] For the state to be an instrument of class domination, however, a certain class consciousness must be presupposed on the part of those who control state power. The "instrument" is not the state in this context, but state power. This is to say, in all state theories that conceive of state power as a thing (instrumentalist theories of power), the state institutions must be unified by a given subjectivity for state power itself to gain coherence and unity.

The most coherent example of this Leninist concept of the state-as-subject can be found in Miliband's *The State in Capitalist Society.* Miliband concurrently emphasizes the institutional fragmentation of state power and the importance of the "state elite" in giving direction and coherence to this potentially fragmented power:

> There is one preliminary problem about the state which is very seldom considered, yet which requires attention if the discussion of its nature and role is to be properly focused. This is the fact that "the state" is not a thing, that it does not, as such, exist. What "the state" stands for is a number of particular institutions which, together, constitute its reality, and which interact as part of what may be called the state system. (Miliband 1969, 49)

> These are the institutions—the government, the administration, the military and the police, the judicial branch, sub-central government and parliamentary assemblies—which make up "the state," and whose inter-relationship shapes the form of the state system. It is these institutions in which "state power" lies, and it is through them that this power is wielded in its different manifestations by the people who occupy the leading positions in each of these institutions. (Ibid., 54)

Having established the fragmented nature of the state and state power, emphasis must be placed on the agency of this state elite in uniting these institutions and "wielding" state power in a coherent way. The consciousness of this state elite is what must be examined, for Miliband, if we are to be able to characterize the state as a coherent actor. To these ends, he examines the class origins, social networks, and educational attributes that characterize all state elites. It is on this basis that he is able to conclude that the state is a bourgeois actor:

> The reason for attaching considerable importance to the social composition of the state elite in advanced capitalist countries lies in the strong presumption which this creates as to its general outlook, ideological disposition and political bias. (Ibid., 68)

> What the evidence conclusively suggests is that in terms of social origin, education and class situation, the men who have manned *all* command positions in the state system have largely, and in many cases overwhelmingly, been drawn from the world of business and property, or from the professional middle classes. (Ibid., 66)

Thus, a central concept for Miliband is what he calls "bourgeoisification," which he uses to argue that even those members of the state elite who do not come from the bourgeois class itself undergo a process of education and socialization through which they learn to think like those who are members of the bourgeoisie.

In its Weberian form, the state-as-subject conceptualization considers the state to be a distinct actor by virtue of the bureaucratic rationality that unites its members and that provides a socially autonomous set of interests such members act to maximize (Block 1987; Skocpol 1979, 1985; Levi 1988). Unlike its Leninist counterpart, such theories posit the autonomy of the state from society because the subjectivity that unites its members is state specific and does not originate within society; state managers have a subjectivity all their own.

Notable contemporary versions of such arguments can be found in the work of Theda Skocpol and Fred Block. Block rejects more orthodox Marxist theories of the state because they assume a class consciousness among the bourgeoisie that he claims is reductionist and remains unexplained (Block 1987, 52–58). As a corrective, he puts forth an argument that does not rely on such assumptions and that, he claims, does a better job of explaining what objective processes determine why the state does what it does. In doing this, he privileges three groups—capitalists, workers, and the managers of the state—as being the principal agents behind state policy. Capitalists and workers are assumed not to have a class consciousness; they are guided by their individual economic interests. State managers are assumed to share a set of interests (namely, the preservation and expansion of the state), given their position within the institutions of the state, and are expected to act in ways that further these interests. This is to say that it is assumed that the individual interests of state managers can be reduced to their institutional interests (bureaucratic rationality). Similarly, Skocpol argues that the state is best understood as having interests of its own that make its rationality autonomous from the rationality of social actors (Skocpol 1979, 24–33).

The fetish in these neo-Weberian approaches is an institutionalist one. State managers, it is argued, share a bureaucratic rationality that explains the given subjectivity of this state-as-actor. This rationality (or, subjectivity) is a function of the institutional position of these individuals. If you or I occupied one of these positions, it would be expected that we too would then "think" and "act" in accordance with this bureaucratic rationality. Thus, we could say that the state as an autonomous social agent exists when those individuals who occupy the positions of state managers share a bureaucratic rationality and act accordingly. However, this relation between the position of individuals within the institutions of the state and their "bureaucratic" consciousness remains unexplained.

It is assumed that the state exists because it is assumed that any person who occupies an institutional position within the state acquires this bureaucratic rationality. At no point do Block or Skocpol explain how this actually happens and what conditions are necessary for this process to be successful.[5] Institutions become substituted as state managers. Such neo-Weberian theories talk about institutions acting "as if" these institutions were thinking calculating agents even though the Weberian assumptions they share place the methodological emphasis on individuals qua state managers and not institutions as such.[6] In this way, neo-Weberian theories of the state-as-subject are guilty of presupposing and reifying the state.

Leninist theories are also guilty of this presupposition and reification because they presume that the individuals who "control" the state share a class consciousness without explaining how this may happen and what conditions are necessary for this process to be successful. A direct correspondence between class origins and consciousness is assumed but never explained or understood.[7] The state-as-subject is presumed by such theorists and the state gains the appearance of an entity that exists beyond the society itself because its existence is not grounded upon any particular set of social practices or conditions.

State-as-object definitions reduce the state to a set of institutions that constitute the site of political struggle and antagonism between various social actors. The state does not act but is, rather, a material site acted upon. Such definitions are common to structuralist theories of the state (or, theories that share a relational theory of power). The early work of Nicos Poulantzas and that of Louis Althusser are prime examples of this concept.

In such formulations, the state and its functions are determined by the reproductive requisites of the given social whole. The state exists as a region of any given social formation and functions according to the needs of the social formation to reproduce its constitutive relations (structure) (see Althusser 1969, chap. 3). In Althusser's formulation, this is accomplished by the combination of the ideological and repressive state apparatuses, which function to secure and reproduce the necessary ideological dispositions and coerce the dominated classes (Althusser 1971). In Poulantzas's version, this is accomplished through a relatively autonomous state that functions to unify capitalists into a coherent class and to separate the working class into individuals (Poulantzas 1973). In both cases, this is a product of class power being mediated through state institutions and forms.

These theories also reify the state because they take it to be a logical necessity that functions according to some omnipotent knowledge of the reproductive needs of capitalism. The state exists as one of the assumed three regions of all social formations (the economic, the cultural/ideological, and the political), whose functions are overdetermined by its relations to the social whole (structural causality). As such, these theories not only fail to question the historical, and thus contingent, material conditions that the existence of the state is grounded upon, but, in formalist fashion, present arbitrary and purely analytical distinctions (political, cultural, economic) as corresponding to real and ontologically privileged relatively autonomous spheres of society.[8]

A Note on Philip Abrams and Ontology

This tendency for state theory to reify the state had been noted by Philip Abrams (1988) in an article, originally written in 1977, that has, unfortunately, engendered little attention from state theory. He argued that political sociology, particularly Marxist state theory, has reified the state by presenting it as something that exists in the strong sense of the term. For Abrams, the true mode of existence of the state is not material but ideological; the state does not exist, what exists is the belief that the state exists. The obvious reason for this misrecognition, Abrams argues, is its legitimating function of concealing the true, class basis and functions of political power.

> The state is, then, in every sense of the term a triumph of concealment. It conceals the real history and relations of subjection behind an a-historical mask of legitimating illusion; contrives to deny the existence of connections and conflicts which would if recognized be incompatible with the claimed autonomy and integration of the state. (Abrams 1988, 77)

Abrams's critique is at once a great advancement and a regression. His critique was the first to take contemporary political inquiry to task for its failure to question the existence of the state and his assertion that the belief in the existence of the state is a fundamental and neglected issue is an important political and theoretical challenge. Nonetheless, the methodological tone and implications of his argument are, in many ways, a regression within social inquiry. By asserting that the state does not exist, by assuming that the belief in the state's existence is simply an illusion, Abrams fails to recognize the state as a social fact, as something with social existence. The important question in regard to the state's existence is not a yes or no ontological one. The important question, as indirectly indicated in the introduction, is not whether or not the state exists per se but whether it exists as a social or a natural fact. The critical task of state theory is to explain and demystify the processes and practices that produce the social existence of the state and thus to negate the state's claim to universality and naturalness.

On this issue, Abrams would have greatly benefited from going back to Marx and Weber or forward to Deleuze and Guattari. Rather than separate the material existence of a given object from the "belief in its existence" or the abstract categories that refer to it, as Abrams does, all of the foregoing theorists emphasize the function of such categories toward the social existence of an object. Marx's analysis of economic categories illustrates this point quite well (Marx 1970, 205–14). Marx asserted that conceptual categories are not simply neutral references to some already (non)existing object but are an integral part of the object itself (cf. Ollman 1971, chap. 2):

> Just as in general when examining any historical or social science, so also in the case of the development of economic categories is it always necessary to remember that the subject, in this context contemporary bourgeois society, is presupposed both in reality and in the mind, and that therefore categories express forms of existence and conditions of existence—and sometimes merely separate aspects—of this particular society, the subject. (Marx 1970, 212)

Weber's famous definition of the state reveals this point if we read it carefully. What is particular to the state is not violence or its territorialization but the legitimacy of such violence and dominating command-obey relationships: "If the state is to exist, the dominated must obey the authority claimed by the powers that be" (Weber 1958, 78). If violence must be legitimate in order for the state to exist, then the cognitive and affectual processes that create this legitimacy must be of primary interest. On this issue Weber, like Marx, stresses the necessity to understand the objectifying function of categories in the production of what we take to be reality:

> It is necessary for us to forego here a detailed discussion of the case which is by far the most complicated and most interesting, namely, the problem of the logical structure of the *concept of the state*. The following

> however should be noted: when we inquire as to what corresponds to the idea of the "state" in empirical reality, we find an infinity of diffuse and discrete human actions, both active and passive, factually and legally regulated relationships, partly unique and partly recurrent in character, all bound together by an idea, namely, the belief in the actual or normative validity of rules and of the authority-relationships of some human beings towards others. (Weber 1949, 99)

> So-called "objectivity"—and Weber never speaks of objectivity except as "so-called" and in quotation marks—"rests exclusively on the fact that the given reality is ordered in categories, which are *subjective* in the specific sense that they constitute the *precondition* of our knowledge and are contingent upon the presupposition of the value of that particular truth which only empirical knowledge can give us." (Lowith 1993, 53–54)

From this, we could deduce that the existence of the state is contingent on the meaning-creating function of such objectifying categories and that these objectifying processes are what must be understood if we are to understand the material basis of the state. Indeed, Deleuze and Guattari, from a radically different epistemological position, have come to exactly the same conclusion:

> There is thus an image of thought covering all of thought; it is the special object of "noology" and is like the State-form developed in thought.... It is easy to see what thought gains from this: a gravity it would never have on its own, a center that makes everything, including the State, appear to exist by its own efficacy or on its own sanction. But the State gains just as much. Indeed, by developing in thought in this way the State-form gains something essential: a whole consensus. Only thought is capable of inventing the fiction of a State that is universal by right, of elevating the State to de jure universality. (Deleuze and Guattari 1987, 374–75)

Of course, these qualifications do not take us very far from Abrams's argument on the importance of explaining the state idea and of noting its delusional effects. The whole set of these concerns becomes recast, however, because the state idea is no longer a mask, "irrational" belief, or false consciousness on the part of those (other than the bourgeoisie, for whom this belief is of great benefit) who believe in it. The state idea is concurrent with the real qua social existence of the state. For example, a great deal of Abrams's claim that the state does not exist derives from his assertion that there is no unity of "state"-institutions that would constitute them as a state:

> We may reasonably infer that the state as a special object of social analysis does not exist as a real entity.... Political institutions, especially in the enlarged sense of Miliband's state-system, conspicuously fail to display a unity of practice—just as they constantly discover their inability to function as a more general factor of cohesion. Manifestly they are divided against one another, volatile and confused. (Abrams 1988, 79)

The assertion that there is no unity of practice between state institutions, by no means a "reasonable inference," presupposes that such a unity could only be the outcome of something inside each institution, some kind of state essence or unity of purpose, that unites them in a substantive way. At the least, Abrams assumes, in surprisingly unhistorical fashion, that state institutions inherently cannot function in a coherent way. This conclusion, however, conflicts with the assumed dominance of the state idea. The conclusion that there is or is not a unity of practice is contingent on our subjective determination of what constitutes a unity of practice. The state idea may create a unity of practice and solidify the role of the state as a factor of cohesion by creating points of view and cognitive categories among citizens and state managers that do function as factors of cohesion and do result in there being a unity of practice. If we believe in the state idea, the state has achieved its function as a factor of cohesion and its practices will be judged to be united given the appropriate categorization of them. Even things as apparently unrelated as wine and sociology may be united by the placing both under the category "French."

A related shortcoming is Abrams's lack of explanation regarding the propensity of people to believe in the state idea. We are left with the image of members of the dominated classes foolishly believing in a fiction put forth by bourgeois propagandists. That even Marxist theorists should have engaged in this reification and misrecognition is in need of explanation and is obviously a crucial part of any attempt to explain the state idea. When Abrams does attempt to explain the propensity of theorists to reify the state, he makes the argument that the belief in the state idea results from some methodological mania and strategic irrationality:

> it is worth considering why marxism generally should have proved so susceptible to this sort of ambiguity. I think it results from an unresolved tension between marxist theory and marxist practice. Marxist theory needs the state as an abstract-formal object in order to explain the

> integration of class societies.... all [Marxist theorists] are hypnotised by the brilliant effect of standing Hegel the right way up, of discovering the state as the political concentration of class relationships.... At the same time marxist practice needs the state as a real-concrete object, the immediate object of political struggle. Marxist political practice is above all a generation of political class struggle over and above economic struggle.... In effect to opt for political struggle thus becomes a matter of participating in the ideological construction of the state as a real entity. (Ibid., 70)

As with the assertion that the state idea is a mask foolishly believed in by the masses, to assert that Marxist theorists tend toward irrationality, that they are "hypnotized," fails to identify any rational causes that might explain these tendencies. A more appropriate explanation for the belief in the state idea is attempted in the next section.

It is important to note that some of the problems identified so far have been at least partly addressed by Nicos Poulantzas in his later work and, subsequently, by Bob Jessop. It is with Jessop and Poulantzas that state theory begins to explain the existence of the state by looking to practices and strategies that might serve as its causes. This not only represents the beginning of a theory that does not fetishize the state but also addresses related shortcomings regarding the unity/disunity of institutions. With Abrams as with state-as-subject theorists (Miliband, Block, Skocpol...), the unity/disunity of the state was assumed. As can be noted from the discussion in the next section, Poulantzas and Jessop understood the substantive unity of state institutions to be historically contingent and thus an empirical question that cannot be assumed away. This advancement coincides with Poulantzas's movement away from the more formalistic elements of structuralism and his subsequent definition of the state as a social relation.

The State as a Social Relation

There is no question that Poulantzas's most famous concept, "the relative autonomy of the capitalist state," tends to be among the least understood. In part, this confusion stems from comparing the concept of relative autonomy to neo-Weberian claims that the state has complete autonomy from society, the resulting assumption being that relative autonomy must imply a limited version of that argument—some, but not complete, autonomy from society. Poulantzas never implied any autonomy of the state from society (he even rejects the state–society dichotomy). Relative autonomy always referred to autonomy from particular class interests, not society as a whole. For this reason, political power is always class power; there is no "state" power in the sense of a power separate or autonomous from social classes.[9] The conceptual problem was to understand how the state can act against some narrow or short-term interests of capitalists in order to act in their general or class interests. In *Political Power and Social Classes,* Poulantzas explains relative autonomy as an outcome of structural causality; the multiple relations of the political to the social whole overdetermine its functions and it will have a relative autonomy vis-à-vis the economic and cultural moments of the social whole because they all affect each other and, thus, will also have a relative autonomy from particular class interests because only in this way can the social whole be reproduced. This explanation was quickly abandoned, however, and Poulantzas's definition of the state-as-object (or region, as he would term it) was replaced with the definition of the state as a social relation.

Poulantzas defined the state in *State, Power, Socialism* as

> *a relationship of forces, or more precisely the material condensation of such a relationship among classes and class fractions, such as this is expressed within the State in a necessarily specific form.* . . . by grasping the State as the condensation of a *relationship,* we avoid the impasse of that eternal counterposition of the State as a Thing-instrument and the State as a Subject. (Poulantzas 1978, 129)

This definition should be combined with Poulantzas's class ontology where classes are to be found only as class struggles and practices: "social classes do not firstly exist as such, and only then enter into a class struggle. Social classes coincide with class practices" (Poulantzas 1975, 14). This represents Poulantzas's attempt to move away from class in-itself and for-itself definitions because social class is a product neither of academic definition nor of the subjective dispositions of "class" actors. Poulantzas's definition of state and class leads to the conclusion that what he terms the "institutional materiality" of the state is a historical product of a multiplicity of class practices and struggles. This allows us to pose the question of what material causes and processes underpin the existence of the state. Thus, in contrast to previous theories of the state, Poulantzas presents a view of the state that does not reify it.

The explanation of relative autonomy and of the unity of the state institutions is revised in light of this definition of the state as a social relation. Relative autonomy becomes a product of the class struggles because, within and between state institutions, various classes and class factions are engaged in struggle, and thus no one class will have complete control of all the state institutions. The product of past struggles will be materialized in the state institutions themselves, their structures, rules, procedures, and so on. The class bias these institutions exhibit because of these previous political struggles is what Poulantzas terms, following Claus Offe (Offe 1973), structural selectivity—the selectivity the institutions display toward and against various possible laws and policies.

The historically contingent balance of forces between the classes represented within the state institutions (what Poulantzas terms the "power bloc") will dictate the particular degree and content of this relative autonomy. If a unity of the state institutions exists, it is to be found in the hegemonic position of one institution (and the class fraction that dominates it) over the other institutions. The hegemonic institution and class interests it represents is able to coordinate the actions of the other state institutions through its power over them as well as the corresponding agreements and concessions reached by the members of the power bloc. In short, the cause of the unity of the state and its relative autonomy is class struggle.

In *State Theory* (1990), Jessop offers the most recent and elaborate discussion within the trajectory opened by Poulantzas. He asserts that the state as a social relation can be analyzed as the site, generator, and product of strategies. First, understanding the state as the site of strategy implies substituting the Offean notion of "structural selectivity" for the concept of "strategic selectivity." Jessop argues that the concept of structural selectivity ignores the differential impact of the state on the capacity of class-relevant forces to pursue their interests; although the state may be more open to some policies and less to others, it does not display this selectivity irrespective of the ways class forces pursue their policy preferences. The concept of "strategic selectivity" brings out more clearly the relational aspect of this selectivity as a product of the relationship between state forms and the strategies that different forces adopt toward the state. In other words, strategic selectivity radicalizes the contingency of the ways by which the form of the state participates in the production of class domination; it is not only the form of the state that plays that role, but also the various strategies and their potential and actual success that condition this selectivity and allow us to identify it. In summary, states are not neutral sites with reference to political strategies of social forces, but are more open to some political strategies than others (Jessop 1990, 9–12). Second, the state is also a generator of political strategies. In order for the state to be interpreted as possessing substantive unity, it is not sufficient, Jessop argues, to establish its formal unity—this is the case with subjectivist theories. The unity of the state, the nature of its subjectivity, and its capacity to act are to be understood in the light of a reinterpretation of the role of state institutions as producers of political strategies. Third, the state's structure is not a set of functional imperatives determined by the societal whole, but it is the product of past political strategies and struggles:

> the current *strategic selectivity* of the state is in part the emergent effect of the interaction between its past patterns of *strategic selectivity* and the strategies adopted for its transformation. (Ibid., 261)

Neither Poulantzas nor Jessop, however, fully overcomes the epistemological limits of previous state theories. Although the concept of the state in Poulantzas is made radically contingent, class, class interests, and class power are assumed to exist as its necessary precondition; that is, Poulantzas never justifies why the practices that produce the state are necessarily and exclusively class practices. Furthermore, it is not very clear what types of practices and mechanisms translate the materiality of classes and class power into the institutional materiality of the state. Yet, by transforming the state into the point of arrival of state theory, Poulantzas's relational theory denies the state any a priori existence. The state exists, for Poulantzas, but its existence is a contingency of specific articulations of power relations.

In Jessop's strategic theory of the state, the inconclusive status of Poulantzas's concept of "social relation" is given clearer contours. He attempts to overcome Poulantzas's class reductionism by assigning materiality solely to institutions. Although these concepts are produced within an immanently contingency-oriented framework—thus denying the predetermined nature of functional imperatives and subjectivity—Jessop's threefold characterization of the state still reduces that concept to the institutional materiality of society. The state, therefore, can only exist when there is substantive unity among state institutions. But how are we to know what "state" institutions are? We could choose a point in time where the state-as-institutional order exists and identify its component institutions, which we could then label as "state" institutions. But, then again, how could we know if the state-as-institutional order exists if we do not know what institutions to look to in order to establish the existence and form of their unity? Obviously, at some point we must posit what "state" institutions are a priori. Ultimately, substituting the materiality qua objectivity of institutions for the materiality qua objectivity of classes does not fully overcome the problems related to Poulantzas's reductionism, nor does it fully overcome the epistemological limits of state theory because it still assumes the existence of "state" institutions, if not the state itself.

From the Reification of the State to Its Explanation

In his analysis of explanations of fire, Gaston Bachelard notes that the object of analysis itself often impedes the production of an objective explanation:

> Sometimes we stand in wonder before a chosen object; we build up hypotheses and reveries; in this way we form convictions which have all the appearance of true knowledge. . . . In point of fact, scientific objectivity is possible only if one has broken first with the immediate object, if one has refused to yield to the seduction of the initial choice, if one has checked and contradicted the thoughts which arise from one's first observation. . . . Far from marveling at the object, objective thought must treat it ironically. (Bachelard 1987, 1)

That the state has been reified by Marxist theorists cannot be a matter of chance or lack of thought. It must be symptomatic of a particular quality that the state possesses that makes it difficult to treat "ironically"; it must be symptomatic of the hold the state has over our theoretical and political imagination. The state is, for political theorists, what fire was for the alchemists of the premodern era. In both cases, the seductive power of the object over the imagination of those who attempt to explain it results in metaphorical and incomplete theories (ibid., 59–82). In both cases, myths and folklore are the privileged form of our understanding. From Prometheus and fire-bellied birds we have gone to tales of social contracts, George Washington, and the Battle of Kosovo.

If, as Bachelard argues, the experience of fire's heat, light, smoke, and so on, limits one's ability to explain it scientifically, then we could also assume that the source of our inability to explain the state in sufficiently objective ways (or, at least, in ways that do not reify it) is our experience of the state. We know from Marx, Weber, Mauss, and, especially, Durkheim that although, in our social existence, we develop commonsense understandings of various phenomena, the first goal of a social science is to break with these preconceived notions and reconstruct them as "social facts."[10] Perhaps a telling indicator of the difficulty of accomplishing this break in relation to the state is the difficulty of identifying "state" experiences. What is our experience of the "state"? Is it the delivery of mail? The presence of traffic regulations? The collection of taxes? The presence of national borders?

Weber, stating that "when we inquire as to what corresponds to the idea of the 'state' in empirical reality, we find an infinity of diffuse and discrete human actions . . . all bound together by an idea" (1949, 99), is not only startling from the perspective of what his concept of the state is usually thought to be, but is also suggesting the sublime quality proper to the state. If Weber is right, it is through the eye and mind of the citizen that the state comes into existence. Moreover, those characteristics of "human actions" that qualify them as inclusive of the state are not inherent to the actions themselves, but rather to the motivations and perceptions of these actions. The assertion that actions may contain within them something beyond their physical characteristics and that this something is to be found within the realm of ideas suggests, in more Marxist terms, that the state exists primarily as a fetish. Here the state emerges as a very different kind of object than that which we are used to. Fire, irrespective of cultural differences, education, ideologies, and so on, is experienced in the usual sense, as an object that, by way of our sensory perceptions, results in a feeling, a change in the physical state of the body: warmth, fear, pain, and so on. This is to say that the problem with fire is presymbolic, it is not a question of the way ideology, or even the symbolic order, maps the terrain of experience. It is not a quality of this or that culture that leads us to misrecognize fire, but rather it is a product of the material characteristics of fire itself that leads us to develop cultural artifacts and ways of thinking that make it difficult to develop scientific explanations of it. The state can never be experienced in such a way because the very categorization of a phenomenon as a "state" phenomenon is necessarily prior to its return in the form of a palpable confirmation of that initial categorization. There is no "state" experience prior to the existence and use of the category "state." Here, we arrive at Žižek's definition of a "sublime object." Beyond the physical characteristics of an object, an abstract quality, one secured by the symbolic order, can come to be ascribed to it—raising the functional status of that object to an acute level of ideological importance.[11]

The ideological and cognitive importance of the "state" in contemporary life is paramount. As Poulantzas notes, "we cannot imagine any social phenomena (any knowledge, power, language or writing) as posed in a state prior to the State: for all social reality must stand in relation to the State and to class divisions" (Poulantzas 1978, 39).[12] Even the most basic of social-scientific concepts, society, seems to be unthinkable without standing it in relation to the state; the state is already assumed as its opposite or its modifier. "Society" has meaning and specificity either in relation to the "state" (state-society or public-private) or in conjunction with a "state" as its modifying pronoun (American society, French society, etc.). These two uses of the state category—to map the internal and external limits of what is thought to be society—indicate the importance of explaining the state idea for any attempt to go beyond the spontaneous and ideological understanding that society has of itself.

Of course, the basic reason explaining the ubiquity of this type of categorization is its functionality toward guiding our actions and behaviors. Althusser may be right when he claims that the public-private distinction is only a distinction internal to bourgeois law, that there is no real limit or absence of the state in the name of the "private" or in the name of "civil society" (Althusser 1971, 144). But it is not a product of naïveté that people tend to think in terms of private-public or American society versus French society. These categorizations are of the upmost importance when filing tax returns, planning a trip, organizing a labor union, and so forth.[13] It is precisely for this reason that such concepts have to be rejected; for, although quite useful to our survival in bourgeois society, they are prescientific and limit our ability to explain the state because they compel us to constantly presuppose it in order to make sense of the world.

Based on the foregoing, we could go further and say that there is no one "state" idea at all. Rather, the state idea always has two distinct meanings. On the one hand, it refers to the production of the political community in national-territorial terms, mapping the "inside" and "outside" of society. On the other hand, it refers to the formal separation within society of political power from economic power, of "public servant" from "private citizen," of sovereignty from social agency.

What state theory has to do in order to explain the state is to explain the causes of these categorizations, the public-private and the domestic-foreign. Poulantzas's assertion that the state is the product of practices should be taken seriously and the material causes of the state idea should be sought. The identification of the practices that result in our "state" thinking, and thus in the existence of the state and the legitimacy of state power and forms, is the next step for the analytical and strategic progression of Marxist political theory; for, if we hope to subvert and overcome the particular spatial and temporal organization of our modern existence that Lefebvre (1991) terms "everyday life," it is imperative that we be able to identify and overcome the ideological effects that everyday life and its corresponding practices have on our consciousness and ability to think. Far from having completed its task, state theory and political theory as a whole are still in the infancy of coming to terms with the state and explaining it. Luckily, Marxist state theory has provided us with the normative foundations and quite a few conceptual weapons for our contemporary efforts to transform reality through the production of critical and demystifying knowledge.

Notes

1. Étienne Balibar notes this point in his discussion of Marx's analysis of the commodity form: "What, then, is Marx's objective in describing the phenomenon in this way? It is twofold. On the one hand, by a movement akin to demystification or demythification, he is concerned to *dissolve* that phenomenon, to show that it is an appearance based, in the last instance, on a 'misunderstanding'. The phenomena just mentioned (exchange-value considered as a property of objects, the autonomous movement of commodities and prices) will have to be traced back to a *real* cause which has been masked and the effect of which has been inverted (as in a *camera obscura*)" (Balibar 1995, 60).

2. Slavoj Žižek has summarized this particular component of Marxist thought: "In short, in Marxism as well as in psychoanalysis we encounter what Althusser calls *topique*, the topical character of thought. This topicality does not concern only or even primarily the fact that the object of thought has to be conceived as a complex Whole of instances that cannot be reduced to some identical underlying Ground (the intricate interplay of base in superstructure in Marxism; of Ego, Superego and

Id in psychoanalysis). 'Topicality', rather, refers to *the topical character of 'thought' itself:* theory is always part of the conjunction into which it intervenes. The 'object' of Marxism is society, yet 'class struggle in theory' means that the ultimate theme of Marxism is the 'material force of ideas'—that is, the way Marxism itself *qua* revolutionary theory transforms its object (brings about the emergence of the revolutionary subject, etc.).... In short, a 'topic' theory fully acknowledges the short circuit between the theoretical frame and an element within this frame: theory itself is a moment of the totality that is its 'object'" (Žižek 1994, 182).

3. See Lukács (1971, esp. 83–110) and Žižek (1989, chap. 1) for an extended discussion of reification and fetishization.

4. This understanding of the Leninist theory of the state goes against most categorizations of it. Most commentators focus on the claim that the state is an instrument of class domination and categorize Lenin's conception of the state as being "instrumentalist," that Lenin considers the state to be an instrument/thing/object (cf. Jessop 1990, 28). There is no doubt that Lenin is an instrumentalist, but, as I will argue, instrumentalist theories of power result in a state-as-subject conception of the state because only in this way can the unity of state institutions and the coherent function of state power be understood.

5. Skocpol makes some attempt to overcome this in her later work when she stresses the necessity that state officials share "a unified sense of ideological purpose" for the state to be an autonomous actor (Skocpol 1985). This, however, remains "outside" of her theory because she is unable to examine how this happens. It remains an unexplained external variable that, at best, qualifies claims to state autonomy by positing certain conditions that are necessary but not sufficient for such autonomy to exist.

6. "For sociological purposes, however, the phenomenon 'the state' does not consist necessarily or even primarily of the elements which are relevant to legal analysis; and for sociological purposes there is no such thing as a collective personality which 'acts.' When reference is made in a sociological context to a state, a nation, a corporation, a family, or an army corps, or to similar collectives, what is meant is, on the contrary, *only* a certain kind of development of actual or possible social actions of persons" (Weber 1978, 14).

7. Pierre Bourdieu's *The State Nobility* (1996) is promising in this respect in that, although not sharing the problematic common to this Leninist conception of the state, it examines the various institutions and practices (at least in France) through which individuals come to be constituted as part of the ruling class that manages the state. This work in many ways overlaps Miliband's emphasis on "bourgeoisification" but addresses the question in a much more detailed way and avoids the fetishizing assumptions noted earlier.

8. Gramsci noted the danger of confusing methodological categories with organic ones in his comments on economism: "The approach of the free trade movement is based on a theoretical error whose practical origin is not hard to identify: namely the distinction between political society and civil society, which is made and presented as an organic one, whereas in fact it is merely methodological" (Gramsci 1971, 160).

9. Even David Held tends toward this confusion of Poulantzas when he argues that to claim relative autonomy and to posit that all power is class power is contradictory: "There are, however, inconsistencies in Poulantzas's formulation ... where

he at one and the same time grants a certain autonomy to the state and argues that all power is class power" (Held 1989, 70).

10. See Bourdieu, Chamboredon, and Passeron (1991, esp. 13–55) for an extended discussion of this issue.

11. As Žižek notes, the most obvious example of a sublime object in contemporary society is money, with its corresponding fetishizing and cognitive functions (Žižek 1989, 16–21).

12. Cornelius Castoriadis illustrates this point when he argues that our understanding of ancient Greek political thought (especially the concept of the polis) is flawed because we are unable to understand without recourse to our modern categories (especially the state) (Castoriadis 1991, chap. 5). This shows not only that "only in relation to the state" can we comprehend social phenomenon, but also how the state reifies itself in thought, making it appear universal and omnipresent.

13. As Bourdieu, Chamboredon, and Passeron put it, "These preconceptions or 'prenotions'—'schematic, summary representations' that are 'formed by and for experience'—derive their self-evidence and their 'authority', as Durkheim observes, from the social functions they fulfil" (1991, 13).

References

Abrams, Philip. 1988. "Notes on the Difficulty of Studying the State." *Journal of Historical Sociology* 1: 58–89.

Althusser, Louis. 1969. *For Marx.* London: Verso Books.

———. 1971. *Lenin and Philosophy and Other Essays.* New York: Monthly Review Press.

Bachelard, Gaston, 1987. *The Psychoanalysis of Fire.* London: Quartet Books.

Balibar, Étienne. 1995. *The Philosophy of Marx.* London: Verso Books.

Block, Fred. 1987. *Revising State Theory.* Philadelphia: Temple University Press.

Bourdieu, Pierre. 1996. *The State Nobility.* Stanford, Calif.: Stanford University Press.

Bourdieu, Pierre, Jean-Claude Chamboredon, and Jean-Claude Passeron. 1991. *The Craft of Sociology.* Berlin: de Gruyter.

Castoriadis, Cornelius. 1991. *Philosophy, Politics, Autonomy.* New York: Oxford University Press.

Deleuze, Gilles, and Félix Guattari. 1987. *A Thousand Plateaus: Capitalism and Schizophrenia.* Trans. Brian Massumi. Minneapolis: University of Minnesota Press.

Gramsci, Antonio. 1971. *Selections from the Prison Notebooks.* New York: International Publishers.

Held, David. 1989. *Political Theory and the Modern State.* Stanford, Calif.: Stanford University Press.

Hyppolite, Jean. 1969. *Studies on Marx and Hegel.* New York: Harper and Row.

Jessop, Bob. 1985. *Nicos Poulantzas: Marxist Theory and Political Strategy.* New York: St. Martin's Press.

———. 1990. *State Theory: Putting Capitalist States in Their Place.* University Park: Pennsylvania State University Press.

Lefebvre, Henri. 1991. *Critique of Everyday Life.* Vol. 1. London: Verso Books.

Lenin, V. I. 1932. *State and Revolution.* New York: International Publishers.

Levi, Margaret. 1988. *Of Rule and Revenue.* Berkeley: University of California Press.

Lowith, Karl. 1993. *Max Weber and Karl Marx.* New York: Routledge.
Lukács, Georg. 1971. *History and Class Consciousness.* Cambridge: MIT Press.
Marx, Karl. 1970. *A Contribution to the Critique of Political Economy.* New York: International Publishers.
Miliband, Ralph. 1969. *The State in Capitalist Society.* New York: Basic Books.
Offe, Claus. 1973. "Structural Problems of the Capitalist State." In K. von Beyme, ed., *German Political Studies.* London: Russel Sage.
Ollman, Bertell. 1971. *Alienation.* Cambridge: Cambridge University Press.
Poulantzas, Nicos. 1969. "The Problem of the Capitalist State." *New Left Review* 58: 67–78.
———. 1973. *Political Power and Social Classes.* London: New Left Books.
———. 1975. *Classes in Contemporary Capitalism.* London: New Left Books.
———. 1978. *State, Power, Socialism.* London: Verso Books.
Skocpol, Theda. 1979. *States and Social Revolutions.* Cambridge: Cambridge University Press.
———. 1985. "Bringing the State Back In." In Peter B. Evans, Dietrich Rueshemeyer, and Theda Skocpol, eds., *Bringing the State Back In: Contemporary and Historical Perspectives.* Cambridge: Cambridge University Press.
Weber, Max. 1949. "'Objectivity' in Social Science and Social Policy." In E. Shils and H. Fink, eds., *The Methodology of the Social Sciences.* Glencoe, Ill.: Free Press.
———. 1958. *From Max Weber: Essays in Sociology.* Ed. H. H. Gerth and C. Wright Mills. New York: Oxford University Press.
———. 1978. *Economy and Society.* Ed. Guenther Roth and Claus Wittich. Berkeley: University of California Press.
Žižek, Slavoj. 1989. *The Sublime Object of Ideology.* London: Verso Books.
———. 1994. *The Metastasis of Enjoyment.* London: Verso Books.

CHAPTER ELEVEN

Global Shift

A New Capitalist State?

Stanley Aronowitz

At the turn of the century, in the shadow of the collapse of state socialism, what has been termed "global" capitalism has taken center stage in world politics. The unexpected emergence of social movements dedicated to, variously, throttling its power, overthrowing it, or reforming its more egregious features may be explained by the virtual free ride transnational capital has enjoyed since the 1990s. Workers' movements have been cut down to size, in some cases impotence. The once vibrant Green parties of Germany and Italy seem securely integrated into their respective electoral systems and now live on as a fig leaf disguising the worst side of neoliberal governments. Once tempered by the presence of Eastern European state socialisms, by national liberation movements in the colonial and postcolonial world, and by powerful working-class movements in advanced capitalist countries, international capital, buttressed by a powerful resurgent neoliberal ideology, moved boldly in the 1990s to reimpose market-driven trade relations, to partially abrogate the prevailing postwar social contract that kept unions at the state bargaining tables, and to strip the state of many of its regulatory and social-welfare functions. In the United States, the stripped-down state became a national security state as a combination of internalized terrorism and the threat of external terrorism reinforced its most repressive functions.

But in the late 1990s, the role of once hidden institutions of international finance and economic terror, the International Monetary Fund (IMF), the World Bank, and the World Trade Organization (WTO), became, under pressure from labor and social movements, sites of political contestation. Once viewed by activists and intellectuals as a distant shore, internationalism has gripped a wide array of trade unionists and social movements. To be sure, the labor organizations' concern for world trade issues is often motivated by protectionism. And rather than identifying the despoliation of nature with rampant capitalism (either in its so-called free-market or state-socialist forms), some ecologists view industrialization itself as a scourge and propose to extend regulation—in effect, to strengthen the state's regulation of capital's ability to consume unlimited national resources. Yet the fact remains that, after a decade of untrammeled attacks against living standards and on the material world in both advanced and third-world countries, in Europe as well as the United States, international capitalism has, for the first time since the early 1970s, come under scrutiny by popular forces.

In December 1999, more than fifty thousand demonstrators (twenty thousand of them trade unionists) descended on a WTO meeting in Seattle and, in the course of their protests, effectively shut down the meeting and much of the city. As if on cue, a coalition of environmental, anti-sweatshop groups, even some of the encrusted American trade unions, and an assortment of organized radicals have turned their attention to the WTO and the other visible international institutions of global capital. By April 2000, the scene had shifted to Washington and London, and, in 2001, to Genoa, where similar alliances staged demonstrations against these institutions and, unlike Seattle, were met with the full repressive force of the local state. Their demands range from some who advocate the abolition of these organizations to a variety of reforms, notably demands on the IMF and the World Bank to reduce or cancel the debts of developing countries, rigorous enforcement of fair labor standards and environmental protections as a condition for making loans or awarding favored-nation trade status, and, perhaps most significant, transparency in their deliberations and democratic involvement of nongovernmental organizations in their governance. In contrast to the reform demands, some now openly identified as anarchists and affiliated to organizations such as the "Black Bloc" named capitalism as the ultimate culprit, a step that went beyond specific issues and reform programs and, in turn, beyond the nonviolent strategic orientation of the reformers.

These events, which have electrified the left and scandalized the media and financial establishments, occur in the backdrop of a major debate in state theory. At issue is whether what is variously termed the "new" imperialism or, in Michael Hardt and Antonio Negri's terms, the emergence of a multinational Empire in which national states play a diminishing role, or simply a new plateau of international economic and political integration under American and Western European dominance, signals the demise or, at least, the advent of restructured but stripped-down nation-states. Or, as some have vociferously argued, all the talk of globalization is so much global baloney with a serious ideological intent: under the threat of capital flight and other forms of deindustrialization, including where to locate investment sites, to subordinate and otherwise contain working-class struggles. On this view we have not left behind the era of sovereign nation-states or interimperialist rivalries. Accordingly, class and other social struggles still occur in a distinct national context.

Without denying the importance of internationalization, as the theoretical debate emerged in the 1970s, Nicos Poulantzas weighed in on the side of those who argue that the national state is not only alive but also well and remains the principal site of class struggles as well as of international economic relations. Poulantzas's later work, *State Power, Socialism* (1978) and particularly *Classes in Contemporary Capitalism* (1978), where he talks of the imperialism question explicitly and at length, may be read as attempts to integrate a distinction between passive and active consent with a more precise understanding of the state in the framework of internationalization.

In *Classes in Contemporary Capitalism,* Poulantzas aligns himself, but only partially, with the Lenin–Bukharin theory of imperialism as an extension of competing national capitalisms but adds the salience of a classic interpretation of *Capital;* that is, in contrast to earlier periods, in which many Marxists understood capital investment and imperialist plunder to be a consequence of the search for markets and for raw materials but tended to presuppose and not explore the sources of imperialism in the logic of capital accumulation and capitalist crises, for Poulantzas contemporary imperialism stems chiefly from the internal contradictions (most notably the class struggle) within national capitalisms of the most developed countries. The export of capital is seen as a solution to the falling rate of profit, which, in turn, results from a rising organic composition of capital, which Marx called a consequence of capital's attempt to solve its problems through raising worker productivity by replacing living labor with machinery. The falling rate of profit thus stems, indirectly as well as directly, from the more or less successful economic and political struggles of the working class to raise living standards.

Thus does Poulantzas attempt to refute those such as Paul Sweezy, and especially Harry Magdoff, who hold to the view that imperialism results from the search for new markets and for raw materials and have assumed the more or less permanent mitigation of class struggle by consumerism, the production of waste, and perfidy of the labor leadership. Nor does Poulantzas support the thesis of *super*imperialism, which derives in a large measure from Rudolf Hilferding's turn-of-the-twentieth-century study *Finance Capital*, according to which international finance capital has become so organized as to eliminate, or at least seriously inhibit, interimperialist schisms and, owing to capital's ability to make concessions to a large fraction of the working class, it can reduce to the vanishing point prospects for world-transforming class struggles. In *Classes in Contemporary Capitalism*, Poulantzas invokes uneven development, which is essentially a temporal category that Lenin suggested to explain the persistence of these intercapitalist and international schisms in the late nineteenth century. In Poulantzas's reflection, the United States emerged from World War II as the most powerful world power. At the same time, he argues, a newly united Europe emerged in the 1960s as a formidable, although subordinate, challenger, thereby setting up the basis for sharper interimperialist conflicts. In short, although multinational capitalism has developed into a world system under American hegemony, it is not without deep fissures.

I want to make two observations here. If, as Poulantzas says, the state "condenses" capital's own contradictions (namely, the permutations of class struggles) and has become, historically, the means by which capitalist social relations of production are reproduced, and if class and other social and cultural movements are constitutive, not merely objects, of power relations on the terrain of the state, then we may say that, within the limitation imposed by its reproductive role, the state remains the chief arena of contestation rather than wholly an efflux of capital, let alone international capital. In fact, a corollary of this conception of state power is that the reproductive and the consent functions may be in conflict; for one of the crucial political shifts of the workers' movements throughout the past century has been to insist on power sharing *within* the state, even as they have deferred the quest for social power in their own name.

My second observation is that states are nation-states. There is, in Poulantzas's reprise of imperialism, no discussion of metastates consisting of multinational capital's own institutions. Or, to be more precise, in his critique of superimperialism, he implies that the thesis of the formation of an international capitalist class with effective political hegemony is mistaken. However powerful are international capitalist arrangements, the nation provides the framework for their realization just as it does for accumulated capital. Despite the prattle about world government and the consultative institutions such as the G7 and the European Union, which offer the shell of representative government but little substance, sovereignty is limited to national borders. Hence, until now, "politics" has remained national. In sum, the *social formation* always refers to the economic, political, and ideological relations of a specific geopolitical space whose boundaries of culture, language, and political forms define the nation. Thus, despite the call of the *Manifesto* for proletarian internationalism and its declaration that the working class has no country, we have no experience of citizenship that is transgressive of national states nor of an international working class capable of cross-national mobilization on a sustained basis. Whether the state is theorized as relatively autonomous, autopoetic (self-reproducing), or is held to be umbilically tied to capital, as its economic, ideological, or repressive agent, all state theories presuppose these conditions. If these conditions remain despite evidence of increasing international coordination among national capitals of differential capacities, the emergence of a truly global capitalism may remain, at best, a tendency, and always subject to the limitations of dominant national capital. However, the question is whether this formulation is a theoretical proposition or one that is rooted in a specific historical period; for Poulantzas insists on the periodization and historicity of forms of internationalization as well as the state. Capital may have, relatively speaking, some transhistorical features (the profit imperative, its tendency to expand beyond national borders, uneven development, and so forth). In this spirit, the question is whether the formulations of the 1970s hold in the period of deregulation, and especially in the era of global capital's ideological as well as economic triumph over its principal opponent, "actually existing" state socialism. What may have remained ambiguous and tentative in the 1970s needs to be reassessed in the postcommunist era when neoliberal tendencies have become dominant in national and international economic and political affairs. Although capital has always been, in part, international, and although Poulantzas's claim that U.S. economic power is, from the 1960s, increasingly challenged within the world system by competitors retains its validity (note the division among the Atlantic powers over Bosnia, Kosovo, and the Gulf War), it would be erroneous to overestimate the significance of these differences and infer a profound political challenge to the U.S. program. Moreover, to ignore mounting signs that transnationalism is progressively weakening nation-states is to miss the significance of unmistakable power exercised by the key institutions of global capital and of the emergent opposition. Although it is true that the leadership of these institutions is composed of finance ministers of the leading powers, especially the United States, and it is, for the time being, inconceivable that the bureaucracy at the helm of the IMF and the World Bank would take steps that directly contravened the will of the ruling circles of these countries, the question remains whether these imperatives are a permanent feature of global arrangements.

Before proceeding, it is important to take account of the liberalization of virtually all Western European socialist and communist parties during the 1990s. The social-democratic and labor parties have long fashioned themselves as parties of government by their broad abandonment of Keynesianism in favor of neoliberalism: they have signaled their willingness to consider measures to "reform" welfare-state protections by reducing benefits, renouncing nationalization of basic production industries as a political program, and reversing their temporary anticolonial stance of the 1970s and 1980s (see especially the despicable conduct of French forces under the command of Socialist Lionel Jospin in Rwanda). But the Communists, long the official opposition in France and Italy and a significant force in Greece and Spain, have responded to the end of Soviet rule and liberal hegemony by renouncing their own revolutionary aims and have declared themselves parties of liberal capitalist governance, and, in the case of Italy, changed their name to the Democratic Party of the Left to signify their altered intentions, and assumed the reins of the capitalist government.

It would be inaccurate to declare the death of revolutionary socialism in a world dominated ideologically as well as politically by big capital. What seems to have died is the close link between the parties of socialism and communism and the labor and social movements. The mass base of these parties is now purely electoral, and in this sense they have become bourgeois parties. In turn, although labor and social movements retain some ties with these parties and with the state, public employees remain state-builders, especially at the local level, the struggle has shifted away from the state to the transnationals themselves, and, when the state is brought "back in" to their strategic agendas, it is mainly to mount actions against the state and its new global institutions. For example, the direct actions principally by public employees and students in France in 1995 were directed toward opposing efforts to rescind elements of the postwar compromise between labor and capital in which workers renounced decisive political power in return for substantial money and social wages. And, as we have seen, the struggle against institutions of international finance focuses as much on their abolition or weakening as on efforts to reform them. In either case, the ideological and economic functions of the nation-state may not be diminished, but certainly are fundamentally different than they were in the regulation era.

Today we are witnessing the merger of the ideological apparatuses with those of repression. In the United States, the role of the doctrine of law and order and the penetration of terrorism as the crucial element of the political unconscious provided a popular base to the apparatuses of the national security state. But this popular base is race and class specific. Having certified youth alongside blacks and immigrants as the "other" is, in addition, profoundly generational. Consequently, it is no surprise to discover that anarchism, the revolt against the state, rather than social democracy has become cutting edge in this new struggle against global capitalism.

Unless a "United States" of at least the advanced industrial societies is able to impose uniform taxes for the purposes of maintaining legitimating services (in the Althusserian mode, some crucial ideological state apparatuses such as social security taken in the wider meaning of the term), the ideological apparatuses of the state (e.g., the social wage of which education and income guarantees are a crucial aspect) are everywhere in retreat. In order to maintain these functions, the tax base has to be relatively stable—which, of course, points to the link between accumulation and legitimation, even absent the state's interventionist role in the economic sphere, which, in any case, seems to be increasingly confined to the manipulations of monetarism rather than of fiscal policy. But global capital has betrayed little taste for shouldering requisite tax burdens and instead has made reverse distribution a condition of maintaining a base within advanced industrial countries. More to the point, transnational capital, the characteristic mode of capitalism since the early 1970s, has sharply challenged state sovereignty.

Globalization has signaled the more or less rapid dismantlement of most of the salient features of the regulation era: in many countries, this has led to the drive to "privatization." In the United States, we have seen the virtual end of major regulatory agencies such as the Interstate Commerce Commission, the Securities and Exchange Commission, and the antitrust division of the Justice Department. French and British privatization are proceeding apace as state enterprises are sold off and neither labor nor socialist governments are inclined to promise to return banks and industrial plants to the public sector. The same is even more evident at the local level within the United States. Although there are few publicly owned and operated utility companies, many states have deregulated electric and gas rates for commercial and home uses and have all but ended their once ruling power commissions; rent control, never strong outside New York and some California communities, is under siege; and, most of all, business regulations of practices such as "insider trading" and other investment restrictions are rapidly eroding.

The ideological attacks against the welfare-state institutions of the regulation era are no more powerful than in the United States and the United Kingdom. The question is whether the underpinnings are to be found *in both* the conflation by libertarians and conservatives alike of freedom with the market and the diminishing funds for public services at the local level produced by the increasingly narrow tax base resulting from capital flight, legal limits on taxation, and the simultaneous reverse redistribution generated by inequitable tax cuts. Some, notably economist Doug Henwood, have argued that capital flight and internationalization generally are overstated and have been deployed by labor's enemies to disarm the workers' movement. There is some justice in this allegation. But it seems myopic to deny or otherwise dismiss the palpable evidence that globalizing tendencies, always a feature of capitalist reproduction and development, have intensified since the early 1980s.

In the first place, many more corporations have become transnational in the scope of investment, in patterns of ownership and control, and through the large number of mergers and acquisitions across national boundaries. National states are increasingly held hostage to capital. The price of retaining plants, and therefore jobs and taxes to run governmental functions, is to withdraw the state's regulatory functions and to shrink the social wage. The state is still recruited to provide infrastructural goods such as roads and water, but not to own or regulate communications, including electrical and gas companies.

Second, the merger and acquisition movement has led to massive displacement of qualified labor since the stock-market crash of 1987, a tendency that continued well into the 1990s. Unlike Western Europe, especially Germany and the Scandinavian countries, which still have an extensive program of education and retraining for some categories of administrative personnel as well as industrial labor, the United States has provided only minimal support. Even training and placement services are largely privatized. In this connection, the emergent federal programs of education aid that were a characteristic feature of the temporary enlargement of the U.S. welfare state in the 1960s have been halted and reversed. As is well known, state and local communities are once more held responsible for education and training at all levels. With the decline of federally supported research, public universities and colleges find themselves at the mercy of an overtaxed electorate as well as right-wing ideologues who, in the shadow of the reversal of fortunes of Democratic state parties, have entered boards of trustees of state institutions on a large scale. At the same time, the local tax base is simply unable to address education and health needs.

Rather than focusing on the state's repressive functions, both Louis Althusser and Poulantzas and the Frankfurt School emphasize the significance of the ideological apparatuses or, in another vernacular, the legitimating functions of the modern state in advanced capitalist societies. Whether derived from Gramsci's work on the theory of hegemony or from Frederich Pollock, Franz Neumann, and Otto Kirscheimer's investigations of the state in democratic and authoritarian political regimes, the argument about the modern state has decisively shifted to determinations of the conditions of consent rather than focusing on elements of force. But, in his final statement, *State, Power, Socialism,* Poulantzas declares, among other new features of late-twentieth-century capitalism, what he calls "the decline of democracy" and the emergence of "authoritarian statism":

> Probably for the first time in the history of democratic States, the present form not only contains scattered elements of totalitarianism, but crystallizes their organic disposition in a permanent structure running parallel to the official State. Indeed this duplication of the State seems to be a structural feature of authoritarian statism, involving not a watertight dissociation between the official State and the structure in question, but the functional overlapping and constant symbiosis. (Poulantzas 1978b, 210)

Ascribing this development to the emerging economic crisis during the 1970s, but also to changes in the relations of production and the social division of labor, which, among other things, is marked by capital's strategy of maintaining profits by an aggressive attack on working-class living standards, Poulantzas points to a steady shift in the state from its "popular-democratic" features to its more authoritarian elements. In contrast to the binary formulation of many state theorists, we may designate his position a "dual" or parallel theory according to which the authoritarian and democratic states exist in the same social space; that is, the formal popular-democratic features of the modern state do not disappear in advanced capitalist societies even as its authoritarian features emerge as, perhaps, dominant. Among these, he emphasizes the widening gap between political democracy and socioeconomic democracy, in particular the rise of poverty in advanced capitalist states, and the increasing role of the national state in favoring transnational rather than domestic capital, especially smaller business and the agricultural sector—to which might be added (from the U.S. perspective) the rising authoritarianism of the ideological apparatuses, particularly education and the fierce politicization of the so-called private sphere, notably the family, which is now subject to the intervention of courts and other repressive authorities.

These judgments are more than twenty years old. But we can see their salience in the United States today. Signaled by the so-called welfare-reform legislation of 1996, and especially by the balanced budget consensus between the two dominant parties, the socioeconomic commitment of the state to alleviate the effects of the economic crisis for those most aggrieved has declined precipitously. At the same time, to adopt the formula of Habermas, Offe, and O'Connor, the outcome of this shift is the discernible decline in the legitimating functions of the state in favor of its repressive functions. In the cities, where jobless rates are as much as twice the national averages and black and other racialized minorities suffer three times more unemployment, the criminal justice system has risen to new prominence. Spurred by a series of Supreme Court decisions, police have gained wider powers of arrest and surveillance. There is a twofold increase in police forces, the prison population has risen to more than 1 percent of the population (two and a half million), and one of three black men will, during his lifetime, be subsumed under the criminal justice system either by incarceration or official surveillance in forms such as parole and probation.

Indeed, the idea of the political *as such* suggests an indeterminate relation between social reproduction and consent; for it is difficult to institute practices of political participation, including its most elementary form, voting, without risking, at least putatively, that citizens will not overflow the boundaries between private and public and thereby insist on a public voice, if not expropriation, in matters of accumulation. In this connection we may cite, not the labor movement—for unions seem appallingly incapable of offering resistance, let alone alternatives, to the drift toward modern authoritarian statism—but environmentalists and urban activists who, more than other sectors, have contested capitalist priorities.

I want to call attention to a neglected perspective, but strikingly parallel to that of Poulantzas, Herbert Marcuse's theory of fascism, developed between 1937 and 1948 in a series of articles and reports written mainly during the period when he was employed as an analyst for intelligence agencies during World War II and then the State Department. In Marcuse's view, at its best, the liberal capitalist state is a "mediator" between the individual and the enormous economic power accumulated by the modern corporation. Through the judicial system, legislation, political parties that are broadly representative of social groups, and, in some countries, formal constitutional rights, the state provides individuals with the means to vindicate their grievances. The *rule of law* has, to an ever-increasing extent, become the medium through which the state operated as a system of national administration, a formulation strikingly close to Poulantzas's insistence that law cannot be reduced to its role as an adjunct to capitalist interests. But, far from agreeing that national socialism is characterized by the emergence of a totalitarian state that, against the will of corporations as much as society as a whole, plays the decisive role in capital accumulation and rules, exclusively, by terror, Marcuse advances the original thesis that under national socialism the state loses its autonomy and, therefore, its ability to mediate through its political and juridical functions:

> "National Socialism" has done away with the essential features that characterized the modern state. It tends to abolish any separation between state and society by transferring political functions to the social groups actually in power. In other words, National Socialism tends toward direct and immediate self-government by the prevailing social groups over the rest of the population. (Marcuse 1967, 67)

In a remarkably parallel thesis to that of C. Wright Mills, but written a decade earlier and published nowhere at the time, Marcuse claims that under fascism society is ruled by a triumvirate of big capital, the army, and the party whose collective will is mediated by, and concentrated in, the Leader who symbolized the drive toward homogeneity and harmony among the various elements of society. Yet, contrary to the usual views, according to Marcuse, however much the individual is deprived of the mediating role of a now totally instrumentalized and subordinated public bureaucracy, individualism is not, thereby, destroyed:

> Fascism manipulates the masses by unleashing the most brutal self-instincts of the individual. The National Socialist state is not the reversal but the consummation of competitive individualism. The regime releases all those forces of brutal self-interest which the democratic countries have tried to curb and tried to combine with the interest of freedom. (Ibid., 80)

Social groups are replaced by the *crowd.*

Here, Marcuse draws a parallel to the early days of capitalism when the ideology and, to some extent, the practices of the free market reduced the state to what Adam Smith termed a night watchman. But even as private corporate power grew by geometric proportions, "the social division of labor and the technological process had equalized individuals and their liberation seemed to call for a union of men acting in solidarity of a common interest which superceded the interest of individual self-preservation. Such a union is the opposite of the National Socialist mass" (ibid., 81). In opposition to this tradition, the Nazis organize the masses guided by the "principle of atomization" within production as much as within civil society. Like advanced capitalist societies today, fascism is guided by what one Nazi edict terms "that mental and physical condition that enables him the highest efficiency and this guarantees the greatest advance for the racial community" (ibid., 82).

It is not difficult to observe the same tendencies in the United States today. Capital has spared no effort to configure technology so that production units are smaller, spatially divided from each other both within national borders and throughout the world, and so the individual worker is more isolated. On the threat of discharge or capital flight, the worker is pressured to achieve more efficiency and to work long hours to the extent that, for many, the weekend has all but disappeared. Moreover, industrial terror, the promotion of fierce competitive individualism, and the "unleashing" of an ethos of self-preservation over solidarity have together produced conditions in which the mediations between the individual and capital have all but disappeared in the preponderance of workplaces. And we have witnessed the decline of the job, if by that term we designate a position that brings with it the amenities of paid health care, work rules that are shaped both by labor and management, and procedures that ensure employment security.

The more labor becomes temporary and contingent, the more the individual seeks "security" through identification with the company. The terror associated with losing a relatively well-paying job tempers the militancy that, in unionized workplaces, is associated with being mistreated. Instead, the union counsels what the worker is often ready to hear: keep your head down and keep your job. In these times, the state has retreated from its mediating role. Any employer wishing to break a union organizing drive need only fire a few activists to show the rest the price of resistance. The union files unfair labor practices charges with the Labor Relations Board, but the employer has many avenues of delay. Meanwhile, the campaign peters out and workers learn that to raise their voices leads only to retribution. As every organizer knows, the rule of law has given way to the almost unfettered rule of capital.

Now, I do not wish to be interpreted as saying that America has entered a fascist era. For example, in recent U.S. history, even as legislatures have become less responsive to the popular will and have revealed their own subordination to some corporate interests, it is still possible, through the judicial system, for individuals and state, that is, local, governments to sue tobacco companies and other manufacturers of unhealthy goods, enter small claims against recalcitrant merchants, and obtain cash settlements in cases of race and sex discrimination. And, even if seriously weakened, health, labor, and other laws and institutions dedicated to ensuring their enforcement still afford some redress. But these protections are conditioned by social struggles and are dependent on maintaining the separation between the state and society, where a public bureaucracy retains sufficient autonomy to act against the most wanton impulses of capital, the reckless and irresponsible use of police power, and hate crimes perpetrated by citizens against each other. But the events of September 11, 2001, have become an occasion for the erosion of civil liberties and for new corporate demands on the public purse. We have seen ample evidence of the usurpation of power by the executive branch. As if on cue, September 11 was followed by a Bush administration–proposed bill to suspend some constitutional liberties for immigrants, and give security agencies the right to detain suspects for an indefinite period without preferring charges. At the same time, Congress did not miss a beat when it responded affirmatively to demands by airline companies for $15 billion in aid to preserve profits that might have been lost after September 11. And the House of Representatives passed a bill awarding $70 billion in tax breaks and subsidies to some of the largest Fortune 500 corporations.

Since the 1990s we have witnessed growing public heteronomy; the state and its institutions are pressed into the direct service of capital when, for instance, the American president becomes little more than a trade representative and, during the Clinton era, an effective means by which discontent was dispersed to the margins of politics in the manner of C. Wright Mills's observation that increasingly public issues were coded as private troubles. In a period of intensifying international economic instability, when capital threatens to massively withdraw from Asia, Eastern Europe, and Latin America unless its profit margins are ensured by the state, the American president and his treasury secretary are dispatched to conferences with the world's financial leaders to deliver a single message: do not try to interfere with the free flow of capital by introducing measures to regulate currencies, restrain large-scale capital flight, and so forth. At the same time, at home, antitrust enforcement, one of the more contentious features of the regulation era, is, with the exception of the upstart computer-mediated information industry, assiduously ignored by the administration, even though it is still legally charged with the responsibility.

As a result, during the 1990s, mergers and acquisitions reached a new historical high. In the midst of a much-heralded economic "boom," each year hundreds of thousands of production workers, technical and professional employees, and middle managers were laid off (the operative term is "downsized") with little or no severance pay, finding themselves without health insurance and, if over fifty, were, for all intents and purposes, retired without pension from their careers. In many instances, downsizing is the result of transnational mergers. Not only are production workers laid off, but administrative, low and middle managers, and even some professionals may find themselves on the job market.

If capital demands that the state stand aside in the economic sphere except to fulfill its function as a valorizing agent, it calls on government to strengthen its police forces at home as well as abroad. In 2000, President Clinton and Congress agreed that although there were no funds for expanding the social wage—indeed, many groups were struggling to prevent further cuts—there was money for only two initiatives: paying down the trillions in national debt to the banks, and a small increase in the huge military budget, which, in the absence of a credible enemy, had to be increased anyway in order to sustain the small wars that continually crop up, especially in the periphery and semiperiphery of the great capitalist states. Although it is still possible in the United States for a victim of police brutality to get his or her day in court, elected officials such as Rudolph Giuliani, the New York City mayor for most of the 1990s, in the name of public safety, flagrantly defend the right of the police to terrorize blacks and other minorities. And many cities have become exemplars of the garrison state. In public schools, many pupils, particularly in black and Latino working-class neighborhoods, are forcibly restrained from leaving the building during school hours, even if they have free periods. Armed police roam the halls to make sure they are in class and, on occasion, administer corporal punishment to offenders, even when the law prohibits such behavior. And, in New York no less than in Midwest cities, elected officials threaten to withdraw public funds from museums that dare to violate the canon of conservative morality by staging art that offends religious and sexually repressive sensibilities.

It would be overly schematic to attribute these developments to shifts in the character of the world and national economies (indeed, ideological conservatism has a long history even in the era of capitalism's steep ascent), but the specificity of the latest attacks on the social wage and on freedom is surely linked to shifts in the relations of production and the social division of labor. Rather than seeking to generate a new power bloc to thwart capital's offensive based on alliances with other classes and social movements, despite the originality of the Seattle events, in the main the labor movement has shown tendencies to draw closer to dependency on its "own" branches of transnational capital, an ominous development in the shadow of globalization when what Poulantzas calls "national" capital has steadily retreated.

This pattern of dependency is thrown sharply into relief by the ominous silence of most of the leading production unions in the wake of capital's economic and political offensive against living standards and hard-won union protections in the workplace. Many sectors of the constantly shrinking industrial working class and its decimated unions have become unable to generate significant offensives on the wage front, against enforced overtime and for the preservation of contractually negotiated union control over the terms and conditions of work. Under the shadow of capital flight, many have settled for job guarantees for the existing workforce and have willingly given up their rights to prevent permanent shifts of jobs away from union control. Moreover, they accept, sometimes eagerly, overtime work assignments on the theory that they must grab whatever benefit they can before the plant shuts down, or, in the alternative, they have become more submissive to management's initiatives as a means to keep the plant from leaving town. Nor, in the United States, does there exist a shorter hours movement parallel to those of France and Germany. Instead, working hours are actually increasing and, despite economic expansion, employers have brazenly, if unsuccessfully, proposed eliminating premium pay for overtime. And, most controversially, many contracts negotiated from the early 1980s through the present day establish two- and three-tier wage systems and permit management to hire nonunion contract labor to work alongside the shrinking unionized workforce. In the face of these concessions, capital is emboldened. Thus, it was no accident that among the more aggressive participants in the Seattle and Washington events was the rank-and-file leadership of one of the more compliant industrial unions, the United Steelworkers.

These developments form the backdrop for comprehending the apparent upsurge in labor's response to globalization and, in contrast to most of the postwar era during which unions were allied with the state and the liberal political parties in opposition to social movements, the willingness of some unions to ally with environmentalists and students. Despite signs of labor's newly crafted outreach, it still appears tied umbilically to hopes for the return of regulation-era benefits, not the least of which is the eroded, but publicly sanctioned, right of workers to organize freely and without employer intimidation. The AFL-CIO has rewarded the neoliberal Democrats with tens of millions in workers' money to elect its presidential and congressional candidates and has refrained from proposing to organize its own political party, even as a pressure on the wayward Democrats. These choices reveal the extent to which one of the more challenging of Poulantzasian concepts—trade unions as an ideological state apparatus—retains its validity even in the midst of some signs of revival of labor militancy.

The validity of theory is by no means assured by algorithms of falsification conducted in the manner of an empirical test. Whether capital becomes more globally coherent and intervenes directly in the affairs of nation-states is a settled historical question. If the IMF and the WTO are coalitions of autopoetic national ruling circles, always constituted by an alliance of leading sectors of capital with the political directorate and key intellectuals tied to them, the institutions nevertheless act in accordance with both the collective interests of national states and of transnational capital, the identity of which is mediated by internal difference. Thus the institutions of world order are constituted by difference, always subject to tension and even fissure. These institutions are anchored to states that provide the military and ideological means that are the precondition of their ability to impose regimes of austerity, sanction authoritarian and totalitarian political and military directorates in developing countries, and maintain capital's world dominance. One might speculate that the relations of dominance in these alliances between transnational capitals and national states are never, a priori, determined. In the first place, interests vary and even collide, and the relation of forces tends to produce shifts; second is the intervention of social movements (which, in relation to capital, are really class signifiers insofar as the struggles increasingly take on a class character). As a condition of the renewal of its mandates, political directorates must be sensitive to popular protests, lest they be replaced or, even worse, provoke radicalization. In turn, if the investment climate is influenced by political and social movements within, say, developing countries, capital may insist on military and diplomatic policy changes in order to stabilize conditions for business.

We can see the operation of this principle in U.S. relations with Cuba. After more than four decades of embargo, repeated attempted assassinations of Fidel Castro, and economic and political isolation of the regime, significant capital fractions have concluded that their interests suggested a policy shift that a section of the political directorate is willing to accommodate. Yet other U.S. corporate interests and the political leadership to which they are tied resist major changes in the relationship with Cuba. The rule of modernization and normalization, which guided some aspects of U.S. foreign policy during the Clinton era, suggests an earlier rather than later agreement. But like the Middle East and the former Yugoslavia, where the United States' allies on many issues have diverged from U.S. direction, the outcomes remain indeterminate, precisely because of the continuing appeal of nationalism in these semiperipheral areas and of the resistance of European states to armed intervention. Needless to say, our estimates of the current period are conditioned by theoretical perspectives as well as historical evidence, by the concepts that guide our understanding of social practice and also by the level of abstraction we employ in the analysis of the state and globalization. For example, what I have just described can be dismissed by the superimperialism theorists as a glitch, confirmed by those who follow Poulantzas as evidence of the importance of interimperialist differences in helping to produce stalemates in international affairs. Against inevitabilists who have noted China, Vietnam, and Eastern Europe's partial submission to the terms of empire, the capacity of the Cuban regime to mobilize its own people to endure adversity and also their ability to improvise a new economy after the collapse of the Soviet Union and their refusal to submit instead to neoliberal solutions, must be accredited in helping to explain the bend in U.S. policy; for, with Poulantzas, I insist that the agency of those bearing the weight of empire are constitutive of its trajectories. At the same time, one must reject every attempt to reify the present as an illustration of ineluctability. Only by maintaining the historicity of social structures based on the vicissitudes of class struggles is this possible.

References

Marcuse, Herbert. 1967. *Five Lectures: Psychoanalysis, Politics and Utopia*. Boston: Beacon Press.

Poulantzas, Nicos. 1978a. *Classes in Contemporary Capitalism*. London: Verso Books.

———. 1978b. *State, Power, Socialism*. London: Verso Books.

Contributors

Stanley Aronowitz is distinguished professor of sociology at the Graduate School and University Center, City University of New York. A former steelworker and union organizer, he has held positions at College of Staten Island, University of California, Irvine, and Columbia University. He currently serves on the editorial boards of *Cultural Critique* and *New Politics* and is author of numerous books, most recently *The Last Good Job in America: Work and Education in the New Global Technoculture; The Knowledge Factory: Dismantling the Corporate University and Creating True Higher Education; From the Ashes of the Old: American Labor and America's Future; Post Work* (edited with Jonathan Cutler); and *The Jobless Future: Sci-Tech and the Dogma of Work* (edited with William DiFazio; Minnesota, 1995).

Clyde W. Barrow is professor of policy studies at the University of Massachusetts, Dartmouth. He is author of *Critical Theories of the State: Marxist, Neo-Marxist, Post-Marxist; Universities and the Capitalist State;* and *More Than a Historian: The Political and Economic Thought of Charles A. Beard.*

Peter Bratsis is adjunct lecturer of political science at Queens College, City University of New York. He is a member of the editorial collective of the journal *Found Object* and has published articles on political theory, nationalism, and Greek politics.

Richard A. Cloward was on the faculty of Columbia University. He is the author, with Frances Fox Piven, of *Regulating the Poor; Poor People's*

Movements; The New Class War; Why Americans Don't Vote; and *The Breaking of the American Social Compact.* He died in 2001.

Adriano Nervo Codato is a professor in the Department of Social Sciences at the Federal University of Paraná (Brazil). He is the author of *Sistema estatal e política econômica no Brasil pós-64* and the coeditor of *Revista de Sociologia e Política.* His research interests focus on theories of the capitalist state and theories of elites; he is currently researching the building of the political institutions during the authoritarian period of the Estado Novo in Brazil (1937–45).

Bob Jessop is professor of sociology at Lancaster University, England. He is best known for his contributions to state theory and political economy and for work on Thatcherism. Among his many publications is the only book-length English-language study of the life of Nicos Poulantzas, *Nicos Poulantzas: Marxist Theory and Political Strategy.* His other contributions to state theory include *The Capitalist State* and *State Theory.*

Andreas Kalyvas teaches political theory at the University of Michigan. His work focuses on the politics of radical breaks and popular foundings. He is currently coauthoring a book with Ira Katznelson on the genealogy of political liberalism.

Rhonda F. Levine is professor of sociology at Colgate University. She is author of *Class Networks and Identity: Replanting Jewish Lives from Nazi Germany to Rural New York* and *Class Struggle and the New Deal: Industrial Labor, Industrial Capital, and the State;* editor of *Social Class and Stratification: Classic Statements and Theoretical Debates;* and coeditor of *Recapturing Marxism: An Appraisal of Recent Trends in Sociological Theory, Bringing Class Back In: Contemporary and Historical Perspectives,* and *Radical Sociologists and the Movement: Experiences, Lessons, and Legacies.*

Leo Panitch is professor of political science at York University, Toronto. He is editor of the *Socialist Register* and a founding member of *Studies in Political Economy: A Socialist Review.* His books include *The Assault on Trade Union Freedoms; Working Class Politics in Crisis; Social Democracy and Industrial Militancy; The End of Parliamentary Socialism: From*

New Left to New Labour; and, most recently, *Renewing Socialism: Democracy, Strategy, and Imagination.*

Renato Monseff Perissinotto is a professor in the Department of Social Sciences at the Federal University of Paraná (Brazil). He is author of *Classes dominantes e hegemonia na República Velha* and *Estado e capital cafeeiro em São Paulo, 1889–1930,* as well as many articles in which he studies the theory of the state from a historical perspective. His research interests focus on theories of the capitalist state, theories of elites, and democratic theory. He coedits the *Revista de Sociologia e Política.*

Frances Fox Piven is on the faculty of the Graduate School of the City University of New York. She is the author, with Richard A. Cloward, of *Regulating the Poor; Poor People's Movements; The New Class War; Why Americans Don't Vote;* and *The Breaking of the American Social Compact.*

Paul Thomas is professor of political science at the University of California, Berkeley. His books are *Karl Marx and the Anarchists; Alien Politics: Marxist State Theory Revisited; Rational Choice Marxism* (coedited with Terrell Carver); and *Culture and the State* (coauthored with David Lloyd). Some of his numerous articles on Marx and Marxism have appeared in *The Cambridge Companion to Marx* and the *Socialist Register.* He is currently working on a book, *Scientific Socialism: Career of a Concept.*

Constantine Tsoukalas is professor of political science and sociology at the University of Athens. He has been professor of sociology at the University of Paris VIII (Vincennes) and has been a visiting professor at the Sorbonne, Princeton University, New York University, and Iztapalapa (Mexico City). His many books include *The Greek Tragedy; Dependence and Reproduction: The Social Role of the Educational Apparatus in Greece; The State and Social Development; Idols of Civilization;* and *Adventures in Meaning: From Peoplehood to Nationhood.*

Index